PT
2668   Härtling, Peter, 1933-
.A3   [Frau. English]
F713   A woman / Peter Härtling ;
1988   translated by Joachim Neugroschel.
          -- New York : Holmes & Meier, c1988.
          xvi, 269 p. ; 24 cm. -- (Modern
          German voices series)
      Translation of: Eine Frau.
      ISBN 0-8419-1046-4 (alk. paper)
      ISBN 0-8419-1047-2 (pbk.)

      I. Title. II. Series.

PT2668.A3F713 1988   833'.914 [19]

                  WaOE   87-8657

A Woman
(Eine Frau)

Modern German Voices Series

Ingeborg Bachmann
The Thirtieth Year

Manès Sperber
Like a Tear in the Ocean

Peter Härtling
A Woman (Eine Frau)

Eric Rentschler, ed.
*West German Filmmakers on Film:
Visions and Voices*

Wolfgang Koeppen
Pigeons on the Grass

Alexander Kluge
Case Histories

Christa Wolf
The Essays of Christa Wolf

Ingeborg Bachmann
Simultaneous

A Woman
(Eine Frau)

Peter Härtling

Translated by
Joachim Neugroschel

HOLMES & MEIER
New York   London

Holmes & Meier Publishers, Inc.
30 Irving Place
New York, NY 10003

Great Britain:
1–3 Winton Close
Letchworth, Hertfordshire SG61 1BA
England

Originally published in German as *Eine Frau*
Copyright © 1983 by Sammlung Luchterhand

The paper used in this publication meets the requirements of the American
National Standard for Permanence of Paper for Printed Library Materials,
Z39.48-1984.

Library of Congress Cataloging-in-Publication Data

Härtling, Peter, 1933–
  A woman.

  (Modern German voices)
  Translation of: Eine Frau.
  I. Title. II. Series.
PT2668.A3F713   1988   833'.914   87-8657
ISBN 0-8419-1046-4 (alk. paper)

Manufactured in the United States of America

CONTENTS

Introduction   *ix*

PART ONE
(Dresden 1902–1922)

1   Childhood or What Remains to Be Found   *3*
2   Father or Five Hands in the Desk   *9*
3   The Garden   *17*
4   Escape with Eberhard   *22*
5   Portrait and Self-Portrait   *29*
6   Mother Gazes at the Sunset or
    Who Wants to Join the Army?   *34*
7   Uncle David's Letter   *39*
8   Elle or The Early End of the Revolution   *45*
9   Sighs of Relief or Hazy Transitions   *56*
10 The First Mirror Image or
    The Young Lady Makes Up Her Mind   *63*
11 A Letter from Carlsbad   *65*
12 Jean Ettringer or The Taste of Death   *69*
13 Frau Perchtmann   *72*

PART TWO
(Prague 1923–1925; Brno 1925–1945)

14 Guest in an Apartment   *83*
15 A Conversation in Bed   *88*
16 Mirjam or The Cat Game   *91*

17	Wotruba's Rage or Curiosity Canceled	99
18	Conversation about Elvira	107
19	The Twins	112
20	Birdseed or Wüllner Adjusts	115
21	Once Again Elvira or Ferdinand Cheats on Katharina	124
22	The Breathing of a Spring Day	127
23	Moving or How Uncle David Lost His Voice	130
24	The Czech	137
25	Perchtmann & Son	143
26	The Trip Back	149
27	Katharina's Circle or Why a Salon?	154
28	Black Friday	164
29	Katharina's Fairy Tale or The Way Time Gets Lost	170
30	Ferdinand Breaks Out	175
31	The Second Mirror Image or The Lady's Not for Burning Yet	179
32	Georg Wüllner's Death	181
33	The Dawn of a New Era or Gutsi Has a New Name	185
34	Prchala's Story	189
35	A Page from the Diary	196
36	Adam Wagner	198
37	Confusion or The End of Katharina Perchtmann the Factory Owner	203
38	The Third Mirror Image or An Anticipation of Obscenity	207

PART THREE

(Stuttgart 1946–1970)

39	A Love Story	211
40	In the Packing Department or So Much for Skodlerrak	218

41 Camilla or You Can't Go Back Again   224

42 An Apartment is Renovated   228

43 Erika Opitz or The Things
    We Can't Learn from One Another   233

44 A Woman Goes for a Walk   238

45 Annamaria or A Son is Made Up For   240

46 The Second Ferdinand   244

47 The Sixty-fifth Birthday   250

48 The Fourth Mirror Image or
    An Old Woman Removes Her Make-up   261

49 Easter in Esslingen   262

50 Annamaria's Letter   268

Introduction

The pleasure a reader experiences when reading the saga of any individual's struggle, awakening, and growth over a long period of time is deeply involved with our basic curiosity about the nature of life itself. While serious literature reflects cultural values and concerns, it also sheds light upon the contradictions, flaws, hopes, loves, and fears that form the web of human experience crystallized within each individual's story. Such is the case with Peter Härtling's *A Woman (Eine Frau)*, published here for the first time in English in Joachim Neugroschel's fine translation. An immediate bestseller in West Germany when it appeared in 1974, Härtling's novel attempts to trace history's silent wave of destruction and despair by depicting the life of one woman, Katharina Wüllner, born in 1902 and still alive at the book's conclusion in 1970, as not only a denial of the futility forced upon so many through two world wars, but also as a testament to the flesh-and-blood survival experienced by ordinary people trapped in extraordinary circumstances.

"Katharina *is* history" is what, in the simplest sense, Härtling wishes to say. Similarly, any theory that ignores the importance of subjective individual experience and memory in shaping the meaning of history also suffers from the coldness and insensitivity at work in the murderous decisions by which history dangles so many fates. In short, Härtling would argue that our only hope of not becoming the victims of history is to recognize that we are its arbiters, each of us defining a version of our own through the memories we feel compelled to share.

It comes as no surprise, then, that much of what happens in *A Woman* is closely linked to the author's own childhood experiences during the Second World War. Born in 1933 in Chemnitz, now known as Karl-Marx-Stadt in East Germany, Härtling grew up as the son of a lawyer who, along with his wife, was severely critical of the Nazi rise to power while also expressing mortification at his son's decision to join the Hitler Youth movement like so many other naive adolescents wishing to aspire to a cause. Eventually, after the family's return to the father's native Moravia in 1942, followed by their flight to the Austrian town of Zwettl in 1945, the father died in the confines of Döllersheim, a Russian labor camp set up in Austria after the occupation. This traumatic period of Härtling's life has been sensitively depicted in his compelling autobiographical book, *Nachgetragene Liebe (Love Paid Back)*, Härtling's endeavor to repay his father with the love he could not give him as a youth. By 1946 Härtling was completely orphaned after his mother committed suicide. From then on his grandmother and aunt were in charge of his upbringing in Nürtingen in the West German state of Baden-Württemberg.

Katharina's odyssey in *A Woman* is similar to Härtling's: her childhood in a suburb of Dresden, married life in Prague and Brno, and finally flight as a refugee to Stuttgart. Her movement between what is now East and West Germany and her long stay in what was traditionally the German-.speaking part of Czechoslovakia also make her life in many ways representative of numerous Germans. For the average English-speaking reader "Germany" means the territory governed by Bonn and the "economic miracle" accomplished after the war and now maintained with such pride. However, what we tend to forget is that language—not just politics or geography—defines a culture. In the heart of every German lies the knowledge that in the case of East and West Germany there exists one culture divided between two countries. Härtling's occasional use of dialects such as Swabian and Saxon in the German (all of which Joachim Neugroschel renders quite successfully in English) not only illustrates the texture of the language on both sides of the current border, but also shows Katharina's sensitivity to the speech and mannerisms that make up her culture. Looked at from this angle, *A Woman* often seems pan-Germanic in its concerns and characterizations, while the issue of Czech sovereignty in the face of German control, which Katharina is made aware of during her stay in Brno, might also be seen as a subtle commentary on the part of Härtling about the resentment and difficulty suffered by any society governed by powers outside of it.

All of this, however, is not to say that Katharina's life is just a facile symbol for what it means to have survived this century's cataclysm as a German. Her life also reflects the struggle with personal identity—and changes in identity—that is characteristic of much of the author's work in his long and productive career. Running the gamut from poems, stories, novels, children's books, and essays to important work as a critic, editor, and publisher, Härtling's literary output has been broad and influential. Two vectors, however, run through almost everything he has written. In celebrated novels such as *Niembsch* and *Hölderlin,* he has been concerned with the meaning and depiction of history as manifested in the genres of autobiography and biography. Meanwhile, a sub-theme to his historical interests has always been the role of memory, especially that of childhood. Katharina's magical childhood and her lifelong return to it via memory throughout *A Woman* represent Härtling's central belief that the history which each of us constructs exists within the intersection of experience thrust upon us and the ability of memory to shape it and prevail.

"It could always only be the garden . . . ," writes Härtling at the start of *A Woman,* "it" being the fusion of Katharina's memory of childhood and the manner in which that memory defines and enriches the story of her life. In a letter to her daughter, Annamaria, she states:

> "It was a remote place in a remote time. I don't know whether you understand me. It's not very precise, of course. My memory has retained the house in Klotzsche and the big garden as an island, as the image of an island. And often, when I've been happy, I've thought about that island, and I've thought that I might find such happiness again later, much later."

That this letter written years later should appear at the beginning of both the novel and Katharina's life is key to the structure of *A Woman.* Excerpts from Katharina's diary and letters in relaying and commenting upon the narrative as it progresses create the eerie effect that there are two Katharinas: one who experiences an event in 1906, but also one who experiences the same event just as immediately, if not more so, when writing about it in her diary in 1932. Similarly, by switching from the past tense to the present no matter when the real action is occurring, Härtling creates for Katharina a consciousness which slips back and forth through time at will. Thus her memory is at all times her real inner life. The reason her childhood garden appears to her as an "island" is that it represents the loss she experiences through time as well as the sanctity of the realm she is able to return to again and again.

But what exactly is Katharina's story? And what significance does it hold for us as readers?

On the surface the facts are quite simple. Like Härtling she is born into the professional middle class, her father the owner of three perfume factories; her mother, the reserved and steady wife despite the husband's numerous adventures and affairs. On the periphery are the three older children—Dieter, Elle, and Ernst—along with the nanny, Gutsi, who in typically Old World fashion becomes the mother more dearly loved than Katharina's own. The most tender portrait, however, is reserved for David Eichlaub, the Jewish brother of Katharina's mother, Susanne Wüllner. In his eccentricity and sadness Eichlaub is the most influential character in Katharina's life. Though his sister Susanne converted to Christianity, gave her children a Christian upbringing, and never seems particularly concerned with her situation as a Jew, David wrestles with his Jewish identity quite deeply, suffering the persecution experienced by so many, often heroically maintaining a precarious balance between hilarity and profound anger. Katharina, on the other hand, stands somewhere between her mother and her uncle. Her identity with and love for her uncle show that she is more sensitive to the issue than her mother is, but because she does not have strong convictions about her relation to Judaism, she never seems completely representative of the victim or survivor. Marrying two men whose views are antithetical to those of her Uncle David, she is Katharina, *a* woman—not a figurehead and not without contradictions.

It is safe to say that Katharina's childhood relatives remain the most central characters in her life. Though she will go on to marry, bear four children of her own, survive the war and heavy losses within her family, as well as have significant relationships with three other men, the immediate adult presences within her childhood are what she will always consider to be her true family. The reason why has to do in part with the garden and the protected, magical world it embodies in her wanderings among the beech hedges, the thicket forever inhabited by wolves after Dieter terrorizes her with their description, and the gazebo with its haven of stories and secrets. Though her memories sometimes drift toward the sentimental and overly romantic, Härtling is careful to keep them in perspective with all that she must suffer in her life. The dramatic reversal that will occur later on is alluded to in an early passage where Katharina reflects on the sensations of the garden and the prized horses given to her by her father:

> At night, when the windows were open, you could hear the animals snorting, sometimes neighing, stamping their hooves on the

grass, scratching—those were the noises she never forgot, dragging them along, talking about them when she sat next to the cattle car in Landshut, twenty years later, waiting to move on, waiting for the two whistles of the locomotive—she spoke about the horses "as if we were at home."

The fact that the cattle car is mentioned here without explanation in the novel's third chapter shows how deft Härtling is at contrasting Katharina's revery with the terror she must survive. Meanwhile, we as readers feel its chilling effects.

"Is it true that one lives several lives?" Katharina asks her brother on the day of her wedding. The answer which *A Woman* provides is that, yes, one does. Beyond the principal locations that formulate the division of the novel into three parts, the people with whom Katharina comes into contact are also a large part of what defines her character. Oddly enough, in a novel very much concerned with German history and culture, some of Härtling's most detailed and sensitive portraits are of non-Germans. Whether it be the wise musician, Jaromir Gawliček, quietly making a point at Katharina's Brno salon, or the journalist, Jan Waldhans, weeping horribly at the German takeover of Czechoslovakia, or the faithful and caring service of the maid, Božena, or the factory foreman, Prchala, hero to both Katharina and her mother—each is as much a part of Katharina's makeup as she is of their own. In fact, one of the most poignant moments in *A Woman* takes place years later in Stuttgart when, after she tells people that the music of Dvořak reminds her of the way Prchala spoke, the narrator informs us that "no one knew who that was." It is as if someone's life has been extinguished before our eyes—our own memory of Prchala becoming just as crucial as Katharina's. For if it is true that one leads "several lives" through other people, it is also true that one suffers several deaths with their passing. Though Katharina never collapses into uncontrollable weeping for the dead, Härtling makes it clear that her life would be all the poorer without the diversity of people who come to inhabit it.

A Woman, however, is also a novel that reflects a specific German concern. Rising above the triad of history, memory, and experience that exists in much of Härtling's work, is the meaning of the German notion of *Heimat*, central to the events in *A Woman*. "Home" or "homeland" work as the proper translation of *Heimat*, but neither captures all that is involved in the original. More than just a localized haven of protection and warmth, *Heimat* also encompasses a sense of community (*Gemeinschaft*) and shared identity on a much larger scale. But just where this identity exists, given the split in Germany's geography, and what it consists of, given the need to confront the deep wounds left by the war, is difficult to determine. In recent years numerous books and films have been dedicated to examining just such questions, Härtling's novel being one of the very first to raise the issue in a work geared toward a general audience.

In the middle of *A Woman*, Katharina reflects on "home" and her life in Brno while writing in her diary:

> "So now I am here, only here, in this house in Brno, with my husband and children. I could write: This is my homeland. Why do I not dare? Is a person at home only once in his lifetime? That is nonsense. But why cannot even the children impel me to say to myself: I am at home with you children. I owe all these strange broodings and insights to Čermak."

Čermak is the Czech factory owner who, in chatting with Katharina while waiting to see Ferdinand, reminds her that "Homeland . . . does not just mean houses, towns, landscapes, or people one is close to. It can be a lot more." Just what it is, however, Katharina finds hard to say. Clearly she longs for the house near Dresden, where she grew up, but she also knows that her feeling of loss and displacement is not limited to one house, one garden, but rather an entire way of life no longer made possible.

Yet the danger of nostalgia is that it can so easily turn into a reactionary sense of nationalism much like the search for the "real" Germany with Hitler's rise to power. Upon the Nazi occupation of Brno and the German takeover of Czechoslovakia, Ferdinand announces with relish that "We have come home," a statement which Katharina wisely defuses by asking, "What home?" Similarly, the fact that her friend Dorothee Neumeister can claim during Katharina's salon that "the Sudeten Mountains have been German since time immemorial" shows how absurd and dangerous such sentiments can become, her ignorant chauvinism making it sound as if the glaciers themselves had German nationhood in mind when carving out the continent.

The answer Katharina may be looking for is actually suggested to her as early as her stay in Prague, though it takes her many years to understand it for herself. In a philosophical discussion with the jeweler Hribasch, whose sad eyes and infinite patience she comes to admire, Katharina criticizes him for worshiping his jewels more than people. Hribasch is quick to point out, however, that he loves his precious stones only to the degree that they are enhanced by the person who wears them. In other words, the objects with which we live and work are sacred to the extent they are utilized by human beings, while even Katharina appreciates the piety in Hribasch's voice when he asks, "Because these things are made by us. All of them. Shouldn't the creators respect their creatures, appreciate them?" If we apply such a question to Katharina's own precious garden we see that, indeed, it is not so much the trees and shrubbery that she longs for but rather the life embodied within them, whether it be Gutsi's voice calling her in, the conversation at summer parties given by her parents under the glowing lanterns spread out across the lawn, or the Bohemian trumpeter at evening from the garden next door.

Unfortunately, objects and gardens, like people, disappear. The most difficult lesson Katharina must learn, the one that accounts for her real growth, is that she too must leave the garden behind in order to find her own true identity within the present. Toward the end of A *Woman,* we see her arrive at just that as she meditates upon a walk:

> She strolls. She runs her fingers along wire fences; her open hands touch the wooden braces of a bench, she rubs the back of her hand on stone. Why does she feel things only now, see them, hold them, discover what she knew but never perceived; now she sees what she never saw: the soft leather of the pony saddle, the bark of the pine tree, paint peeling on the garden fence, porcelain, rustling, fragrant textiles, the tweeds that Ferdinand preferred, the flannels that Wagner wore, Rossman's tarpaulin jackets, stone balustrades, stair landings, the summer-warm metal of Ferdinand's Tatra, the handle of the baby carriage, a strange, usually sticky rubber, the bomb splinters in the garden, shards, glass shards, the noise of the bombs, the swelling howl, the clattering tank tracks—she makes up for the past, gathers.
> That's her too.

A litany sung to the objects which anchor the human reality of her past and present, one can almost see Hribasch nodding in silent agreement at Katharina's realization that within her power to imagine the lives she has lived out of the things that surround her lies her own identity, her own specific history, and the only *Heimat* she can claim. Sentimentality, however, has no place within such a notion. Since the lives of which it consists are as fleeting and variable as the objects she gathers, Katharina's *Heimat* must remain a place fixed only within her language and memory.

For though it is true that "she is free, she was freed, bit by bit," it also holds that she must endure her freedom."

That Ferdinand Novotny, the last man with whom Katharina falls in love, should work in the Ministry of Justice is no accident. Justice in the face of history is central to Härtling's novel. We need only remember that the author's father was a lawyer to consider how important justice might be to him, while for Katharina it is the only thing which can give her life meaning. Studying herself, she realizes with horror that "this person lived and suddenly she discovers that she has been lived, that she herself did little to lead her own life." Justice can come only with her emancipation from the forces that have controlled her life thus far. Traditional notions of family, motherhood, sex, and politics—anything that has kept her trapped as a puppet dangled by the beliefs of others—all of it must be swept away in order that she come to know herself for who she really is. Hence, there is little in her which can accept a grand and sentimental celebration by her family on her sixty-fifth birthday, Katharina choosing instead to tell it as she sees it:

> We got together for this celebration, not because we loved each other, but for one single reason: Because my memory encompasses all of you. You are in my brain as you were and as you will never be again. And now the party is over.

What on the surface may seem cruel and unappreciative here is, iron-ically, an act of selfless love. Like herself, Katharina's children and grandchildren must come to terms with their own history as she has with hers. By releasing them from the responsibility to take on her story and relive it, she grants them the freedom which she herself sought throughout her entire life. As Annamaria says at the end of the novel, "She always needed people who required her love." It is to Härtling's credit that he shows us just how triumphant and liberating such a love can be as Katharina Wüllner survives her own saga to secure an identity of her own—a sign that miraculous change is still possible in an all too unmiraculous world.

Peter Filkins

A Woman
(Eine Frau)

PART ONE

(Dresden 1902–1922)

1
Childhood or What Remains to Be Found

It could always only be the garden, the beech hedge, its shadow perforated by wandering lights, the gazebo, the leafy hut under the birches, or the evening solo of the Bohemian trumpeter, who was the gardener next door, it could only be the garden when she described her childhood, and her sentences came from a song, as if she were unwilling to believe it all now and yet could not find a more perfect truth. And the large, white house, always in a summery mood, was also given a stanza.

"It was," Katharina had written to Annamaria, her youngest daughter, "it was a remote place in a remote time. I don't know whether you understand me. It's not very precise, of course. My memory has retained the house in Klotzsche and the big garden as an island, as the image of an island. And often, when I've been happy, I've thought about that island, and I've felt I might find such happiness again later, much later."

Katharine Wüllner was born in Klotzsche, near Dresden, on February 7, 1902. She was the youngest of four children, and her birth was celebrated by the factory owner Wüllner with several buddies in the living- and dining-rooms of the spacious house. The merrymaking went on for three days and three nights, during which time the almost dwarflike little man never even looked at the whimpering object of the festivities, and he visited his wife only once. Susanne Wüllner, emerging over and over again from a jittery sleep, heard the racket, the howling,

3

the singing, and she asked the nurse to close all the doors downstairs on the main floor, so they wouldn't be disturbed up here.

She lay in her room, high on her bed, a pale, beautiful person, her dark eyes gaping, as if she were tumbling from one terror to another, her black hair spread over the pillow. She frequently received the physician, sent for the baby, and told the other children what to do on that day—all this in a soft voice, which everyone gladly listened to. She entrusted Elle, the older daughter, with the most important tasks. The twelve-year-old girl, tall for her age, precocious, often overbearing and stubborn, maintained the contact with the household, the kitchen, and also the father, to whom she was closest.

"I miss you all," he had written to his wife from Piešťány, where he had been forced to stay for a long cure, "but I wish Elle were here, together with her temper tantrums. She understands me; we have the same feelings."

Elle, laughing, ventured among the tipsy, worn-out men and whispered into her father's ear, transmitting her mother's wishes, which he cheerfully registered and rejected: Tell her—and he was always loud—that we're doing it for her and the child. Besides, they would all be leaving soon, going to the White Stag. A breath of air, girl, morning air! And Elle was infected by his laughter and hugged him, finding him weird, the delicate man, whose movements looked balletic—an artist, not a businessman, people said, and yet they feared his mercantile skill for he had, after all, turned a drugstore into a huge corporation: three factories, two in Dresden, one in Bodenbach. An inventive mind devoted to beauty, manufacturing colognes and creams, especially the world-famous Combella Cucumber Milk. I caress millions of women, he sometimes cried, a tender lover. Yes, I understand. Go up to your mother and tell her the house will be peaceful soon. The party's ending.

The men leave, their voices can be heard from the garden. They laugh. The noise moves away. The house heaves a sigh of relief. The baby's crying can be heard, the calming hum of the nursemaid, the calls of the mother, and of the children too. Light from the garden penetrates through the windows, a soft green becoming visible in waves—"I've never found that light again anywhere, I inhaled it, it sated and cheered us."

She was baptized in the village church of Klotzsche, Katharina Susanne Leonore. Her godparents were the father's brother and sister-in-law, whom Katharina never saw again: they emigrated to South America, occasionally sending exotic gifts. The Wüllner family was represented in large numbers at the christening. Only one of her mother's relatives came—her brother, the pharmacist and singer David Eichlaub, who, unlike his sister, had never converted. In front of the church he made sarcastic remarks, which his brother-in-law laughed at, for he was an atheist anyway and regarded all this as a continuation of prehistoric shamanism, with which David disagreed, but Wüllner ignored him, or said: Well, I don't want to get into a fight about your faith, we all have a little of it anyway, old friend. So let's go to the christening.

Uncle David sang.

The pastor was moved.

Susanne Wüllner wept. She had said: This is my last child.

Only the baby emitted no sound when its thin, black hair became wet from water. Now it had names, which it had to put up with, grow into. Uncle David strode over to the choir again, terrifying everyone, for he hadn't announced what he'd be performing, and the organ was no match for his melancholy when he sang the first song from Schubert's *Winterreise*, "I came here as a stranger; I leave, a stranger still." Let's hope it's not a bad omen, said a member of the Wüllner clan, and the father of the child who had thus been sung about complained after the service: What the hell are you doing, David! It's not the baby's fault! Just don't start philosophizing again! Which David didn't; instead, he took the baby from its mother's arms, cautiously carried it ahead of the group, along the avenue, to the garden entrance. That's a *park*, Wüllner would say, but his wife insisted on calling the vast grounds encircling the house a "garden." The uncle carried the niece, cradling her, humming Figaro's aria; he occasionally turned toward the parents behind him, showing them the child.

It was, according to Katharina, a sunny morning in late May.

"Georg was full of warmhearted courtesy today," Susanne Wüllner wrote to her very old mother in Breslau, "he hasn't been so considerate in a long time, but he does have to make up for his all-male festivity. He's as capricious as ever."

Katharina was given a room on the second floor, under the roof. It remained hers. Later, she was also given the small chamber next door. So she had a small apartment.

What she knows, what she knew and then told, filled with a nostalgia to which she succumbed: The faces bending over her, bright from the rays of the sun falling through the gathered muslin curtains; the face of her mother, whose voice she enjoyed, always wanting to hear it whenever possible; the nursemaid, Gutsi, who could calm her down with funny doggerel and ditties, a coarse, attentive face, in which watery blue eyes floated over a ski nose. There were constant cries: Gutsi! Where are you, Gutsi? My teddy bear's gone! Come and help, Gutsi! Everything's spoiled, the color's running! And Gutsi always managed to help. Katharina was really closer to her than to her mother, who sometimes withdrew or traveled with her father, and who could become inexplicably alien to her, very remote, almost inaccessible. *"Ma bonne maman,"* Ernst used to address her, quite seriously, in a love that could not give up a certain aloofness. But Katharina called her "Mummi," discovered her warmth, her loneliness: "Don't be sad, Mummi, don't."

She runs breathlessly through the house, down to the second floor, across the gallery, down to the main floor. She stands in the living room, two stories high with a strangely cubic dome; she shouts; she's scared of ghosts, which Dieter has made her believe in. Gutsi comes, Mummi comes, both women take care of her, take turns hugging her, and she enjoys the warmth, the help, which drives out all fear. Now it's good. Yes, it's good, and her father asks what all the fuss is about, he comforts her too, spirits a small chocolate bar from his pocket, the paper smells a little of tobacco; when she is back in her room, sitting on the window seat, she will sniff at it again, because it is a smell that women don't have.

She is small and frail, does not grow as fast as Elle. She's inherited her mother's full hair. It will soon be curled into locks that look like puffed pastries, which she likes. She finds herself pretty; she peers into the mirror, pays attention to her clothes. Dieter, whom she loves more than anyone else, "her brother," scolds her for being "finicky;" she doesn't mind for he also calls her "cute." He leads her along the street, to the village square, taking the road to foreign places as if they were new continents, saying: Loschwitz is over there. And there's Dresden.

She was in Dresden: on Prager Strasse, and in the factory, one Sunday in the Zwinger, where Mummi let her ride a stone figure in the fountain.

She hides in the gazebo, hears the shouts of the people looking for her: Katharina, Kathi, say something, child! Where are you! She doesn't stir until it occurs to Dieter or Ernst that she might be hiding in the hut, and one of the boys opens the door: What a so-and-so! He pulls her out: We've found her! We've got her! Everyone laughs. But you could have said something, child, Gutsi rebukes her. Okay, okay.

"I sometimes get fits of 'sentimentality,'" she writes in her diary during September 1932. "I then envision landscapes or rooms, very specific situations with myself at the center, all alone. Then again, I feel poignant or I sing particular tunes such as 'I have Lost Her Now, Alas,' or the beginning of Tchaikovsky's piano concerto. It's really crazy. I enjoy these diffuse moods."

They celebrated her fourth birthday. Father had been away for a long time; inexplicable things were upsetting the household routine—the parents had a fight, Gutsi was more fidgety than usual. Elle cursed the "goddam mess" she'd gotten into, which angered Gutsi, who said that a sixteen-year-old girl ought to know how to behave, such language was unworthy of her: No, Elle, you're going too far, you ought to behave like a young lady.

And what about them down there? Elle shouted.

Forget about it. It doesn't concern us, said Gutsi; she had tears in her eyes; she sniffed loudly. Everything runs its course. That was her maxim. She used it on all occasions, and she was probably always right.

Father had left home; mother withdrew, spending little time with the children—Elle didn't need her anymore, she was almost seventeen, attending high school; she had decided to become a painter, move to Hellerau, which no one tried to talk her out of and no one even believed. Dieter, one year older, had already graduated from high school; he wanted to study mathematics at Leipzig. Ernst, wrapped up in abstruse plans, a daydreamer, saw himself as a big-game hunter in Africa or as an adviser to the king; you'll see, he furiously smashed through their disbelief, you dunno nahthin' (his Saxon accent was stronger than Gutsi's).

They had a party for Katharina's fourth birthday. Georg Wüllner had returned from an "investigative tour" of America, full of ideas for his production; he said he had discovered new essences, which he was sure would be all the rage. Everything seemed to be straightened out.

A table was set for the children on the lawn, between the house and the gazebo; girls the same age and older had been invited from the neighborhood; Gutsi was directing, two hired waiters were serving; Peter, the gardener, and Asta, the cook, were in charge; only Father was missing.

The presents piled up on the grass—dolls, clothes, doll clothes, a toy clock from Mummi.

She asked where Father was.

Coming—he has important plans for you, Kathi, only for you.

She wriggled so much that Gutsi whacked her.

Calm down, he'll come. Now just drink your chocolate and entertain your friends, okay?

Oh, she's a real live wire! And the murmuring of the grownups. She runs into the gazebo, closing the door behind her, snuggling up on the couch, wishes Father were here, until cheerful noise lures her out again. Father comes toward her, leading a black pony, that trots docilely alongside him: C'mon, Kathi! Look, Kathi! This is for you. As black as coal! It's for you! Mount it!

Father lifts her up, she wedges the pony's back between her legs, whispering: Hold me tight, Papa. His hand presses her gently on the swaying, living seat.

The pony was christened Alexander; it was given an enclosure behind the house, a stable for the night, a small wagon. Katharina soon learned how to ride; she had the pony for twelve years, until after the war began; then it was taken away.

She wanted to sleep with Alexander; they wouldn't let her. So the next day she rose early, before Gutsi, sneaked into the garden, sat down in front of the fence, and, still timid, watched the pony grazing.

During those years, no one had to remind her to take care of Alexander. He was her companion, her pride.

It was, she told her children, my loveliest present—nothing surpassed it—a daring surprise that Father pulled off.

The past trickled away in her, image for image, stored away, for later. By the time she could have evoked everything, only shards remained. Individual scenes, more bitter and more precise: in a cold, run-down factory apartment, birdseed weighed into small pouches, another specialty of Father's.

Come home. Go away.

She hears only the Bohemian trumpeter next door, over and over, the nocturnal sentimentality, Moldau and Elbe, she sees herself running through the house, the curving stairway, she feels the cool bannister on the palm of her hand; the bannister is much too high, she shoves against the front door, calls for Gutsi, dances across the lawn, which smells of constant summer, she is four years old, she owns a pony with a red saddle.

The landscape is missing as yet, the cities are unknown as yet.

2
Father or Five Hands in the Desk

People said that if Georg Wüllner had not found a wife as short as
he, actually about an inch shorter and also beautiful, he would have died
of empty boasting. But this way, he at least applied some of his energy
and imagination sensibly and successfully. He was short; his papers said
5'3", but he had managed to hoodwink his way up by at least one inch.
Nevertheless, he looked "fully grown," masculine and sovereign, and it
was clear that any man who didn't take him seriously would have to
reckon with nasty consequences. Friends at the university had called him
Perkeo. His head looked strangely huge: under the thick hair, an overly
high, overly round forehead; under the eyes, dark circles which, as even
close friends said, were due to his not very restrained life style—an
erroneous if understandable explanation; the dark circles were really a
physical peculiarity, which had already caused the five- and then seven-
year-old to be dewormed, even though no worms were ever found and the
circles never vanished; the temples under the hair, which was tightly
combed back and smoothed with his own pomade, seemed hollow, highly
sensitive; Wüllner was conceited about his nose, its straight, slender
bridge—his mouth, however, was small.

He always dressed meticulously, *à la mode,* and preferred going to his
Czech tailor in Dresden's Neustadt, partly because he could gossip there.
For years now he had been going to spas alone, or at least not accompanied by his wife, to Carlsbad, Franzensbad, or Piešt'any, and his
amorous doings made him both a pampered and feared figure in Dresden
society.

9

Katharina loved him very much. He shook the house; his Jovian, joy-hurling laughter drew her whenever he was at home, and she was soon granted the privilege of visiting him in his study ("but you've got to keep quiet, baby") and watching him during his experiments. He worked magic. This'll be fine, she heard him say, this can be blended beautifully, the women'll go crazy over it. She silently observed her father's work, watched the larger glasses into which tinctures, milky substances, and schlierens were poured, mysterious and disgusting. He moved playfully, sometimes hopping from one foot to the other, rubbing his hands, leaning his head to one side. He never stayed still for an instant; that was part of him. That is how she'll remember him.

When he felt like it, he wallowed in the Saxon dialect, but he also spoke High German, as well as impeccable French and Italian. He attributed his linguistic talents to his ancestry: Hungarians and Italians, a few Saxons too, but more Bavarians and Czechs. Although Katharina met many of his relatives, she could never fathom these people: they evidently couldn't get along without adventures and catastrophes. I gratefully greet the Janissaries, Magyars, and Mongols among my forebears!, he had exclaimed during a birthday speech, embarrassing no small number of people. He could, if cornered, not give a rap about conventions; he was basically free of them and ignored social rules.

Grandfather Wüllner had owned a pharmacy in Penig, but after leasing it out "with a wife and five boys, so to speak," he served as a ship's apothecary for six years. The children could then repeat dozens of marvelous tales they'd heard from their father. They barely knew him, they knew their mother all the better; she kept them well disciplined amid fits of hysteria, as a result of which three of the five boys ran away at an early age and could not be talked into choosing socially suitable professions. Georg Wüllner went to high school and university only because he was very sickly and dependent on his mother's care. At home, he imitated his brothers' distant pranks, and his mother's curses went deep. When his father was finally discharged from the ship, he took back the pharmacy, successfully selling countless homemade patent medicines; he said right out that cat shit was more effective than this stuff, but when it came to faith and disease, you could cure someone with wind. He died at fifty-two, leaving the pharmacy and the factory, so that the family could plan for the future almost without anxiety.

Katharina knew her grandmother; she avoided the whining woman, who often fought with Georg Wüllner. Katharina was born in the house in Klotzsche; only Dieter had known the small apartment over the pharmacy, in Dresden's Altstadt. It was impossible to cook in the kitchen since Wüllner always did his experiments there, successfully as it turned out: he soon had to expand the output and distribution of his beauty products, rent factory buildings. He discovered the house in Klotzsche during a stroll; in lengthy, drawn-out negotiations, he managed to talk the owners into selling him the villa. He left everything else up to his wife.

But for Katharina he was not only the father who loved surprising his children with crazy presents, who did not run his house, he was also the constant homecomer, the story-teller about whom stories were told, the egoist who drove his wife to the wall, threatening to divorce her or flee: What am I supposed to do here, Susanne? I'm being killed by comfort. You do everything calmly because you find it pleasant. The children, cowering, heard the arguments; only Dieter occasionally had the nerve to interfere; he was put in his place and told to mind his own business. The parents were right, for their queer relationship endured.

I love her more than ever, Wüllner had later said to Katharina, when she knew his amorous affairs by heart; laughing, she reprimanded him, and he cited his age: Who else would have me now except for your mother—that's how insidious I am, right?

She recalls the hands, those repulsive casts of polished bronze that he kept locked in his desk, until Mother happened to find them, pulled them out of the drawer, and lined them up on the desk, five right hands, very diverse, one narrow, the other a bit coarser, with protruding veins on their backs, but clearly female hands—she waited for her husband until he came home late that evening, found her sitting in front of the hands. Unruffled, he sought refuge in laughter: What a tableau, you and the hands of those ladies. Susanne said she was ashamed, especially in regard to his heartless reaction, she didn't find this funny, whereupon he tossed his coat on the divan, pulled a chair over to the desk, and sat down opposite her as if he were visiting himself: Do you really want to know the details, Susanne? And when she didn't answer, he began in a low voice: They're not laid out in the right order, Susanne. Shall I help you? He leaned over and began to rearrange the hands: I don't want to torment you, for God's sake, so please interrupt me if I am draining you; but you did know about it, if not from me, then from others—or at least you had inklings.

He stands up, looks at the casts (rocking on his heels, a habit that is supposed to make him look taller): I admit these things do not reveal good taste—no, for me they're trophies, mnemonic devices, but they don't work.

All at once, looking at him directly she said: Sometimes, like now, I have the impression that you're not normal.

He sits down again. That could be. Do you want to listen to me? She nods.

Philosophy aside, Susanne, I don't appreciate this chat. I only want to give you the factual data about these objects you've found.

He is speaking like a government auditor. Let us begin with the first hand. On the left from your point of view.

She interrupts him: Do you really think, Georg, that I care to listen to your fairy tales?

He does not look up; he pushes the artificial hands a bit closer together and says, These are no fairy tales, Susanne.

She leans back, invites him to begin with a "Go ahead."

Here, this hand emphasized the words of Emilia Galotti. It was eighteen years ago, we had been married for only one year, 1889, do you remember, we saw Teschner perform, she was a wonderful Emilia Galotti. "Violence! Violence? Who cannot defy violence? What we call violence is nothing: seduction is the true violence. I have blood, my father; as youthful, as warm as any woman's blood. My senses are senses too. I stand for nothing. I am good for nothing." I can still hear it, I know it by heart. A bit later, I met her at a banquet. You had a migraine, I think, and begged off. David happened to be visiting, and he came with me. He left the dinner earlier. He found the situation embarrassing, as he told me later. When the company began to break up, I asked her whether I might see her home. She ordered her carriage, and when we arrived, she asked me to accompany her inside. Our affair lasted more than three years. Did you know about it?

Yes.

Who told you?

Does it really matter?

No.

Elise Teschner, he says, is responsible for all these hands. When she was rehearsing Schiller's Mary Stuart, at home, in front of the five full-length mirrors in her bedroom, he concentrated purely on her hands, and when she, exhausted, withdrew into the salon, he said that her art resided in the eloquence of her hands. She agreed with him, stood up, removed this hand, "this hand!" from a dresser drawer, and placed it on the table, saying: You can have it. Should I go on, Susanne?

Of course.

He pushed Elise Teschner's hand aside.

Did you ever see her again?

A couple of times in Berlin. She married again, an aristocratic officer. We see one another occasionally, we're on good terms.

And the second hand?

I don't like it. I've never liked it. It's coarse, do you see? The fingertips are too broad.

It's an experienced hand, it's no longer all that young.

Do you know it, Susanne?

Yes.

It belongs to Marianne Winterhoff.

I know.

You knew about it?

Yes, dear, from the very first day.

It dragged on terribly, he said; it was unpleasant toward the end. It had no beginning; he had slid into it, he had been flirting with her, granted, but not with her alone.

That's not like you, Georg, no.

They met occasionally, at social gatherings, in Kreuzkamm, at the opera.

She's almost one foot taller than you.

You're exaggerating slightly.

The Winterhoffs happened to be in Carlsbad at the same time as Wüllner. He had run into them at the Hotel Pupp; they planned to go on joint excursions and spend a few evenings together. A telegram summoned Winterhoff to Dresden.

He's a pompous ass, Susanne, he thinks that without him the world's going to collapse—or at least his paint factory will. He was agitated, ranting about some mistakes made by his assistant, and he left. He recommended Marianne to my care. I called for her every morning. We played, only hinting at our mutual interest; we teased each other with ambiguities; sometimes she made me look ridiculous by emphasizing her tallness with her clothes, her hats and shoes. I sensed what she was doing, but my anger was mixed with desire. I wasn't the first man with whom she'd so openly cheated on her husband. He was so thoroughly absorbed in his business, he didn't notice anything, refused to notice anything. He's an efficient buffoon, she said whenever his name came up.

Wüllner hoped his wife would interrupt, but she didn't help him out of his growing embarrassment.

We sent the coachman away. More than a week had passed. She expected her husband the next day. A decision had to be made, both of us wanted it. We sent the coachman away, near Ellbogen. We walked up a forest path; she kept stumbling, I took hold of her arms, helping her along, then she held me tight, and we fell to the ground, carried away, forgetting everything.

He had stood up, walking back and forth along the bookcases. I find it disgusting, Susanne, let me stop.

Did Winterhoff come the next day?

Yes.

And that was the end of your dalliance?

On the contrary—Wüllner was talking easily again, she had again succeeded in dispelling his inhibition, making him think he was telling her about everyday things.

We met in her home. We didn't wait. It was the adventure, our response to the propriety we should have observed. But it couldn't last. We returned to society, for which our affair remained just a rumor. The only odd thing is that we've really forgotten each other. When our paths now cross, we aren't troubled by the memory.

Susanne Wüllner said: How silly. And the hand?

What do you mean?

How did you get hold of her hand? If I know Marianne Winterhoff, it couldn't have been so easy talking her into doing something so tasteless.

We had a date in Loschwitz. She wanted to visit an artist, a weaver; I took her to the sculptor who had cast Elise Teschner's hand. She liked his work. I showed her some casts and asked her whether she wouldn't like to "immortalize" her hand. She looked at me, astonished: Why the hand? I flattered her, said her hands were beautiful.

And this one, the third? asked Susanne. It's really attractive, very delicate, a child's hand.

Yes, a child's hand.

A frivolous whim—or?

Her tone had changed. Now she sounded hurt.

No frivolity, he said, it was more like a dream. You don't know her; I only saw her a few times. It was four years ago, in Nice, just before the outbreak of the war. Bertrand had invited me; he wanted to lease a few of my patents. A charming fellow, cultivated, an attentive host. I was staying at the Negresco. April was sweeping the boardwalk with a soft wind. I felt so exhilarated, so strangely free of everything. The day I arrived, Bertrand took me through the old city. We were planning to negotiate the licensing rights that afternoon, in the presence of a lawyer. We had separated after lunch, in the finest spirits. I wanted to rest for an hour, and I even fell asleep.

I woke up, bathed in sweat. I could barely move, my arms and legs were almost paralyzed. I obviously had a fever. I rang for a messenger and wrote a brief note to Bertrand, asking him to send me a doctor. Bertrand arrived with one in less than an hour. I had food poisoning. The doctor prescribed a few things, sending out a bellboy. Bertrand calmed me down, promising to notify you. We could finish our negotiations in a couple of days. The doctor felt it would be better to have a nurse in attendance. An elderly woman in a nurse's uniform came; I didn't understand her French, and there was also a girl of sixteen or seventeen, who introduced herself as the doctor's daughter. She told me to call her Denise. When the old woman washed me, the girl discreetly vanished into the small adjacent salon, waiting until the nurse called her.

The old woman kept talking away at me, I didn't understand a word. I could barely shake my head, every motion was painful. Denise interpreted: The nurse had said we could expect another bout of fever. I shouldn't worry. They would take turns watching me. The fever came as announced. Toward evening, when only a small candle was burning, I woke up again, I was shaking. I tried to call out, a hand settled on my forehead. Denise was sitting next to me. Slowly, as if she assumed I knew very little French, she said: Are you cold, Monsieur? I nodded. She gave me herb tea. It had probably been brewed by the old nurse. Is the tea helping? she asked. Not especially. I watched her as she walked over to the window with short, silent steps, drew the curtain, went to the door, turned the key, and without disrupting the resolute flow of her movements, stopped at the chaise longue opposite my bed, pulled her dress over her head, put it down neatly, as she did her underwear and stockings. She came over to me naked, slipped into bed with me, and said she would warm me up, I would soon feel better.

Her father visited me that evening. The old woman had replaced Denise. He was amazed at my enormous improvement but said I should still take care of myself tomorrow. (The next day, I nevertheless negotiated with Bertrand. I was satisfied with the results. The war spoiled everything. I haven't heard from him since.) I asked the doctor if Denise could have a farewell lunch with me: I said I was grateful to her, she had tended me so charmingly. He agreed, but warned me not to seduce the girl, that would come soon enough. We dined in a good restaurant on Rue Masséna. I was afraid she'd be restrained, the memory of the previous evening might embarrass her. She listened to my stories about Dresden, my family, the factory; her childlike quality confused me, for she often seemed more sophisticated than I. She took her leave at the park, unexpectedly; she said she had a date with a girlfriend, she'd forgotten all about it, she had to hurry. She kissed me, saying: Now you have to remain healthy for a while, Monsieur.

What about her hand? asked Susanne. How did you get it?

At lunch, I had told her it was her hands, they alone, that had healed me. She smiled, holding them out to me. They're small, she said.

Father always says they're going to remain a child's hands. Would you like to take one along? Should I have the cook chop it off? Should I call the waiter?

Amused, I begged off. No, but one can have hands cast, by a sculptor.

Then it will be cold, it won't be able to heal, she said.

But I can remember, I said.

A few weeks later, a package arrived, containing this hand; there was no accompanying letter.

His story had drained him, yet left him in a good mood. He wanted to go to bed. As he rose, Susanne pushed him back into the chair. And what about these two hands, Georg?

He pointed to the fourth hand, pretending aloofness, which she noticed: It's big, rough. It wasn't much. A maid at the Luisenhof. She was coarse, but not stupid. It didn't even last six months. Susanne asked whether she had really been "coarse," or whether he had only imagined it because of her social position. You're disgusting, Georg. You retell your stories, worming your way out of them. You inveigle your way out. What about the fifth hand?

She had sat down opposite him, as at the beginning; but now, *she* was directing the conversation. When he tried to speak, she waved him off: You don't have to introduce her to me. She lives in an apartment in Neustadt, you pay her rent. I don't know how often you visit her, I don't spy on you. She's the divorced wife of an officer in the Royal Bodyguard; her henna hair and her beautiful bosom are famous in certain circles. You keep her, but you no longer know what to do with her. She's become a headache. The hand—well, yes, it's well-groomed, overly manicured out of boredom.

She smoothed her dress, a gesture he was familiar with; she said, Thank you, Georg. Good night.

Years later, she told Katharina she had sobbed all night, repeating the stories over and over again, learning them by heart, and she had resolved to leave her husband as soon as possible; but she had been too weak; she had loved him more than ever, she had been ashamed.

As a child, Katharina happened to stumble on the hands in the open drawer when she was allowed into her father's study. Gutsi, when asked about them, mumbled that it was stuff and nonsense. The adolescent girl received hints, forgetting them, until the aging mother told her the story of the five hands exactly as if she had memorized every sentence, using the intonation of the man she had loved, and who had died in the meantime: I admit these things do not reveal good taste.

3
The Garden

Until her marriage in 1923, the garden was Katharina's true home. Not the white villa, the vast living-room, which, cold and pompous, remained eerie for her; nor her two rooms in which toys and old furniture gradually accumulated. She said she had never been able to fathom the garden fully; if she were asked, say, to paint its layout, she would keep getting confused, there would be "blanks," undiscovered or forgotten things.

But, she said, even at the age of four, she had felt "redeemed" when, holding Gutsi's hand, she returned from a walk and arrived at the garden gate. If it was locked, they had to ring a bell (she couldn't reach its iron handle until the age of seven), and Peter, the gardener, eventually materialized with a huge key. The house was barely visible from here. The driveway divided at an erratic block, the two ribbons vanishing in the dense green. People always followed the right-hand path (because it was customary?), just like the carriages and, later, the cars. Katharina's favorite tree stood right behind the block: an ancient weeping birch, she could conceal herself behind its drooping branches, a hall redolent of moss and damp wood.

Gutsi shouts! Her shouts are part of the many diverse noises of the garden. Like the cries of birds. She doesn't always have to obey the shouts; they keep the nanny close by.

If she continues along the path, toward the house, which gradually

17

becomes visible (but never entirely until you're in the forecourt, since trees and bushes keep blocking your view), a vast lawn opens up to the right, sloping down in gently springing waves to a pond. The few clusters of trees arranged asymmetrically on the lawn make them look as if they were wandering slow and dignified across the grass.

The meadow had changed over the years. Father had planted birches, quickly growing trees, and set up a wooden platform by the pond, with white chairs, benches, and tables on the platform (they often danced there, the wood eventually became black and shiny); a few duck couples and their offspring swam on the pond; in the middle of the war, a small castle had been built for them on a pilework, with bull's-eye panes and lots of useless turrets; during the war, between the pond and the "woods" bordering the garden, Mother had her chicken farm, a rather rickety wooden coop hammered together by Peter, and a wire lean-to in which the poultry could run around; the chickens, Mother's pride and joy ("Other people have to go hungry, all they have is turnips, but we have fresh eggs every day!") were a special robust breed; Katharina remembered that they were called blond or black or giant leghorns. The cackling flock vanished between 1922 and 1923; Gutsi insisted on getting rid of the chickens, for she and Susanne Wüllner had assumed responsibility for them, and ultimately, Gutsi had to take care of them alone.

The "woods"—she didn't know every nook and cranny; her childhood fear, imbued by Dieter, remained: he had told her that two grizzly bears lived there in a hollow tree and that sometimes there were also wolves. She was afraid to go into the woods unless she was holding Gutsi's hand, even though Father had given Dieter a good scolding and tried to instill courage in her: The only predators there, he said, were maybe three mice and two squirrels, and she did like them, after all. No, there were no grizzlies; it had been amply proven to her, and Dieter would have forgotten his fantasies long ago if she hadn't come to him before her wedding and asked him and Peter to get the benches from the woods, she didn't have the nerve, whereupon he laughed, asking whether she was still scared of the wild bears. Wolves, too, she replied, laughing, I know they're not there, but are they really not there? As a result, she knew only the main path through the small grove, not the twisting trails of the boys, the dilapidated tree houses and the clearing, where the boys had their meetings, protected from the displeasure of the grownups; the grass was six feet high now, it was too difficult for Peter to mow there.

Her first big party took place against that dreaded background, that trap set by a brother's fantasies for scared little girls; to be sure, in their childhood, they had already been allowed to join the adult soirees on warm summer evenings; the children were nicely dressed up, they were

offered petits-fours or other pastries on silver trays, and skillfully eluded
the delighted flattery of ladies and gentlemen. Katharina could hear it,
the humming, the music of the small orchestra, especially the waltz
violins, which she loved, to which she danced just like the grownups—
"just look at the little doll!"—the lantern light, colorfully dispersed by
the evening wind, the flames of pitch torches that Peter had driven into
the ground—she did know how parties were planned and given here, but
when they celebrated her eighteenth birthday in February, Father had
spoken about a "belated birthday party in summer." That could be
arranged, he said, despite the bad time, he would dig up wine, there'd be
no lack of guests.

The problem of what to wear kept her busy for weeks; Gutsi and
Mother suggested, she rejected, she had moods and stage fright, worrying
that rain would spoil everything, and Peter expressed the opinion of the
masses: It wasn't proper splurging in such an earnest time but it was
typical of the Wüllner life style, always ignoring the general taste. The
war had ended a year and a half ago. Let them squawk! Father didn't let it
bother him; he indulged her excitement by talking about surprises,
assuring her she'd be amazed: You'll be amazed, little princess!, yet she
was a couple of inches taller than he, "Little Princess!", and he got the
entire household excited, involving everyone in the preparations, the
great secrecy. Don't worry about a thing! Gutsi had sewn a frock of lace
and cambric, designed by Mother: as if you'll never wear anything else,
they said when she tried it on; she attempted to walk in a floating,
haughty way.

Mother, Gutsi, and Cook made open sandwiches with vegetables,
yeast marinades, eggs, and a smidgen of sausage. There was more than
enough wine. Lanterns were suspended between the trees, Peter still had
a store of torches; last of all, he waxed the planks by the pond, singing at
the top of his lungs; Mother thought it was crazy of him to wax them, but
he's doing it for you.

They had done it for her, and before the first guests came, the seven
men from the opera chorus, hired by Father, filed past her in their
tuxedoes, introducing themselves, bowing; the rehearsing violins could
soon be heard through the garden.

It's your party, Father had said, I'll give a speech, if it's appropriate,
otherwise just enjoy yourself, dance. Carry yourself well, Kathi, you're
the center.

The family waited for their guests at the meeting-point of the two
driveways, Dieter and Ernst had come from Leipzig, Elle had left her den
in Hellerau for this evening, but she was accompanied by a rather bizarre-
looking elderly man, whom Father, casually sizing him up, nicknamed

"Trapper-Vulture-Beak." Katharina said she had felt as if her arms and legs were dying, she was growing stiff, she would never again be able to stir from the spot, she hadn't caught a single name or known any of the faces. But the tension had dissolved; when Kasimir Bülow turned up, she knew her party was a success, no matter how much the others might criticize the next day.

She had met Kasimir through Elle; he really wasn't her type, a brawny guy with indolent, almost lurking movements, his blond hair very short; he worked in a printing press and was planning to become a publisher; his political views were far crazier than Elle's, but he skillfully held back such remarks from her parents, so Father thought her "second love" was smarter and more educated than poor Eberhard.

The small orchestra had begun to play; taking Father's arm she preceded the others down to the pond, where she settled at the head of the large table, between Father and Kasimir; Gutsi suddenly appeared behind her and placed a stole around her shoulders.

Father had the first dance; after that, she didn't care in whose arms she lay.

When had she learned to tango? Kasimir had taken her hand, and they had run over to the ponies; the shadows of the animals stood out against the lighter sky, they snorted, pranced toward her, up to the fence; she softly called Alexander II, who resembled his predecessor like a twin; she hugged him until Kasimir drew her away, saying it wasn't time for the pony. They hurried to the gazebo, sat down on the small veranda, kissed, and stared at the wooden filigree of the porch. She can't remember what they talked about, probably just silly things, and Kasimir vanished from the Hellerau circle a short time later.

Gutsi called, called her back to the party; she danced until morning, until one lantern after another went out, the torches shrank down, the laughter turned into whispering, and Kasimir vanished after bowing perfectly to Mother. Katharina thanked her father; it was light out, they were drinking coffee in the living room. That was one of our best parties, said Mother, and Gutsi walked her to her room, helped her undress: Sleep through the morning, don't run away from us, Kathi. Nono.

But the garden: A narrow footpath runs from the driveway, to the right, past the house, under a rose trellis flanked by two benches hewn out of tree trunks; the path melts into the "back meadow," with the corral at its extreme edge.

Alexander had soon gotten companions; his airy shed was replaced by a stable for five horses, two large and three small ones; the children rode out together, with friends too. Father had "gifted himself" with a horse, as he exaggeratedly put it; all but two had been requisitioned in the war; now there were three again.

At night, when the windows were open, you could hear the animals snorting, sometimes neighing, stamping their hooves on the grass, scratching—those were noises she never forgot, dragging them along, talking about them when she sat next to the cattle car in Landshut, twenty years later, waiting to move on, waiting for the two whistles of the locomotive—she spoke about the horses "as if we were at home."

I've left out the gazebo, she said; it gathered stories that I cannot tell; it was a refuge for Dieter and Elle, just as Ernst claimed the woods for himself. The pond belonged to me, the meadow, the paddock.

She said: The meadow behind the house, the apple trees and plum trees were Mother's precinct; the beech hedge shielded us from our neighbor's property, and Mother made sure it was always correctly pruned: wide below, narrow on top, almost like a pyramid. The party shut out almost everything from her memory; it made her forget that Ernst and Dieter had been soldiers, that Kasimir limped because a bullet had smashed his knee; she didn't remember Father's nimble evasions and maneuvers, his attempts to have cucumber milk declared vital to the war effort, or Mother's skill with turnips in the kitchen, or the potato patch in the back meadow, the vegetable beds, the shooting in the street, which prolonged the war, or Father's farewell address to the Kaiser.

She had seen the garden only once more, after her parents had been forced to sell the house. In 1929, she had stood at the gate, trying to convince herself that her home was somewhere else. Now nothing was the way it used to be.

4
Escape with Eberhard

The reason was awful: The war had deprived the house of men and it needed help. For the garden and to replace Peter, who was lying in the army hospital a second time, they found Herr Kowinetz, who didn't look even close to seventy; Susanne Wüllner had a hard time discouraging his landscaping ambitions. Eberhard Brodbeck, a high school student from Radebeul, reported for minor chores; he turned out to be a lazy dreamer, who charmed the women. Herr Kowinetz couldn't stand him and rejected his help. So Eberhard made himself useful in the house, in the kitchen, running errands and constantly entertaining the girls.

Fifteen-year-old Katharina succumbed to his transparent spell. Nearly all his stories were subsequently exposed as flimflam, but in the beginning she believed everything he told her: Apparently, he had traveled quite a bit with his affluent parents, he had been to Oriental countries, and, needless to say, Italy, France, Russia. It was quite reckless sending an entire family on incessant secret missions that were useful to the Kaiser.

Mother made her cutbacks; whenever Father was home on furlough (in the third year of the war, cucumber milk could no longer keep him out of uniform), he listened to the boy and laughed, urging him to give his best regards to the Kaiser. He told him not to overdo his adventures for the Fatherland. These comments embarrassed Eberhard, but, no

22

sooner had Wüllner left the kitchen than Eberhard continued his anecdotes. Katharina was annoyed by her father's "bad taste."

Although Eberhard was only a few months older than Katharina,
there was nothing childish or immature about him; he was a well-
proportioned young man, fairly tall for his age, with a narrow, elongated
head. He wore his hair in waves down to the back of his neck.

She received her first kiss from Eberhard.

She had begun her diary with him and continued it, with interrup-
tions, or rather abridgements; after the birth of each child, she would jot
down its name, weight, size in abbreviations, then the first emotions,
sounds (she was more detailed about Annamaria: in 1929, when her
marriage with Ferdinand was on the rocks, the notes on her sorrow
helped to ease her dead-end existence). She had started her diaries with
Eberhard; the first two, 1917/18 and 1919–22, in oilcloth albums, the
subsequent ones in normal, unlined school notebooks, the pages of
which she creased along the edges in order to enter the dates:

> He kissed me! I nearly fainted. Mummi must not notice any-
> thing. Gutsi will keep still about it if she finds out! Yes, my life is
> beginning!

This life, which she now wanted to lead independently, began with
the cajolery of a notorious liar, whose cloud castles had a solid founda-
tion for her. Whenever Eberhard could escape from his chores, which
were few and far between anyhow, they met in the stable, and lay in each
other's arms, trying out each other's lips, their own lips, fearing someone
might surprise them, touching each other cautiously, and, minutes later,
returning with flushed faces to a public that remained unaware.

She said she had become more and more confused, losing her
surroundings of which she had always been certain, she could no longer
confide in anyone, not even Gutsi—she distanced herself. Furthermore,
Eberhard kept criticizing her parents' life style; he found it extravagant
and thoughtless. These people stuck their heads in chests of gold, he
said, and didn't know how awful things looked in the world, how much
poverty there was. And they ignored the war, he said. She felt he was
exaggerating: after all, the men were away, at the front; some had been
wounded, like Dieter and Peter, and if they hadn't had Mother's chickens, they would have gotten sick of turnips long ago—but Katharina
didn't have the nerve to retort; eventually she adjusted to Eberhard's
furious stupidities, made them her own. But she did except her parents.

Eberhard always knew the latest news from the front. Katharina recalled that in 1917 there had been a peculiar about-face in the boy's comments. At first, he had babbled on about victories, the invincibility of the German troops; he had deified Hindenburg and Ludendorff, reeling off a litany of battle names; she said she could still hear the constant refrain of Chemin des Dames. But then he had seen through the machinations of the crowned heads, the generals, the tycoons; they came to terms, he said, on the backs of their nations, and the proletariat was always humiliated, bled white. The sufferings caused by the war would unleash the proletariat's energy once and for all. He said he was attending a discussion group and had made up his mind to join the Social Democrats.

She had gained a certain distance that made her more alert. Without admitting it, she realized that Eberhard was little more than a pretext.

Whenever he was in the house and the garden, she was with him. His declamations became more heated, but also more cogent; he could quote now, cite names, especially Rosa Luxemburg, whom he worshiped like a saint. He said his group had petitioned the government to release Rosa from prison; she was the only one, he said, who knew where the path of the working masses was leading, she had the vision, the knowledge; they had to follow her. Katharina asked him how his father was reacting—wouldn't the Secret Envoy throw him out of his home? But Eberhard waved it off as a bagatelle, which she understood only after they parted company: his father, an optician, knew nothing of the monarchistic feats that his son, while still in his imperial phase, had saddled him with. Now Eberhard needed no more heroic deeds from his father; Brodbeck, Sr. had been replaced by Rosa Luxemburg. Katharina was haunted by her erotic sensations. She dreamed about Eberhard, and also other boys, and she was ashamed of these unconscious fantasies, but Eberhard had helped her attain a level of freedom that separated her from Gutsi, Mother, and Father; she thought Elle enjoyed that freedom in a different way and she considered it important for her own future. Father's business know-how, his crazy projects, now struck her as questionable, Mother's domesticity as petty. She decided to "give herself" to Eberhard; she instantly found her decision comical, but couldn't hit on any other solution, and thought hazily about her first period, the terror that had been strangely unphysical, not really a bodily disruption, even though she had felt the blood and suffered cramps. She had avoided talking about it to her mother; the women, Gutsi and Mother, had registered the event with tacit understanding, had been a little more tender, Gutsi had brought her some gauze, hoping she would manage on her own.

She envisioned that her closeness with Eberhard would be similar. She described all this in her diary, and also what followed: the flight, and Eberhard's helpless collapse.

August 2 (1917)

Everything is coming to a head now. Eberhard plans to go away with me. I am leaving the family. I do not feel quite comfortable about it; it need not be a permanent solution, of course. But it is an attempt! I am squandering my life. . . .

As long as we are on vacation, we are free. He also thinks we ought to know one another better, test one another properly. That is true. Tomorrow morning, when Mummi is in town, we will sneak away. Eberhard has explored an as yet uninhabited new building in the garden town. One can enter it through a basement window. He has spent the night there several times. How does he work it out with his parents? He won't tell me.

And after that? We shall see. Mummi will probably be worried. I really do not care. Perhaps she and Gutsi will find everything merely eccentric.

August 4

I am in a tiny, absolutely empty room (no; there are three blankets, two suitcases, and I), I am kneeling at the window seat and writing in my diary. Eberhard has been out for two hours now, obtaining food. However, I believe he is impelled by a hodgepodge of feelings, not an empty belly.

The house is pretty, we have tried out all the rooms—this one here, with the window facing a tiny garden, is the one we like the most. I like the kitchen too, but we won't be able to use the stove.

I left home as if I were not doing anything special. No one noticed. I do not know what I packed in my suitcase. Eberhard waited for me at the trolley stop, and we took the seven o'clock trolley to Hellerau. A trip! Something like a wedding trip! If Mummi had seen us, or Father; the other passengers paid no special attention to us. Eberhard chattered like a madman. I did not listen. The streetcar could have driven into a tunnel, I would not have noticed. I noticed how awkwardly Eberhard was behaving.

Perhaps he had already lost courage. But he was also able to laugh charmingly.

I now know that there is no such thing as happiness, only its harbinger. Or what? I am writing nonsense.

He is away. He will come any moment. We will eat together, squatting on the floor like Moslems. Then we will place our arms on the window seat and wait for the evening. We will snuggle together as we did yesterday evening.

He had no courage. I did not expect it.

Yes, we were both clumsy; I a lot less. Eberhard still had his glibness. He repeated long-winded conversations he had with his friends, he told me about Rosa's sufferings, then he started talking about Hellerau. How wonderful it is here, he said, the inhabitants had started an association, or else an association had been started, made up of tenants. They cannot be evicted, they can move out only if they want to. Tenancy can be bequeathed. And rents cannot be raised. That is socialism, he said, even though it is only for well-to-do and educated people. Now I suddenly realize that I am alone— no, I realize how alone I am: I don't know why Eberhard is not back. He cannot need all this time to shop.

We made love yesterday. (When I imagine this diary falling into someone else's hands, Gutsi's or Mummi's! It is unthinkable!) Eberhard was spirited at first, but then he grew timid when I lay down on the blankets. The floor was pretty hard. At first, I was embarrassed, but beyond a certain point my fear was gone, and I did not care what Everhard might think of me. After all, he wanted to also! Only it was not the same as in the stable where we had to worry about a surprise visitor. Here we were really by ourselves. And everything changed. I discovered how childish Eberhard is, how comically he behaves.

He lay down next to me like a log and did not stir. I caressed him, took his hand, nestled against him, and finally kissed him. His lips were dry. I wanted to ask him whether he was feeling all right, but I did not. (Can a girl show that she wants to make love? I am certain that Mummi would despise me. Not even Father would understand me. Maybe Gutsi, but she has probably never had such feelings.) After we had been lying like that for a while and Eberhard never even thought of turning to me, I stood up, looked down at him—his eyes were closed—and I asked him why we had run away in the first place. He did not answer. Fine, I said, if you don't know, then I know. I love you. That's why. I took off my skirt and blouse. He did not open his eyes, but he did hear me undress, and he said in a pleading tone: Don't do it, please don't. I kept only my panties on. Gutsi has often admired my bosom. She says I have beautiful, opulent breasts. Now I was a little embarrassed again. I lay down next to him, took his hand, and placed it on my breast. His hand was heavy, stupid. At that moment, I despised him. He waited a long time before kissing me. His hands caressed my back. I said to him: Get your clothes off too. He undressed lying down and acted strange again. I decided simply to overlook all these stupidities.

All at once, he pounced on me. It hurt. Saliva dribbled from his lips to my neck and it disgusted me. The pain vanished very slowly and I moved with him. But the feeling of happiness I had looked forward to did not come. He was alien to me and I was alien to myself. All at once, he pulled away and said: We can't afford to have a baby. If he remained with me, I'd have a baby, he said. I preferred not feeling his weight anymore. I probably do not love him. I have probably made a mistake. But I want to remain with him. We will get used to one another.

It is evening now. Eberhard is not back yet. I am hungry. I drank water in the kitchen. Where can he be? I will sleep, that makes time pass most swiftly.

August 5, evening

I am home again!! Eberhard humiliated me. I am going to handle my life differently. Not be so naive, so rash. Mummi did not scold, although she had suffered terrible anxieties. Father had ordered her not to call the police. He was quite monosyllabic when he saw me. Gutsi stayed with me until half an hour ago. I asked her to leave me by myself. She kept saying: I just can't. Now I am crying.

Eberhard did not come back that night. He must have sneaked up to the apartment door in the morning and slipped in a letter. I did not find it until I was about to leave. I did not have to reflect for long: I had no choice but to go home. I decided to act above it all. When I packed my few belongings into the valise, I discovered the letter, the note. I want to copy it here. I will never see that bigmouth again! The note says: "Dear Kathi, Our goals were too big. It won't work. Let us wait until the world no longer puts obstacles in our way. Kisses! Your Eberhard!"

Toward evening the household had gotten more and more agitated First, they had called out Katharina's name, then looked for her in the surrounding area. Gutsi had checked with Katharina's girlfriends, and finally Susanne Wüllner had gathered everyone in her small salon: Gutsi, the kitchenmaid, Herr Kowinetz (sighing adroitly); they voiced all sorts of conjectures, they envisioned rapes, which only Gutsi argued against; why shouldn't Kathi have run away, perhaps even been kidnapped? She's only a child! cried Susanne Wüllner. She's no child, Gutsi corrected her, she's a girl, precocious and certainly with fantasies of her own, which Mother then argued against. She simply couldn't conceive of that, Katharina still acted very childlike. Because that's how you want to see her, Gutsi retorted, bringing the circular debate to an end—that was how Wüllner found them; he was quickly drawn into the perplexed group, but he was much calmer. He agreed with Gutsi: if no man was involved, it would be best to send Kowinetz to Eberhard's parents; if their offspring was likewise away then the conclusion was obvious. Kowinetz promised to hurry and then returned surprisingly fast; however, the waiting had now made Wüllner nervous, too. The boy, Eberhard, was perfectly fine, he was with his parents. Since yesterday afternoon. He claimed he hadn't seen Katharina, much less taken her for a walk. He was very worried and had asked whether he should look for Katharina. Kowinetz added that he had rejected the offer. They would really have to call the police now. Wüllner waved the idea off again. If he knew Katharina, he said, she'd find her way home.

(So Eberhard had betrayed her; she didn't learn this until weeks later, and it no longer hurt. The whole business made her distrustful: love could be easily aroused and even more easily forgotten.)

Wüllner had kept telling the others to go to bed, or at least rest a bit, it was enough if he stayed up; but the group did not disband. They stopped speaking. Wüllner pulled out his watch at regular intervals and, whenever vague noises came from the garden, Gutsi and Susanne Wüllner would jump up, peer through the windows, stand anxiously in the doorway for a while, and then return to their places. Long past midnight, Susanne collapsed. Weeping, she knelt before her husband, begging him to call the police. He said he didn't want to compromise himself and the child; he would wait until morning.

When Katharina timidly rang the bell, Wüllner left, asking Kowinetz to leave too; he said he would thank him for his assistance. Thus, Katharina found only her mother and—a broad shadow in the background—Gutsi: she was surprised at the cheeriness, the composure of the two women, although their eyes were red from fatigue and weeping. She was welcomed without rebukes, like someone returning from a long journey, as if they were terribly delighted at her slightly late homecoming. She didn't see her father until later.

August 6

No, I am not ashamed. Gutsi was of the opinion that I should be ashamed. No! Yet I cannot be proud either. Had it not been Eberhard, but someone else, my life would have changed. I am certain.

5
Portrait and Self-Portrait

Katharina was developing at a tempestuous rate. Susanne Wüllner had written her brother David; she was somewhat anxious watching this burst into adulthood, for Kathi was still a teenager and could not possibly cope with all these new sensations.

"A sweet creature," I tell you. You haven't seen her for a year, and you won't recognize her. I'm enclosing a photograph which was taken with difficulty. Katharina refused to be photographed. She finds Matthias (you know—our old family photographer in Altstadt) silly, and she says none of his photographs come out right. You have to keep posing, she says, until you get cramps and you look so ugly in every photo. Georg, who has been absolutely in love with her ever since he's been in the army and seeing her only on short furloughs, talked her into it: he said he wanted to carry a likeness of his beautiful youngest daughter at all times. She prepared meticulously for the session, which led to new arguments, for I advised her to dress up, while she preferred everyday theatrics; I yielded to her taste after Gutsi appealed to me. Katharina had decided on an airy muslin blouse and a dusty pink taffeta skirt. She had gotten Gutsi to make the blouse, and it really shows off her figure, as you can see. Nevertheless, Kathi is right when she says that the picture actually distorts reality. Her face is far too lively, no single moment is enough to capture what it can express. She looks pretty in the picture, but she is more than just that. Georg may be exaggerating when he calls her beautiful; there are more attractive girls among her school friends, perhaps more fiery ones, too. Even Elle, I feel, is more striking. The delightful thing about Kathi is the clarity of her emotions. I really don't know why I am writing you all these things. Why am I praising my daughter to my brother? I am a slightly crazy matchmaker. Presumably, her face will not change much more. It is oddly completed, mature. She is the opposite of Elle in every way, yet she is drawn to Elle's high-flying urge for freedom; she so greatly admires her elder sister. Elle has her red hair from Georg's family. Katharina's black hair comes from us. Granted, her blue eyes are alien to me. She does have a Jewish touch.

Sometimes I catch myself gazing at her, totally absorbed. She is used to it. I am fascinated by her manner: She reacts abruptly to everything that happens around her; she cannot dissemble. Her face plays with great sensitivity, alternating between tension and indolence. Sometimes guests are astonished at her narrow head. When Katharina wears her hair combed back tightly, she looks like Nefertiti, that Egyptian queen whose bust was recently found. Her eyebrows, straight lines, are nearly blond—which always amazes people. She has a small birthmark on her upper lip, which we often tease her about.

You can have a look at her soon. Her inner feelings, however, are not very open. She can feel joy like none of the other children. She can also close herself off completely, and I fear she has a great number of secrets.

When the war broke out, she was beside herself. She was swept off her feet by the general euphoria, indeed so intensely, that we we were afraid this twelve-year-old girl would go off with the military transports just to be near the jubilant warriors. She changed in 1917. Dieter had been wounded; she visited him at the military hospital in Albrechtstadt and returned with the opinion that animals can never be as cruel to each other as human beings. Ernst encouraged her along these lines. His political eccentricities, which she had previously smiled at if not mocked, were now decisive for her. She read Socialist pamphlets, and believed in the slogans of the pacifists. And then there is Elle with her lunatics in Hellerau! None of this reaches Georg. He says that the children have to learn how to live and that they seem to be learning zealously and effectively.

I have to break off, my dear. Gutsi is summoning me to my duties. It is becoming more and more difficult filling the pots for this gluttonous crew. The newspapers say that the situation on the

Western front is stabilizing. I do not have that impression. This war is getting more and more horrible. Thank goodness Georg is not stationed right at the front and Dieter has two more weeks' medical leave. They still have to get Ernst. He received his draft notice several days ago. He will not exactly be the most eager soldier. Gutsi is pressing me!

Mother had asked her to come to the salon for a "confidential conversation." This room was Katharina's favorite in the entire house; it was barely larger than a cell, with very few, light-mahogany furnishings and a wonderfully soft, crunchy couch, which you could sink into, burying your face in the pillows. In summer the windows were always open; you looked at the garden, the light flowed in strands across the red carpet, with its strutting peacock-like birds. Susanne Wüllner was sitting at the secretary, her back stiff, tense. She had barely looked to the side or greeted Kathi.

What's wrong, Mummi?

(It must have been some kind of embarrassing matter.)

Have I done something wrong? Is it so bad?

Oh, no.

She turned the chair halfway round to the girl, leaned forward, folded her hands on her knees, didn't look up.

She said she had to speak to her a little about everything.

Everything? Has so much happened?

Such conversations were necessary from time to time, said Susanne. She spoke in a stilted way and was embarrassed. She didn't glance up.

Come out with it, Mummi. Is it about Eberhard again? Do you or Father have something against the discussion group? Have I misbehaved? Do you want to tell me about it?

Susanne Wüllner sighed: Katharina, you have a certain tone which I cannot cope with. Now that you mention it, I do want to enlighten you about something. You lead a life that few girls of your age and social background can lead. The same is true for Elle. You are fifteen. I consider it possible that country girls of the same age are having certain experiences. Most likely apathetically and under the pressure of circumstances. But you? Don't you notice that your schoolmates are keeping away from you? Their parents find you irresponsible. You are bringing us (she glanced up for the first time) into disrepute. I must reproach myself for not having looked after you properly. Gutsi is a dear, to be sure, but too indulgent, and she can seldom say no to you children. What has become of Ernst? He is a political guerrilla, a lunatic. Perhaps it runs in the family. When I think about your father.

But Mummi, said Katharina, you're exaggerating, you're afraid of things that are strange to you. I'm supposed to be a child, I know, I'm supposed to remain one for a long time. In three months, I'll be sixteen. Am I supposed to be a child for another three years? So you can marry me off well?

You're precocious. You all were. Dieter, Ernst, especially Elle. I had hoped you'd turn out different. Come here. Sit close to me.

Now her voice was again as Katharina would keep it in her memory: full of protective warmth. Come here! Kathi.

You gave away something that you will never have again. Do you fully realize that? She paused: Don't you want to answer me, Kathi?

Of course.

She pushed the girl away. Sit across from me. You do not have to answer if you do not wish to.

Katharina had the ability to become unexpectedly childlike for others, to seem hurt. Now she protected herself in that way. But it was also possible for her to be more adult at times, almost superior to her mother.

Keep talking, Mummi.

Your indifference is driving me mad.

But I'm not indifferent.

You might have a baby.

I don't know.

At sixty, Katharina said—and she clearly remembered that moment—she would have loved to burst out laughing; but her mother's anxiety kept her from doing it. She was the child, not I, although I really didn't even know how a baby is conceived—whether a single time is enough, perhaps just a kiss—and even though she had made me completely unsure of myself. Then she began to speak, spoke past me, to herself: when I met your father I didn't know anything about all that, no, I knew nothing, only rumors, and above all, the feelings, child, which in this stage are probably more accurate than any knowledge, at least that is how I remember it, and our wedding night was terrible; he was gross, ignored me, ignored my fear and pain, he thought only of himself; when he fell asleep next to me, I hated him; he was a stranger who had violated me, whose kisses were different from the ones I had experienced before. Now he was my husband. No one had ever so much as hinted at what lay in store for me, my mother could not have let such offensive things cross her lips, and I learned nothing from that, nothing. I left you alone. I should have explained a few things to you. But how? Who taught me, for goodness sake? It could be so natural. But it's not. It embarrasses me just to think about it.

Why? asked Katharina.

Her mother kept talking, ignoring her: You're too young. It's a bad way to start. We couldn't shield you, not even Gutsi could. You didn't trust us—or else we didn't worry about you, I didn't even realize how much you'd grown. But you're a child, for me you're a child. What should I do with you? And if a baby comes . . . Katharina said very loud, and felt heartless: Can a baby really come, Mummi?

It was as if Susanne Wüllner could see her daughter again after a long absence: Yes, if you—

There were words she didn't know, didn't dare speak.

If we were naked together, said Katharina.

Yes.

But he said we mustn't have a child and he went away.

Perhaps he knew it, says Susanne Wüllner, lost in thought again.

What should he have known?

You would have sensed it.

That he was with me.

There's something, in the end—

"That was not all," Katharina wrote in her diary. "Eberhard cheated me once again, without my knowledge. There is a very high peak, I know retrospectively that I waited for it. He was cowardly in every way. Here too. How wretched."

What, Mummi?

It is hard to explain, Kathi, I just can't, no, no, I can't.

She had gotten up, walked around Katharina, and now stood behind her.

It can be very beautiful. You both just have to be in love.

I did love Eberhard.

Of course, child.

After a helpless pause, her mother said: I don't want to keep you, Kathi. But if you don't bleed as usual, you must come to me.

But I've been bleeding since yesterday, Mummi—whereupon Susanne Wüllner burst out laughing, fell back into the chair, impatiently slammed the backs of her hands against her lips, and snapped at Katharina: Well, then go.

In 1964, after visiting her mother in Stuttgart, Annamaria, in great confusion about the aging woman's life style, wrote to her sister Camilla: "She almost arrogantly considers herself young and free. Sometimes she's even vulgar. And she has no restraint in conversation. Mama was always peculiar—how often did we enjoy that in our childhood—but now she overdoes it. Her makeup is obnoxious. A few days ago, I discovered that she wears black lingerie. An old woman!"

6

Mother Gazes at the Sunset or
Who Wants to Join the Army?

Sometimes, at lunch, they spoke about a possible war. Wüllner made light of the rumors: after all, he traveled a lot and he found everything generally peaceful. Fine, one can understand that the Kaiser feels uncomfortable about the Entente Cordiale; now even the Czar is against us. But did that mean war? No. But none of the adults believed him, despite his knowledge of the world; and Uncle David, usually not a skeptic, lamented a hysteria that he said had attacked everybody, threatening to blind them; Mother agreed with him—besides, one could see more soldiers in the street than usual, and Gutsi simply spoke about "a bad feeling," which she said had never deceived her, no.

Dieter was waiting to be conscripted. The house changed during those days. Everything seemed provisional. No one saw to it that things remained where they were; they were treated more carelessly, more forgetfully, and so the family was always looking for them.

On Sundays they were always on the move: Katharina remembered the intensely expectant moments on the Brühl Terrace, the light, the voices of many people, gulls soaring across the water, the river with boats and steamships. "Look, here comes our steamer!" "It can't be, we're too early." "Is everyone here?" "Where's Elle?" "Who's got the picnic basket?" "Mummi, can you hold my parasol?" Only their voices and that incomparable backdrop. They are taking the steamship to Saxon Switzerland, to Schandau, Dittersbach, Königstein. Someone has

34

handed out paper flags; the children wave them tirelessly, small automatons of patriotism. They sit on the terrace of the Gold Angel in Schandau, the Elbe behind them; ships keep gliding up, men keep shouting orders, "the White Fleet!", and the ships keep spewing day trippers into the mountains, the guesthouses.

They wander (no one must be absent) through the Grand Garden, "no zoo today!", too bad, they wander to the Grand Pond, "now to the Pikardie and then back to the pastry shop, and you can stuff your tummies"; Father is in a generous mood, they drink as much chocolate as they can stand, they feel ill anyway; they are allowed to do anything they like, "as if we were enjoying the hour before the end of the world," says Uncle David, a frequent guest.

Life changes.

But it is still lovely.

She gets away with a lot, and no one scolds her.

Even though Gutsi should tend to the others, she is usually near her. "Do you have any plans, Katharina?"

Her schoolfriends are often in the house, small clusters of shouting, excited girls; "Leonie is still missing!"

First it was a rumor. Mummi had brought it along; it was unbelievable, she said, dreadful if it were even to be attempted. She didn't want to talk about it. She had gone to her room, slamming the door behind her, she said she didn't want to confide in anyone for the moment, she wanted to wait for Father, she hoped he wouldn't be too late. Susanne Wüllner was very excitable, "built close to the water," as David put it. But she said she didn't weep all that often; if others wept, especially Elle, who usually wept out of anger, she would mock them as "crybabies."

Wüllner, contrary to his wife's expectations, came early, as agitated as she, but less offended than triumphant. He said it had to come like this, the fire had to be set somewhere. Dieter held Katharina in his arms, Elle and Ernst remained in the background, full of expectation. What had happened, anyway? Mummi was utterly confused. Why didn't she show up? Where is Susanne? Gutsi stood on the stairs, shrunken, pressing her fist to her lips.

They ran after Wüllner. The situation made him big. We cannot escape history, he said, so we must take control of it.

He asked everyone, including Gutsi, to sit down. He took his place at the head of the repulsive Old Teutonic table as if chairing a business conference; he clapped his hands without looking at anyone, took several deep breaths without launching into a speech, and then, with all eyes on him, he rubbed the ball of his thumb on the edge of the table. He straightened up, pressing his upper arms against his body, and placing his hands side by side on the table. He then said that the rumors they had heard were correct: Balkan scoundrels had assassinated Franz Ferdinand, the successor to the throne, in Sarajevo. Why, they had killed him in cold blood! He sucked his breath in very loudly, which made such a deep impact on Ernst, sitting to his father's left, that he imitated him. Father in turn swiftly lunged out and smacked his face. You clod! Do you think I'm gonna let you make fun of me, at such a time?! It was inevitable, he went on, war was imminent, the German Empire would support its Austrian brother. The Balkans had been seething for a long time, given the chaos prevailing there (!), and one could have foreseen when the pot would boil over. Now it had happened. There will be war, children, war! His voice trembled. A grand national awakening could be expected; nevertheless (he lowered his voice as if embarrassed), he would not put off his trip to France. After all, everything had to run its course.

Katharina scarcely heard her father. She was bothered by the theatrics of the scene. And she still felt like laughing. So she observed her mother, who was leaning back, staring straight ahead, her lips moving. Susanne Wüllner was obviously not listening to her husband (Peter and Dieter were the only ones giving him their undivided attention; Ernst was bewildered by the smack, Elle was plaiting the tassels of the tablecloth into thick braids, Gutsi was busy choking back her sobs).

Wüllner terminated the session, shooing everyone out of the room with impatient gestures. He told Dieter, the eldest, to remain with him. C'mon, hurry up.

Katharina ran after her mother. Susanne Wüllner walked down the corridor to the small sitting-room, turned, saw her child, held out her arms, received her, hugged her, pushed her into the room, let go of her. Katharina stood in front of her mother. She later said she could not think of anything to say, so she sat down on the couch, waiting to see what would happen. She said after a while Mummi talked to herself; Katharina did not understand everything, but she could recall one or two sentences verbatim: Everything will change, Kathi, nothing will remain. This world will go under, mine, yours. People will pursue a different kind of happiness, a different justice, a different meaning and purpose. I don't know whether there will still be emperors or kings. Many will fall. When I think of Dieter, and also Ernst. . . . I've never bothered with heroism and honor, Kathi, as little as your Uncle David. And your father too is a very civilized man. He lets go only in certain moods. He has just had his great hour. I don't know what will become of this home, of us. We had too much happiness.

Katharina said she wanted to tell her: Mummi, you're being too pessimistic, it won't be all that bad. We still have Father and Uncle David and Dieter and Gutsi. They're all here. But she didn't have the nerve to break the silence.

The sunset afterglow, she said, lasted until they gathered for dinner on the terrace, brooding deep into the night, with Father silently presiding over them; Gutsi, said Katharina, then took her to her room, later than usual.

Wüllner left for Paris and Nice.

Katharina said she felt as if time were contracting and this state of affairs would never end.

She often went to town with Gutsi.

The diary entry for July 25, 1914, in the twelve-year-old's hasty, narrow, rightward-sloping penmanship, says:

> If things go on like this, then I will care more for Gutsi than Mummi. She is always with me, takes me along everywhere. The streetcar conductors know us. They always greet us in a friendly way. Mummi even takes her meals in the small sitting-room, and I do not have the courage to go in there. I am not really at home here. But the town is beautiful, the excitement of the people, the joy of the soldiers. Dieter says that Austria has sent a final ultimatum to Serbia, and since we intend to help, war is bound to come. Dieter is going to be a soldier.

The day the German Kaiser declared war on Russia, Katharina and Gutsi went to Albrechtstadt. Katharina had put on her most beautiful dress, against Gutsi's opposition; it was hot, the trolley was crowded; she held tight to Gutsi, who was sweating miserably in her gray dress, constantly wiping her face with a handkerchief. Groups of men kept singing in the streets. Katharina says she felt cold and warm, she had fever and a sense of happiness that was transmitted to all mankind; "as though I were the tiny, burning focus of the world." At Albrechtplatz, they fell into a maelstrom of young men who kept waving their caps and starting songs that they never finished; they were carried down Alaunstrasse and to Alaunplatz; there they ran into a barrier of bodies. Katharina was scared she'd be crushed to death. But Gutsi shoved men and women aside, smashing her way through, shouting: No, girl, we'll never see anything like this again. This is a divine moment! An elderly man grabbed Katharina under her arms; she struggled, he lifted her high: "Look, child, look!" And finally, she saw them, eight abreast, the soldiers, gray and red, and flags, bouquets; someone shouted, "That's the

177th, here comes the cavalry, what gorgeous horses, oh my, and the cadets! God, how young, oh my, how young!"

She smelled the dust, scorched by the heat, said Katharina, it tickled her nose, she kept sneezing over and over; Gutsi slapped her on the back. You haven't caught a chill, have you, that often happens on such hot days.

The soldiers sang "The Dutch Prayer of Thanksgiving" and "Watch on the Rhine." When an officer marched past, she pressed her nose into his uniform for a few seconds and smelled it; it reeked of rancid fat and mildew; she was scared. She told Gutsi she wanted some flowers. Where could I get them, Kathi? There had to be stands. All the people have flowers and they're throwing them at the soldiers. "Hey, look, the Guard!" Gradually, the crowd shifted around the marching columns, making way for them; there were shouts to make way. She shuddered under the commands. Eventually, someone began to sing *Deutschland über Alles*. She joined in. Gutsi wept. Katharina managed not to weep with her. They followed a column. They're marching to the railroad station, said Gutsi. They're going to the front lines. Those young boys, oh my. And at twilight, when drunkards were reeling through the crowd, they got into a mobbed streetcar and headed home. Now they realized how exhausted they were. You're tired, girl, said Gutsi. They were squeezed into their seats, and she nestled her head against Gutsi's arm. She was so drained that she felt as if the war had begun a long time ago and would never end.

7
Uncle David's Letter

Every now and then, Katharina read this letter to her children. She said she didn't know of any letter that moved her so deeply, and she was thankful that Mummi had left it to her and not to Dieter or Ernst. She said she had been surprised by David Eichlaub's handwriting. She remembered him as big, overbearing, a physical appearance that tried to leave its mark on everyone; yet the handwriting was so neat and tiny, evoking the very opposite effect. Although not a Christian, but an enlightened Jew, he had sung at her christening—a song from Schubert's *Winterreise,* and it had become one of her favorites, she said, no, not because it had been sung at the start of her life. She knew the *Lied* by heart, and sometimes she sang all four stanzas:

> I came here as a stranger
> I leave, a stranger still.
> May showed me its favor
> With many a bouquet.
> The girl spoke of love,
> The mother of marriage—
> And now the world is dreary,
> The road is wrapped in snow.
>
> I cannot choose the time
> For my wanderings,

I must find my own direction
Through this darkness.
A shadow of the moon
Is my companion.
And in the white meadows,
I seek the traces of deer.

Why should I tarry
Until they drive me out?
Let their hounds howl
At their master's house;
Love loves wandering
(That is how God made it)
From one person to the next.
My darling, good night!

I will not disturb your dreams,
You need the rest,
You shall not hear my footsteps—
I gently close the door!
And as I leave, I write
"Good night" upon the gate,
So you can see that I
Did think about you.

She said that whenever she scoured her diaries for remarks about Uncle David, she realized again and again how fascinating he had been for the children: a grownup who had fallen from the adult order, a trickster, a marginal man. Elle may, perhaps, have made fun of him, I can't remember, but the rest of us were completely devoted to him, for, unlike Father, he didn't hide behind raptures, he seemed close and vulnerable despite his constant merriment.

The six pages of fine, soft, handmade paper had yellowed only at the edges. The handwriting, however, in violet ink, had faded, and it was not easy deciphering the tiny letters. Katharina used a magnifying glass. After reading Uncle David's letter to her mother so often, she knew it by heart anyway, and she recited it like a dramatic poem; she virtually performed with Uncle David.

Glauchau, 3/5/18

Two days after the Peace of Brest-Litovsk

I have never prided myself on being a prophet, dearest Susan [David often called mother "Susan," pronouncing it the English way; he was an Anglophile, he had attended an English university for a time and, before the war, he had spent a long period in London or Bath every year: I can still hear it today, that somewhat sarcastic "Susan"] and I would never have dared predict that Georg too would now be put into a military uniform. However, I am not worried; he will manage to keep himself out of the danger zones. You have depicted the problems of your household graphically: your husband is away, Dieter is wounded, and Ernst too is at the front—things have been quiet there for two days, I hope; Elle is running wild, and Katharina is apparently indulging in a freedom that you deeply mistrust. Let her be!

You are complaining. You should have complained earlier, and the whole nation should have complained too. Did I not leaven your intoxication four years ago, and did you not all gang up on me? In one of these debates, Georg, as I recall, reproached me for thinking like a Jew, not like a German, not for the benefit of the Empire. To which I retorted: I am a Saxon, and he settled the matter with a hearty laugh. All these banalities. All these enumerations of victories. All this concealment of defeats. A chaos of feelings, which has turned us into killers. You made things too easy for yourselves. What is left for us but the choice between black and red, between monarchy and socialism? I feel queasy, I admit it. I am no revolutionary, I am not a man who overthrows the status quo; I clutch at things that I am familiar with, that I love.

As for being a Jew: If I denied myself, they would force him upon me—the Jew whom I refuse to have anything to do with. How often have I been viewed and treated as an exotic being in Glauchau! Do you remember when we were in a Leipzig hotel with Father and Mother, and we recoiled when a lady, or rather, a fat woman lolling in an easy chair, clucked ecstatically upon seeing us and commented: "Ah, these darling little Jews." I held your hand tighter. We both realized at that instant that this honey was poisoned. Our parents apparently had not heard anything. It did not matter, they could not have helped us anyhow. Those few words had made us alien, set us apart. Did you cry afterward? I did, several days later, when I thought of what had happened. From then on, I was resigned to being "almost a stranger." I was respected. I had my circle at the university, and later as well, like here in Glauchau, where "crazy David" is accepted by polite society, an esteemed pharmacist, a popular singer and entertainer, an eccentric with "insane ideas," a sought-after bachelor, who is not quite up to marriage. He has his affairs all over the place. Let him be and keep an eye on your daughters.

That's me Susanne. You have escaped. A Wüllner has rescued you from all that. And I hope it will not happen again to your children. I know I am revealing a great deal.

If our parents knew, they would be unhappy, albeit silently, for they also adjusted and concealed themselves. They remained faithful to the tradition only at home.

Do I really know what Jewish is? It is different, that is all. It is irksome. It forces me to be different from different, and different from others. I am sick, Susan, sick of dissembling. And now, during this absence of peace, I am completely on the outside. What can I rejoice over? The braggadocio of Ballin, the court Jew? Should I prove my true grit as a soldier? Show it to them? How? By slipping into a further role created by the others, for the sake of the others?

I had a horrible dream, probably under the impact of all this news about constant destruction. I seriously wonder whether I should tell you my dream. I have to get rid of it, I would suffocate if I remained alone with it. It haunts me, as if I had experienced it in oppressive reality. And basically, I did.

I was standing in a vast square, and I cannot recall any enclosure, any structure delimiting the space. A wide circle of people surrounded me—strangers, peculiar, lifeless, virtually frozen. Their clothing was neutral, inconspicuous, and they all looked alike. They stared at me with half-open mouths. Their gazes hurt me. They made me extremely tense, so that I finally came out of myself and saw myself next to me, intimidated, wearing only trousers and a shirt without a tie, my head drawn in, my eyes lowered. It was like the outbreak of a disease. The oldest of the people surrounding me, a bald-headed old man, obviously their leader, took one step forward, tried to speak, stopped, letting the silence become a strain on everyone, and then shouted: "Jew! Jew, David Eichlaub!" The moment the words reached me, I felt them injure me visibly, on my skin. My skin was burned; it contracted, like an ulcer. I looked at me and saw the ulcers, I had images of lepers. What I saw was the same. A woman stepped forward right after the old man, a beautiful lifeless woman next to him, and she shouted: "You womanizer, you Jewish whoremonger!" And once again, the words leaped under my skin, devastating it. A child shouted: "Bachelor! Pill-Jew!" One after another. And I saw me shrinking under their invectives, into a single wound. My face vanished in a disgusting red protuberance, in which only the mouth struggled for air. My shirt unraveled over a gangrenous chest. My arms shrank to crusty stumps. I knelt before the crowd. Slowly, step by step, keeping their eyes on me, they drew back, vanished. All that remained in me was a pain that did not come from any life. I watched me losing my balance, falling forward on my face, a shapeless clump of flesh, and I knew I had lost my powers of speech. All I could think was: That's me. That's me.

I will not try to interpret the dream for you, Susanne. Analyze it yourself, my dear. But that is the state I am in now; all my merriment, which you all delight in (Uncle David is full of fun, such a happy-go-lucky dear) is deceptive and will keep deceiving you.

Lately you have often written to me about Elle and Katharina, and their political views. Why are you indignant? Should we not have expected the young to turn away quickly in order to save their bodies and minds if our world came to an end? Lenin and Liebknecht are certainly no greater swine than Kaiser Wilhelm and Ludendorff. And their ideas point ahead. Not that I believe true justice can be established—ah, Susan, they can call me a fool already—but I do believe in a little more fairness or in a flexible humaneness. Not even the hawkers of better truths have an inkling of where that will lead us. They have to be taken seriously. They will hardly make me a socialist. But the damn war and the meanness of a losing class have given me pause to think.

Here in Glauchau, everything is at sixes and sevens. A few war invalids have formed councils and are making the factory owners quake in their boots. Loherr—you know him, the most elegant in the bunch—has fled to his summer home in the mountains. *Après moi le déluge,* and with me my bag of money. It makes me puke. I am worried that the boys on the street will finish off my pharmacy the next chance they get.

You have lost Elle, Susanne. Forgive me, but you did not pay enough attention to her, and when you could have called her back, your nagging drove her away once and for all. You do have influence on Katharina. She is no longer a child, I can tell, I notice it; but she trusts you. She is deeply involved in the family, she admires Georg, she is very fond of Dieter. But bear in mind that she is tougher and more independent than Elle. She will leave you all, soon, and decisively.

I am foolish, I am making myself a prophet. I hope Georg will manage to goldbrick his way out of the army very soon. You need him. He is cunning enough to get you all through any situation.

They are not likely to shoot Ernst down, and Dieter's wounds will heal. What more do you want? You have me as a nightmare.

Love,

David

P.S. We will soon have problems with medical supplies. Write and let me know what you need, what you are lacking, including bandages and tape. I will bring some along next time as a present.

Uncle David's dream, said Katharina after reading the letter, provided me with information about myself and my background. Mother bequeathed the letter to me shortly before her death. It too casts its spell, like everything that came from Uncle David.

8
Elle or The Early End of the Revolution

During the final year of the war, Elle's influence on Katharina became overwhelming for a while. Her influence was strengthened by her companion, Kasimir, whom Katharine was very fond of. As emphatically as Elle propagated free love, horrifying the family, she nevertheless remained faithful to Kasimir. Her flirtations, pursued chiefly for the sake of her theory, had a touch of violence, repelling her suitors within a very short time.

Elle was small and squat; she was proud of her beautiful bosom, which she left uncorseted beneath hand-woven blouses. She hennaed her naturally ginger hair.

Wüllner could not relate to his eldest child, nor did he try. He called her a crazy kid and predicted that, short of some miracle, she'd go to the dogs. In their highly infrequent conversations, she repaid his coldness with sarcasm. But Wüllner learned a great deal about her circle through friends. She measured her own freedom against his and felt she was better off. Wüllner was cunning in his use of the forms that hemmed him in—he never broke through them. Elle, by contrast, despised the laws of her society, and her only approach to the "others" was her parents' home.

Gutsi had never particularly cared for Elle. "She was a sneaky kid when she was six, and it's gotten worse over the years." Gutsi was therefore all the more disturbed by Katharina's interest in the confusion at Hellerau. She could picture Elle's life only in her terrified imagination, and she described it as a living hell. "They're destroying themselves," was one of her cant phrases, "the reds, they're worse than the plague! Just think of Rosa Luxemburg, they've locked her up in the fortress!"

Hellerau was anything but hell. Even in Katharina's later stories, it remained a realm of unknown freedom, as natural as breathing. Elle had been hesitant about liberating the sixteen-year-old from the house; she feared conflicts with their parents. But when circumstances permitted (Father having been drafted, Mother counting turnips with Cook in the kitchen, and Kowinetz pulling out potatoes in the park), Elle kept bringing Katharina to Hellerau more and more often. There was some resistance. Gutsi wouldn't let go, she stood behind Susanne Wüllner. However, Elle saw to it that Katharina attended school regularly (against Wüllner's ideas: What are women doing at the university anyway? Do you want to send Kathi to Leipzig all alone?); Katharina did not seem the least bit spiritually crushed; and for the moment, Hellerau's sole effect was the hand-woven clothing. So the resistance at home gradually yielded.

After all, Katharina first had to learn the rites, practice them. Kasimir assisted her; she trusted him, his tact and delicacy helped her whenever she felt left out. To people meeting him for the first time, he seemed uncouth, always raring for a fistfight, probably an ambitious worker. During the Hellerau period, Katharina's diaries, which she kept in an almost intemperate manner, were dominated by Kasimir, until he was replaced by Skodlerrak, with no datable transition. She denied that she had ever been truly in love with Kasimir. He belonged to Elle, she said, he was Elle's boyfriend. When she was still spending only her days in Hellerau, returning to Klotzsche at night, Kasimir was usually with her. He introduced her to his friends, took her to their apartments in the attractive Riemerschmid houses, brought her to the Dalcroze Educational Institute, where she was so enchanted by a group of dancing girls that she signed up for gymnastics courses, assuming her father would pay for them (which he did without her hearing even one word of protest).

They hiked in groups through the Dresden Heath, gathering around a campfire at night, singing, debating. Only later did she learn that the carefree scene could be devastated by differences of opinion, relentless hostilities.

The garden around the villa went to wrack and ruin. Kowinetz had given up the fight against its decline, retreating to the potato field. He also proudly harvested tomatoes and lettuce, and looked forward to a large crop of beans the following year. Susanne Wüllner was grateful to him for his zeal. Katharina found the overgrown garden beautiful; the grass in the corral was knee-high, which inspired Kowinetz to acquire a couple of goats. "That's the way it goes," he said, "we've gone downhill, from horses to goats."

Whenever Gutsi left her after listening to her Hellerau stories without commenting, Katharina would sit down at the desk and record the events of the day.

2 August 1918
Hellerau

Today, I finally met Herr Jakob Hager, Kasimir's employer. He is a very impressive-looking man. A black shock of hair, like a prophet, thick lips, a cigar usually dangling from them, and gigantic hands, veritable paws. He is said to be very rich and supposedly started the printing shop purely as a hobby in order to produce expensive books for his publishing house. Kasimir is learning a great deal there. He behaves almost humbly toward Herr Hager even though he usually acts like a know-it-all. I am surprised, for Herr Hager does not care much for politics; today, when we were sitting in his small office, enjoying some fabulous coffee he had prepared, he said he did not give a damn about politics, we would have to wait and see, he was sure we are about to have a great blossoming of literature. Man needs feelings, he needs certainties. Kasimir did not say a word. If Hager were not his employer and if Kasimir did not have such great respect for him, he would have given him a piece of his mind! Hager, in a booming voice, read aloud to us from a book by Theodor Daübler that he published three years ago, and he allowed me to copy these lines:

Averroes, mangler of the soul, I fear you! And yet, I must now own up to my sinister insight! We souls perish, waft away! I exist only once! And the miracle is that I exist now of all times! And not only now, but also here. I have my homeland, a piece of myself into which I was born. Sea, sea, I see you and yet yearn for you! For you too, wind, sea, wish to waft into my being. Sea, sea, here I am, alone with you, and my peace; and my peace—which is no longer I, because it darkens, dark, darker than dark, where I can never see— feels the heaviness of the ocean and is eased by the knowledge of constellations reflected in the ocean. For ocean, ocean unrolling yourself, I am a poet, and you do not resemble me! You shall abide, but eternity speaks from within me!

Herr Hager looked at us expectantly. I could not say anything. The lines struck me as obscure and also a bit silly. Kasimir had bowed his head, avoiding Herr Hager's eyes, and I noticed that the reading had left him ill at ease. Outside, I asked him what "Averroes" meant. I don't know, he said. It's some kind of educated word. Däubler just tosses them around. But you ought to meet him. He looks like a god that's come down from the mountains; he's always reeling about, drunk on his own opinions. Hager is wrong, he says Däubler sits in a cloud-cuckoo-land, and we're bringing the revolution. A short time later, he added: I like him, I admire him.

Visited Elle early that evening. Again a dozen people in her room. Including Skodlerrak, the potter, whom I greatly admire. He seldom joins the discussions. Once he remarked: "We should live in large fraternities and practice socialism; the stuff we chatter about here has no substance. And Rosa's in prison."

Rosa was the watchword. Kasimir and Skodlerrak had introduced it. The other young men and girls, dancers, art students, commercial artists, loafers, premature invalids sent home from the war with experiences that they seldom revealed, by no means all Socialists, there were also monarchists who had started wondering, military minds, dreamers—they lived in groups or alone as subtenants in romantically appointed garrets, reading any new books they could get their hands on, singing together, one of them always strumming a guitar or a lute. Some were known only by their last names, like Skodlerrak, others only by their first names, like Kasimir. Kasimir's last name was Bülow. His father, legend had it, was a big shot on the Supreme General Staff, and he had kicked out his son. But Kasimir must have been getting support from somewhere. Meanwhile, Elle was earning enough from her workshop, in which she employed one potter and two female weavers. "Of course, who's gonna buy our stuff anyway in such times?"

It was the almost animal warmth and closeness that attracted Katharina the most. She had never known camaraderie in this form. Such a life simply had to be new. It could never have existed like this before.

We young people [she wrote] are rediscovering life. We will change it. We will topple authority. We do not need it. We will build a world of grand and useful solidarity. Skodlerrak read to us from Leonhard Frank's *Man Is Good* and then from a letter that the author wrote to him from Switzerland. He knows what moves us. He is young, like us. He can be one of our voices. Skodlerrak had tears in his eyes when he read us the most important sentences: "Mankind today is on the threshold of an enormously decisive universal change. Anyone who does not see this or does not want to see it will go under with the old era: even if he is a *bel esprit* and poet, he is nevertheless a reactionary; an enemy of mankind. What should the modern writer be? . . . Yes indeed! That's what I am! And I will not deal with what emanates from the central authority; instead, simple and naked, so that everyone can understand me, I will fight against the focal point of authority, whose downfall is nigh. World history has stopped; human history is starting. Between them, authority, the status quo, lies toppled." These words are for us. I know them almost by heart. Or Barbusse! Or Heinrich Mann! These are fan-fares. The world is being shaken!!

Skodlerrak read aloud from the newspaper. The end of the mon-archy, the establishment of the republic—these events, she said, glided past her as in a dream—shredded images, hastening sentences. As did the first confrontations between the army and the councils, the workers in Dresden. A film, she later said, which I understood only partially, the collapse in which we were all involved, we, too, who assumed we were carrying the present and the future.

They were sitting in a large circle on the floor of Elle's workshop. They had consumed a watery soup from clay bowls. Someone had brought liquor. The bottle circulated; no one had the courage to wipe it before putting it to his lips. Wanda, a tubercular girl, whose melancholy was catching, had played the guitar; they had hummed, getting into the right mood; four or five candles provided light; the boys had their arms around their girls, Katharina leaned gingerly against Skodlerrak.

Kasimir told about his meetings with the soldiers' councils. They feared that the Social Democrats would establish a bourgeois republic, they were too weak. Hadn't the Social Democrats voted for the war loans?

And what else?

The soldiers, the workers, and the progressive intelligentsia would carry the day.

It was time for Lothar to enter the limelight. He was rather new, a boy of nineteen, the son of a court official, whom he repudiated. Katharina did not like sitting near him ("Lothar has an electricity that affects me directly," she wrote, "he could ask anything of me. I often want to touch his skin, see him naked. He would be horrified at my fantasy.") Lothar was the acknowledged expert on the October Revolution, the apologist for Lenin. Kasimir claimed that Lothar made up most of Lenin's statements only to show off. Lothar said in his hoarse voice that Lenin's demand that the parasites be eliminated had to be carried out here too. The Revolution could brook no compromises. It had to identify its opponents and wipe them out.

The group was always amazed that when Lothar attacked with such sharp remarks, he did not sound like a fanatic, he seemed completely relaxed.

Elle got a few people to stop murmuring, and she said: It would never end, Lothar. You will always find new opponents. Ultimately, the proletariat will become its own enemy. I do not know that statement of Lenin's. Perhaps he did make it. But what do I care, even a genius can make a mistake, and we don't have to regard his utterances as sacred. The Revolution requires not only faith, but also constant doubts.

No! No! Lothar broke in. You're committing treason when you doubt.

Rosa, Elle continued, wants the political opponents to be respected. The Party has to be that strong.

Those are remnants of bourgeois thinking, said Kasimir.

But it's fair, it's human. Katharina was frightened by her sudden protest. Skodlerrak turned to her, ran his fingers over her hair.

A new humanity will come only through the Revolution.

When one Socialist strikes another?

Which republic is the right one, a girl asked, Ebert's and Scheidemann's or the republic of the Spartacists?

There is only one, Lothar shouted, the republic of the councils. Didn't you read the proclamation of the central council of the navy? Do you realize how far things have gotten? He held up a document that had been folded and refolded over and over, and was now tattered.

Just one passage, that's all! So that you finally understand the indignation. This is what things sound like out there: "We've had it! With a profound sense of resistance, we watched the leaders of the majority Social Democrats mobilize the bourgeoisie in the struggle against the class-conscious proletariat. Every day, every moment, we hear news about more victims in the harsh war between brothers. An ocean of dreadful lies has poured over the capital of the German empire. The bourgeoisie is triumphant, and the proletariat is bleeding, bleeding worse than ever! Socialists! Awake! Socialists! Unite! What has happened so far? We ask and accuse: What is happening? Only one thing is happening? A new mass murder! The pure in heart, those who love the people, can never rely on brute force. Comrades Scheidemann, Ebert, Moske, Lanzberg, Eichhorn! Do you still love the people? Did you ever love the people?"

Only his chronic hoarseness prevented Lothar from hollering.

It was too bombastic for her, said Elle.

Kasimir shook his head: The Spartacists will gather their forces soon, the workers will stand behind them. It won't be long now before Scheidemann is swept away. This situation cannot hold. The government is backed by the industrial magnates. They haven't surfaced yet, but their filthy power is tangible again.

Father has been back home again for several days [Katharina had written on October 14, 1918]. We gave him a wonderful welcome, we even had champagne. But then he buried himself away. I have not seen him for days now. He takes his meals in his room, and when I wanted to visit him there as I used to do, he asked me to leave him alone. Things are not so simple, my girl, he said; I sense that he is not so worried about the collapse of the empire. At the moment, he does not know whom to talk to or act with. He has entered an alien world. That is how he is behaving. But I care for him very much. I feel sorry for him. Yesterday he was visited by Fritsche, his chief clerk. They were together for a long time, until late at night. Then I heard them talking in the garden, outside the front door. Mummi said the factory in Bodenbach had been occupied, only for one day. Father is going to shut it down, she said. One Dresden factory is enough. Mother said (and I had the impression she was trembling with fear): He'll get us through. He just has to pull himself together. Why did I say: We really don't need him. Because I was annoyed by Mummi's weakness or father's whining? After staring at me aghast for a long while, she said: You're all heartless and egotistical. You've forgotten what he did for you."

It was time for Skodlerrak. Everyone else had voiced his opinion or what he considered an opinion, and, according to ritual, Skodlerrak, a man of few words, had the last word.

Skodlerrak was the sort of person who makes an impact by means of self-confidence that is never flaunted; he aroused trust and never lost it. He could be a Leader, Elle philosophized, he has that mystical attraction; but there's a clod inside him who doesn't want to be a Leader. Katharina disagreed: He knows, but he doesn't want to be one. He's more of a thinker than a doer. That's probably how he talks himself out of it, said Elle. Despite their affection for Skodlerrak, they could never agree about him. He probably prefers boys, said Elle, but hides it behind his intellectuality. You're disgusting. In contrast with Lothar's lashing hoarseness, Skodlerrak's voice sounded pleasant. It doesn't matter who runs the State, he said, Ebert or Liebknecht: he will be the State with its anonymous power, which is so terrible for the individual. He will be the State with its bureaucracies and its army. He will be the State, which decides on war or peace.

Kasimir wanted to interrupt, but Elle quickly put her hand on his mouth.

I could read aloud to you, as Lothar has done. I don't want to. But I suspect that quite a few people near me dream about a freedom that does not need a State, that has no power or violence, a freedom that creates the equality of all people and justice for all and mutual help. Killing people is not the same as abolishing institutions. We have only one power—the power of the Idea. By acting on our own terms, in order to bring about a freedom without power, we will transform reality without using force, without murdering.

You're a pacifist, said Elle.

No, an anarchist, said Kasimir. The stuff that Skodlerrak's preaching is Bakunin and Proudhon—nothing but old chestnuts. How, my friend, can order be created in a chaos of freedom, as your prophets see it?

You understand order only as a fiat, Kasimir. It's been drummed into you. Either the order of monarchs or the order of the proletariat. But either way, it's an order imposed from above. Can't you imagine an order without authority, an order created and established from below, by many people working together? Without a ukase and without liquidations? I didn't really want to read to you, like Lothar. He pulled a brochure out of his pocket and, without leafing through it, found the passage,

Bakunin—Bakunin! Didn't I tell you, Kasimir crowed. Skodlerrak ignored the interruption. Bakunin wrote on the basis of his experiences with the Paris Commune: "The social organization of the future can be set up only from below, through the free association and federalization of the workers, first in associations, then in communities, districts, nations, and finally in a vast international and universal federation. Only then can we establish the true and life-giving order of freedom and universal happiness, the order that does not deny the interests of the individual and the society, but instead affirms them and harmonizes them. It is said that such a concord and universal solidarity of the interests of the individual and the society can never be truly realized, because these interests supposedly contradict each other and can never be balanced or come to any sort of terms. But in response to such objections, I say that if these interests have never been harmonized before, then that is the fault of the State, which has always sacrificed the interests of the majority to the benefit of a privileged minority. . . ."

Skodlerrak had spoken against an increasing resistance. Lothar said that those were the visions of a man who didn't understand the world. The interest of the individual could no more be diverted or broken than the interests of groups. So there had to be some sort of organization, some sort of party. I'm not ignorant of the world. But Bakunin's model has never been tested.

Elle went into the kitchen; she said it was time to adjourn, she had to go to the workshop at the crack of dawn and take care of the kiln. Do you think the girls see to it? Forget it!

Skodlerrak offered to walk Katharina home. She had a room in Frau Blüm's place, didn't she? He didn't say a word en route.

Spartacus was defeated. Kapp mounted a putsch. Lothar vanished. They heard he was working for *Rote Fahne,* but they couldn't find his name in it. He must have changed it. Did you really know his name? Was his father really a court lackey? Rosa Luxemburg was murdered. They came together to mourn her. Sentences and images clustered in Katharina's mind, confusing her. She dreamed about street fights, persecutions; she saw Father digging trenches in the garden, in front of the portal. There were new faces in the group. Young, elegant people, attending schools in Hellerau. Kasimir was still politicking. Skodlerrak showed up, but remained silent, sucked on his pipe, left early. Elle, whose life was speeding up peculiarly, kept finding new, wrought-up friends, and she dragged Kasimir along as a good escort. Her parties were renowned; she threw many. More and more mediocre people joined her circle: war profiteers, discharged lieutenants, fancy hookers. Elle, badgered by Katharina to be more selective about her guests, wouldn't listen: I want everything to be wild and woolly, sister dear, like life. I'm fed up with politics anyway, and Kasimir can try his luck with these broads. Yet she was jealous whenever Kasimir flirted with one of the girls with bobbed hair.

Katharina soon noticed, and exploited the fact, that she was one of the attractions at these parties. She did not drink much, she was intoxicated by the compliments and the dancing. Elle had dug up a rather out-of-tune piano, and there was usually someone who could play it. Katharina enjoyed the "morning constitutional" after a long night, when small groups of them hiked into the moors at dawn, and the boys held hands with the girls. She had "almost let herself go" a couple of times, but, still thinking about Eberhard, she kept the men at arm's length. Several times, she had surprised Elle in bed with Kasimir, during the day, which didn't bother the couple. The first time Katharina had run off in embarrassment; but Elle had pooh-poohed her embarrassment, explaining "how natural such things are." Later, Katharina walked past the lovers, greeting them, and found something to do in the kitchen or the workshop; but she was agitated by what she had seen. She would have liked to be in Elle's place, but she wasn't free enough.

Skodlerrak came to her rescue. He, of all people, who was rumored to be ascetic, to like boys, at best. He had long since made a habit of seeing her home. After a while, they started going on walks and hikes. The two of them went to Meissen, visiting Moritz Castle, strolling on Der Weisse Hirsch. He was a good listener; she didn't break into his monologues with arguments. Sometimes he surprised her with small acts of tenderness, casually placing his arm around her shoulders, or grazing her hand with his. She thought these things were accidental. He was a good ten years her senior, and his natural authority kept her at a distance. One evening, after a walk, he invited her to his home.

He used no fancy rhetoric, he just said: Why don't you come to my place, Kathi? I was speechless, all I could do was nod. I had pictured his apartment as Spartan. It was attractively messy, a home and workshop in one. He had absolutely crazy old furniture. A lot of great paintings by artists he was friends with, such as Kirchner and Mueller. He does not keep his books in cases, he piles them up on the floor. There is a large, wide bed behind a screen. He made tea. Sit down in that chair with the high back, he said: It suits you nicely. The gray slipcover behind your black hair, that's lovely. He sat down on the floor, next to me. I lost all my self-consciousness. I was no longer embarrassed by the situation. I asked him what his first name was. He answered: Call me Skodlerrak. I don't know how much time we spent drinking tea in silence; then he got to his feet, lifted me up, and kissed me. It was not a real kiss, his lips brushed across mine. Then he carried me behind the screen, put me down, and undressed me like a child. It was fun. I did not help him. I would have loved to undress him too, but I did not dare. He embraced me, I felt his clothes, then he put me on the bed, saying: Don't cover yourself, and he undressed. He touched me with light fingers, all over, here and there, on my cheeks, my forehead, my throat, my breasts and belly. It was all new. I had never known how alive my skin is. His lovemaking was very tender and vast. I can't quite put it into words.

Katharina wrote this entry on July 22, 1921. It was the only time they slept together. She did not ask Skodlerrak whether she could visit him again. The tension between them came to a head one afternoon on the terrace of Loschwitzhöhe: she had a crying jag. Skodlerrak ignored the other people. He caressed her, moved his chair next to hers, held her, ordered an apple cider for the young lady and a cognac for himself, and said: Listen, you don't belong with us. I made a mistake. But you were waiting for love, and I like you. So go away now. You'll be all right.

The next day she moved back to Klotzsche. Her parents exulted. Gutsi, who, having replaced Asta, now did the cooking, quickly came to her aid with comfort and goodies. Wüllner suggested a few weeks in Carlsbad that fall, or else next spring.

Hellerau dissolved. Her Hellerau. It changed. Now, the schools dominated the picture. Parties were still given; only politics retreated; as though people had decided to banish the drearier reality from paradise.

Elle had met an ex-officer, Werner Oelze, who took her away from Kasimir. He talked her into leasing out the Hellerau workshop and moving in with him. He lived in an elegant floor-through on Kaiser-Allee in Blasewitz. She left Kasimir "in the lurch" (as he himself used to describe it), which aroused suicidal fantasies in him. Hager thoughtfully rescued him by getting him a job with Drugulin in Leipzig. So Kasimir vanished. Elle, however, adjusted briskly to her new environment; the former guardsmen, the petty aristocrats and reactionary parvenus soon made her forget the revolutionary speeches of the Hellerau circle. She had a sort of amnesia that helped change her into a chattery demimondaine. She and Katharina occasionally got together in Dresden. (After failing her Gymnasium exams once, Katharina had finally passed. Father, of course, was dead set against her attending the University of Leipzig: she'd go to the dogs there. "So you'll get hitched straight out of school.") Katharina found her sister unbearable, a caricature because of her complete lack of confidence.

Elle died in early March of 1922. She and Oelze had gone driving with two of his friends—an "outing." Oelze had taken a wrong turn. According to the newspapers, they had ended up on some miserable road near Porsdorf; there had been a very thick fog, and the car had veered off the road, plunging into the flooding creek of Porsdorf. The men had managed to get out of the closed automobile; the lady accompanying them in the back seat had drowned. Wüllner spoke of the unchivalrous behavior of those would-be gentlemen. Katharina penned a single sentence in her diary: "Elle is dead, because of Oelze, that creep."

At the funeral, Susanne Wüllner collapsed. People crowded around her, they had to call a doctor. Uncle David stood at the edge of the grave, tears running down his cheeks. He took Katharina's arm, saying: Let's go home alone, child.

9
Sighs of Relief or Hazy Transitions

Katharina finds the house again. The plaster is still peeling, gray, the garden still doesn't have its old look, and even the light over the scenery seems dimmer. But Katharina's memory is gathering: She drives the ponies together behind the house, piles up patent-leather shoes and ruffled dresses. She recalls Gutsi's stock phrases: "Everything will turn out for the best," "Leave your father out of it," "You can get through anything with bread and a little love,""There is always only the first man, child; you need the second one to survive." She grants the garden its wilderness, even though the successor to Kowinetz, who retired once and for all, and to Peter, who died in the final battle on the Somme, has done a lot of trimming and pruning. She sends Elle in front of the house, in the evening. She confuses Dieter's and Ernst's voices, two boys, laughing, arguing. She has Mummi sing upstairs in her room, and she waits until Father, returning from a trip, gets the presents out of his suitcase. All this will never come again.

The house cools off.

Dieter is at the University of Leipzig, studying medicine now after economics; Ernst is at Berlin, studying law.

The house ages with the parents, and it becomes too large.

She converses now and then only with Gutsi, Mummi remains dazed.

Wüllner travels a lot. Business is flourishing again. His foreign

56

contacts are useful. He dresses fashionably again, leads his usual outside life, full of fantasies and affairs. But the Wüllners no longer entertain. Family festivities are modest, without the agitation, the naive pomp of childhood.

Locked up and yet not, she only waited, she says, for someone to come, or she resembled a cocoon, her memory gradually diminished, the images of her departure were lost. There was little variety, aside from the conversations with Gutsi.

She told her father she wanted to have a talk with him. He promised they would, but he kept putting it off day after day; and he was saved by his travels.

She didn't dare approach Mummi.

However, Susanne Wüllner made a start—quite surprisingly after years of lethargy—by yielding to her old love of theater and opera. She went to Dresden at least twice a week, the first few times accompanied by friends; then she asked Kathi to come with her. Her mother told her that if she didn't pull herself together for some conversation, she would utterly deteriorate—"and that reproach from Mummi, who buried herself for three years, hibernating far too long. And, bang, she broke out, she's got a new lease on life! She lets me run along, embarrasses me, calls me dull and lazy. What can I answer her?" They avoided talking about the state of the household, about Wüllner. Kathi's past was not mentioned, nor her future.

She ran into people she had known in her childhood, she saw that Mummi had many friends. Kathi was taken up by "high society," she grew accustomed to its chitchat, to the way it shut out any current events, aside from its exclamations of terror ("one hundred twenty-two billion gold marks in reparations—Where are we going to get it?!" "Just look at what Rathenau's negotiating in Rapallo. . . . We're being sold to the Bolshevists!" "Erzberger's been assassinated—now, I'm certainly against killing people, but that traitor. . . ."). Katharina read, she heard what happened, and she was repelled by the occasional comments. She wondered what Kasimir or Skodlerrak would say; at such moments, she longed for the Hellerau Circle, for its fever, its sincerity. Everything was happening far away, nothing happened to her. On the contrary, the old society was renewed, dazzling her with its brightness and its posturing. Susanne Wüllner, aging slightly, was a woman to confide in, but limits had to be respected—and Katharina acquiesced.

Basically, it was because of a shock, Skodlerrak's rejection and Elle's death, that nothing touched me anymore [she wrote fourteen years later, in 1936]. I had become a child again, a kind of sleeping beauty—and during that period of all times! After all the experiences I had had! And someone had to come and awaken me with a kiss! Mummi was obviously looking for my prince charming. It's odd: when I think of our evenings at the theater, the opera, I focus on "tracings" so to speak. When I go out into the square, accompanied by Mummi and her friends, all of us festively garbed, I see the silhouette of the Royal Church strangely delicate, as if under water, the Castle, the Monument, the curve of the Frederick-August Bridge dissolving in chiaroscuro. These things are actually more palpable than the people, at least in hindsight. . . .

The man whom Mummi found for her was not at the theater, but at the Art Gallery in the Zwinger. She said they met in one of the rooms on the second floor, right in front of Van Dyck's *Portrait of a Lady,* for which Mummi had a weakness. He was waiting for her there, with a friend, snappy and dashing, in a somewhat ludicrous knickerbocker suit (his friend dressed the same way, like a twin). He bowed curtly to Mummi, as did the friend; he kissed Mummi's hand, then hers, Cadet Sergeant Werner Leberecht; Mummi beamed at him. Then, for Katharina's sake, she kept her distance as they continued through the Gallery, so that her daughter could converse easily with him.

She couldn't get used to him. They strolled along the Elbe, sat in coffeehouses. The conversations, usually monologues by Leberecht, were demure and in some way dangerous.

You are a lover of the modern theater, *gnädiges Fräulein?*

That is perhaps an overstatement. I was impressed by *Salome, Elektra,* and especially *Der Rosenkavalier*—the music is marvelous.

Superb, but decadent, don't you think?

Perhaps. I think it's more than that. But being a soldier, you probably don't deal with art that much, Herr Leberecht.

A soldier! I am and am not, as you see. I do have my mission, although it is not official, and nothing could be worse than an unintellectual military man, don't you think?

I've never thought about it.

There is probably little talk about soldiering in your home, *gnädiges Fräulein!*

True, oddly enough.

What about your brothers?

They were in combat. Dieter was wounded twice.

And now?

He's studying at the University of Leipzig. Ernst is at Berlin.

Do your brothers stay in touch with their fellow soldiers?

I don't know. I don't believe so. No.

That is regrettable, my Fräulein, for nothing endures more solidly than friendship forged in fire.

Perhaps.

I must tell you that I am a confidant of Captain Ehrhardt. . . .

Really?

You know about him?

No.

You will hear about him, my Fräulein, he is one of the ethical men who will make up for the betrayal of Versailles, one of the people whose actions will help bring a renewal of the nation. Isn't it wonderful that the true German spirit won out in the election in upper Silesia? We shall fight, as we did in the Baltic. And if it comes to civil war—the reds have to be held down and beaten. This is not Germany in which we are living.

Were you in the Baltic, Herr Leberecht?

Of course.

One hears dreadful things. . . .

It was fierce. The struggle will go on.

And now the assassination of Rathenau. There is so much injustice, there are so many things I can't understand—why did he have to die?

For the sake of justice, dearest Fräulein. A Jew and a traitor to the Fatherland! Our comrades Fischer and Kern acted out of profound conviction. They are martyrs. What does Ernst Moritz Arndt say: "Do what you must. Win or die, and leave the verdict to God." A favorite saying of our captain.

Does it mean anything?

You will see, my Fräulein. Our cause will be victorious or our Fatherland will perish.

Leberecht haunted her dreams, bowing snappily, cannoning out from behind corners, patrolling nocturnal streets alone, talking about riots. She resisted her mother's request that she spend time with him, the poor boy was a bit confused, like all soldiers who'd fought at the front, but he did have class, Mummi said; his background was excellent. Katharina refused: Not Leberecht.

Susanne Wüllner, her spirits revived, began entertaining again. Wüllner was present more often, he cut down on his traveling—"all those lousy transactions are useless, the money's worthless"—and Uncle David, who had come to an evening of songs and crooned Schumann's *Dichterliebe*, remarked with his usual self-irony that his stove was only smoldering, so to speak, and if things didn't improve, he'd have to shut down his pharmacy. He did shut it down several weeks later, moving to

Dresden, where he earned a livelihood by writing music reviews and giving musicales in the homes of the *nouveaux riches*, who paid bargain-basement prices to rent the "charming *causeur*" as a parlor ornament. But now, he was warming the Wüllner home; "for no reason at all, he had brought along a nice assortment of fireworks, and that evening, flitting through the park like the shadow of Councilor Crespel, he lit the fireworks, and turned them all into children. Georg Wüllner stopped philosophizing about his business, and Susanne was as breathless as in the past. Katharina never budged from his side. She begged him, as in the old days: Tell us, Uncle David, tell us about the Marschallin with the gigantic breasts. Well, you know (she had heard the story a dozen times), I don't want to mention her name, it's better not to. Let's forget about her obesity. She had a wonderful voice. She still had it. She was replacing Siems, who always sang the role at premieres. Yes . . . the first act has its problems for a pompous Marschallin, doesn't it? Lying in bed with nothing but lace on, plus that dainty Oktavian—if he is dainty! "How you were! How you are! No one knows it, or suspects it!" David vocally sketched the scene: "Are you complaining, darling? Do you want many to know it?" And our diva stretched out in her pink chiffon. It was breathtaking—it went on for miles, and sweet little darling simply vanished. If her voice hadn't been so enchanting, the audience would have cracked up. The colossal legs, still horizontal, were struggling, hunting for solid ground. Little darling had his wits about him, he tried to shove the mountain across the edge. To avoid any possible accident. Ah, dear girl, I was squealing inside. What a woman! The Moor enters, carrying breakfast. The Marschallin got up, my child, she did it! The miracle happened. She wasn't all that big, as the audience realized to its surprise, she was simply as tall as she was wide. But her bosom, girl, phenomenally corseted and heaved up. An unbelievable décolleté. And on the bosom lies—horizontal! horizontal!—a cross the size of a hand, sticking its beam into the void. That was too much! There were titters, they turned into laughter. The curtain dropped. Someone began to applaud, then someone else, then the entire audience, frantically. After a long interval, the tremendous singer appeared in front of the curtain, her makeup softened by tears. She bowed, the curtain rose, she stepped back into the scene and, with no cross on her bosom, she resumed singing, in a marvelous voice. Oh, dear girl!

Now the house was almost its old self again. The soiree was a success, the guests were having a good time. Uncle David sang well and was an even better conversationalist.

To me it seems as if we are merely catching our breath. Things won't stay this way. People are talking with fear in their voices. Only

Father seems to have been liberated by the general catastrophe. He is focused on the here and now, even though the situation at the firm must be disastrous. Fritzsche told Mummi so in strictest confidence: We have to be prepared for the worst. A certain mismanagement is simply the dot on the *I*. I don't understand anything about it. I'm only worried about Father and Mother. How can we help them if everything falls apart?

The hell with everything, Wüllner had said after the party and after David's departure, we're taking the waters in Carlsbad. And you're coming along, Kathi. It was his game. He could still play it.

We had to unpack again [Katharina wrote on August 18, 1922]. Something unfortunate has happened to Father. I'm not letting everything get screwed up, he had cursed before leaving the house with Fritzsche. He has to go on a business trip, it seems. I don't see him, I only hear him in his study. He has actually gone out of town. Too bad—but why should we of all people be better off? [And two days later:] Father is back. We are packing. Mummi says we've always been crazy. I cannot say why I am suddenly worried about the two of them. On the other hand, I am looking forward to the change.

Finally, dressed for the trip, she got hold of her father. She simply had to talk to him. She said she had been waiting for weeks.

They sat down at the large table in the dining-room, far apart, as if after an exhausting conference.

Well, what is it, Kathi.

I can't keep vegetating at home like this, Father, I'll go crazy or end up an old maid, or—

No one's asking you to vegetate here.

I'm grown up.

Well, in some respects.

I've got my Gymnasium diploma, Father, I could do something, and it's no longer that impossible for girls to attend the university.

That's true. But it may be impossible for you.

Should I run away again because you're keeping me prisoner?

Oh, child.

Well, then what are you planning for me?

Let's think about it calmly.

We've had more than a year.

What about Hellerau?

That's a different story.

Well, we'll think about it, I promise you.

Couldn't I help you in the office?

Absolutely not.

Then what *do* you want?

You should get married, my girl, that's all. That'll put an end to our problems.

10
The First Mirror Image or
The Young Lady Makes Up Her Mind

There is no such thing as time when she stares into the mirror; when she stands there, waiting and waiting, until she is nothing but that image. She likes it; when she was a child, she begged for a mirror for her room: a big one, a real one, which I can fit into completely! And she got her mirror, albeit after a delay.

Now, in the hotel room in Carlsbad, she is an old hand at mirrors. And she is satisfied with this one triple mirror, which surrounds her almost entirely. It must still be daytime; she wants to see herself without a beautifying artificial light. She turns the key in the door; no one is to disturb her for half an hour.

She loses all time, she is weightless from concentrated gazing, only her image becomes sharper and sharper, a girl, a woman, whom she considers beautiful, yet whom she despises in a moment of self-contemplation, as if her gaze were injuring her skin. She feels tenderness, voluptuousness, and a touch of self-love. You're over twenty, Katharina Wüllner, she says. She slowly undresses, following the movements in the mirror. She tosses her clothes and underwear about heedlessly. She watches the muscles and sinews tensing and loosening in her arms, thighs, and belly. When she sees these things, she feels them. She feels things she never feels ordinarily.

She has combed her hair back tight, putting it up in a bun as she often does, in order to bring out the narrow shape of her skull. Her eyes see her eyes. She opens her lips without a sound. She runs her splayed fingers over her cheekbones.

Uncle David says my head is like Nefertiti's; it's true, she says.

My skin is soft and tight, she says.

She reaches under her breasts, gently, lifts them, sees the nipples grow, and excitement pulses in quick strokes from two small points into her body.

She sees her belly stiffen, she sticks it out, looks at herself in profile, rubs the cool, solid surface of the body, pinches skin, twirls it, watches the hand reach into the pubic hair, which crinkles around the fingers, she looks up, into the eyes, responds to the gaze in the mirror until she is all image, she notices the thighs parting slightly, she sees the hand slip between the legs, stay there quietly, press the warmth back into the belly.

She hears her breath. It is no longer the image in the mirror that is breathing. She has returned.

She lies down on the carpet in front of the mirror and gazes at the ceiling. She is slightly dizzy. Her head is now her body.

After a while, she stands up, relaxed; she takes a bath, dresses, visits her parents in their room. She tells them she feels fine, she is looking forward to their stay here.

11
A Letter from Carlsbad

Hotel Pupp, Carlsbad
2/28/22

Dearest Uncle David,

I am no poet, alas, for I sometimes have visions or whatever you want to call them: I feel as if I were on a stage. And now, that feeling is stronger than ever. I was last here in 1914 with Father and Mother and found everything grownup and elegant. But now, something I regarded as unsurpassably grand and beautiful has shrunk down considerably, and the world has become a stage set (still charming!), where others perform. Did you notice: I started my letter with the word "I"! I did so intentionally, for, when I tell you things, am I not the hub around which everything turns?

So: contrary to Mummi's (admittedly notorious) anxieties, we are lucky in regard to the weather. How does the phrase go? The air is silky . . . and it has not rained even once this week. Which, of course, greatly spruces up our stage set, especially nature, the granite rocks; you can see shadows wander across them when you pause for a while during a stroll—not to mention the absolutely crazy architecture! Every house here aspires to being a palace, and if it has not managed to become one, then it vegetates as a crippled little castle, still ostentatious. And are the people any different?

We, for instance? Papa moans daily about the decline of the mark (yesterday, one had to pay 6,800 marks for a dollar) and at the same time, he congratulates himself for having a "nice tidy sum" in

Prague, which "is being squandered left and right." And why do we have to stay at the Pupp? Are we princes or parvenus? Father cannot help it, and I enjoy it. Honestly: Can't I walk through the lobby with the eyes of all the men on me? Can't I settle on a park bench with Mummi in such a way that countless male stars instantly start orbiting around us? Can't I arrange the scenes according to my taste? I can! And how!

The *déjeuners* here are celebrated. Our table is quite prominent and it is noticed. The reason, to be sure, is a bit vulgar: evidently, the only people taking the waters here are elderly gentlemen and their rather voluminous wives—or to put it more grossly: fat women. So people like us stand out. And Mummi *is* attractive, isn't she? Whenever we enter the dining room, people start whispering. The gentlemen sit up straight; the ladies, piqued, stir their forks on empty dishes. It is lovely!

Father is enjoying himself, as you can imagine. He is a charmer. Father and Mummi have met two friends from Dresden, the Winterhoffs: he is a scatterbrained man who prattles on and on about his business, and she, although nice to look at, is prematurely aged, wildly, gaudily dressed, and forces Mama back into her reserve, while Father, nonchalant as he is, always gives Frau Winterhoff tit for tat. Oh well, I don't really fit in.

(To keep my melancholy from becoming too loud, let me write the following sentences in parentheses. They are meant for you, and you alone, since I am certain that you understand me, dear Uncle David. Why do I see Carlsbad as a stage setting? I really feel as if I were on a different planet. There are reasons for this. I keep thinking of my Hellerau comrades—if they could see me here! Would they merely find it funny? I do not think so. They would be furious with me. For them, I would be a traitor. Of course, I am bourgeois—but this is too much! All this *morbidezza*, this hypocritical and often inauthentic wealth . . . and countless people used as lackeys . . . they would have no sympathy with such diseases, they do not care about the Marschallin or the Lady of the Camellias. I must admit, I am sometimes delighted by this atmosphere. I act numb and yet I am also sure of myself. This too can be pleasant. It is wrong to say so, yes indeed . . . do you understand me, Uncle David?)

I was interrupted here two days ago, even though I had not told you the most important news. No, I am fibbing. No one interrupted me; I was too lazy to write, I got distracted, and ultimately the "object" of my report can also demand his rights.

Dearest Uncle David, I am getting engaged! Isn't that sensational? Hadn't you all given up on me already? Not you, no. But the others! An old maid who absolutely wants to go to the university, an emancipated bluestocking. . . . What? What's that? And what's wrong with that? Except that I just can't, it's not me, that's what's wrong with it, that's all.

What's his name, I can hear you ask excitedly, what is he, where does he come from? Patience, Uncle David. His name is Ferdinand Perchtmann, he is eight years my senior, and an assistant executive in a knitwear factory near Prague, but he is to take over his father's firm in Brno. What does he look like? Can I draw his portrait? You know, he actually looks a bit silly. No, that is not correct. Only the two of us together might look funny if each of us were not enough of a person. For he is a beanpole, almost six feet six! And I am a dwarf next to him. Furthermore, he is blond, with a thin mustache on his upper lip. He has friendly blue—I sometimes tell myself: naive—eyes and a relaxed boyish face. Being so tall, he hunches slightly when he walks. He is always dressed impeccably, unpretentiously. What amuses me most about him is his accent. He talks like the Bohemian trumpeter at our neighbor's. Do you remember him? That Austrian flavor, and the funny use of prepositions. Isn't that impossible, Uncle David? I'll wean him away from all that, you can bet your life.

There is still a certain gap, one does not get accustomed that quickly to a stranger whom one suddenly considers a lover, who arouses troubling emotions. It will work out. But he has struck something in me: trust. This too, like many things concerning the emotions, is hard to explain. I have known him well for only a week now. And the way I met him! Very much in line with the conventions of this curious town. I occasionally noticed him during the first week, in the covered walks of the spa, in the hotel lobby, and at the *déjeuner* (he sat with his father—his mother died in a horseback accident—just three tables away from us; our table and his exchanged greetings). I liked his friendly way of watching over the sickly old man, accompanying him; it was unpretentious, coming from an inner strength. Is that how it is phrased? Goodness, I am having such a hard time with this letter. But I want you to know everything!

Since father is acquainted with several gentlemen here, he was invited to join a club, where, as I was informed, they discuss the disastrous currency conditions or instruct one another. They are all manufacturers, businessmen—Germans and a few Czechs. The group includes the two Perchtmanns, whose factory is supposedly highly respected. Its name is Moravian Knitwear. It does not matter to me at all. I know it should. Should it not? We shall see. We met and there was some kind of spark. I fell in love—almost. And I am ready to cross out the "almost" soon, very soon. We shall get officially engaged in November and marry before any comments prevent it. In February; for the "boy," as Father Perchtmann calls him, needs a wife, partly for the sake of his public image. I am that wife. I will be that wife.

Am I happy, am I really? Oh, dearest Uncle David, why do I always seek a happiness that probably does not exist? Or is happiness something very different from what I have always believed it to be? And why do I so easily forget what I have been? Am I fickle, frivolous? What do you think?

Hugs and kisses from your loving niece

Kathi

P.S. I am about to go riding with Ferdinand. The dollar supposedly already costs eight thousand marks. It is getting scary. We are planning an excursion to Ellbogen tomorrow.

12
Jean Ettringer or The Taste of Death

The story has a real beginning; only the ending remains open. The house is filled with children, it is loud and lively. In Katharina's room, a piano is being shoved, with great effort; Mummi, Peter, and Gutsi heave it across the threshold. It's yours, now you can start taking lessons. At seven, you're already a bit late.

The teacher who applied for the job was named Jean Ettringer, a young gentleman from Metz; he was studying at the Royal Conservatory, and, not very well off, he had to give private lessons. He was cordial and charming, yet he made Katharina uncomfortable from the very start. There's something about him, she told Elle, but could not explain what "it" was. Elle, being a lot older and acting superior, did not share Katharina's reaction; she hit it off with Monsieur Ettringer instantly and took him away from Katharina now and then. This infuriated Susanne Wüllner! Ettringer, she fumed, is not being paid to converse with Elle. He was an excellent teacher, and Katharina made fine progress. During her lessons, she forgot her qualms about him, she absorbed herself in the work and eagerly allowed him to correct her. If he himself played (he loved Chopin), she would observe him. He was of medium height, very agile in his movements, he had finely articulated "pianist hands," which he was clearly proud of, and his face was more funny than disquieting—in later descriptions, she called it "bulbous." The cheeks, nose, chin, forehead, why, even the lips looked oddly sinewy. But she was pleased that he did not treat her like a child, condescendingly; he took her seriously.

He came three times a week, punctually at three-thirty, leaving the house at five. Usually Gutsi would take him upstairs: often Susanne Wüllner would sit in a corner, listening to the practice session. Katharina made such excellent progress under Ettringer that a "small recital" was scheduled after only six months. A few friends were invited; the entire family was present. Katharina and Ettringer played several pieces from Bizet's *Jeux d'Enfants* as duets; then, by herself, she tackled the much-hated Czerny, and quite respectably at that. If she flubbed, Ettringer, who sat next to her, turning the pages, gently touched her arm. That was the first time she ever liked him. And during subsequent lessons, she was less sulky; he spoke to her more often, bringing her candy now and then. A certain closeness developed. He happened to tell her that he sometimes had fits: She didn't have to worry. It wasn't serious. Although it *was* serious for him, he added softly, for it seriously jeopardized his career. During a fit, he might fall to the floor. She didn't have to be scared or help him, she should just place a pillow or blanket under his head. The fit would pass. It would presumably never happen, for he could feel it coming and would then cancel the lesson.

Later, in Prague, she wrote to Uncle David: "Music helps me recover. I often go to the opera or to a concert with Ferdinand. To think that all my knowledge of music comes from Jean Ettringer! And how anxious he made me! Why, I even had the dreadful idea that his disease had slipped into me in some enigmatic way. . . ."

That was only partly true; the twenty-three-year-old was still repressing the shock and knowledge of the seven-year-old.

When it happened, he was sitting just two feet from her, at her right, but hunched away, so that she had to turn her head in order to see him. That was how he always sat whenever he asked her "to play a piece all the way through." All at once, he said, "yes," and then "yes" again. "Yes!" She stopped playing, turned to him. He sat on the stool, his torso stiff, his eyes gaping. He looked as tight as a spring. Are you all right, Monsieur Ettringer? she asked. First he nodded, then he shook his head. Should I keep playing? Did I do something wrong? Now his face twisted. No, she said, please don't, Herr Ettringer! She didn't dare stand up from the stool. Is this a seizure, Monsieur Ettringer? He didn't react. She stood up, hoping to get to the door. She didn't succeed, for no sooner had she moved than the spring in the paralyzed man uncoiled, and Ettringer flew in an arc from the stool to the floor. She shrieked, leaping to the side. Ettringer's face twisted into a grimace. His head rhythmically whipped back and forth, banging on the floor. The thing lying in front of her did not look human. A bitter taste gathered in her mouth. She finally managed to scream; she screamed and ran to the door, down the stairs, out of the house. It was snowing. She ran through the garden, into the grove, which she usually avoided; she fell down several times, got caught in a thicket, cowered under it. She didn't hear Mummi and the other children calling her, or Gutsi approaching her. She says she either fainted or fell asleep. Meanwhile, they had instantly called Dr. Schnabel, the family physician, and he had gotten Ettringer calm again. Dieter found her. He had almost missed seeing her. She was cool and all rolled up. It was a shock, said Dr. Schnabel, she had probably caught a chill. They didn't undress her, they put her to bed under a mountain of blankets. She became so feverish during the night that the doctor advised taking her to a hospital. Susanne Wüllner wouldn't hear of it. The fever lasted almost two weeks. She had pneumonia. Dr. Schnabel was nearly always in the house. She says she can't remember anything except this: Whenever she awoke, her mouth was filled with the bitter taste of Ettringer, and she knew she could not yet recover. She knew that this was the taste of death. Your mouth gets so bitter. When the taste was gone, she said later, she recovered.

Ettringer no longer came to give her lessons. He had asked to stop. She sometimes ran into him in town and felt as embarrassed as at the start of their acquaintance. Her new piano teacher was named Gottfried Mertens; he had no seizures, but was nowhere as inspired as Ettringer, and she learned a great deal less.

13
Frau Perchtmann

You still have to try the dress on! Why are you so pale, dear? Father wants to see you before we go over to the church. You'd better have a bite of something. Were the Perchtmanns satisfied with the hotel? You should give Gutsi a goodbye present. Have you packed already? Who was the last person to talk to the Luisenhof about the luncheon? Dieter ought to take care of it. It's almost time, child.

She hadn't wanted to get to the church by walking through the village. The walk would be embarrassing for her. It was a custom, she was told: she of all people should not flout it; "people" expected it of her. Now, at the window of her room, where some of the furnishings had already been pushed together and the closet door stood open, the inside plundered as before an escape, she felt indifferent about it. She was waiting for Ferdinand, she heard voices from the house; Gutsi, breathing loudly and asthmatically, sat on the bed, waiting to help her into the fur. The day was cold and clear. The garden lay under the snow, and she could hear the crunching tread of the gardener, who was at the gate, waiting for the Perchtmann automobile. She couldn't stand that noise. She would walk, crunching, through the streets. "Hey, getta loada that! The Wüllner girl! She's getting hitched! Time flies!" She wanted to remember events from her childhood. Her head remained numb. Her only thought was: Too bad there are no more ponies. Is that all I can think of? she asked herself. "Is that all I can thing of? I asked myself."

Gutsi sank her skillful fingers into the folds of the dress: Wasn't the waist really still too wide? And she was to let the veil drop loosely over the décolleté. After a great deal of effort, they had managed to dig up two nieces of Wüllner's to carry the train. "We've always been deficient when it came to a sense of family. But it's not so bad." Wüllner was content; he was obviously struggling with the pains of parting. "She *is* lucky, after all." She sees the gardener pulling the gate open, bowing before a black automobile. Now Ferdinand came to fetch her. He was accompanied by his father and his father' sister, a dragon, as Dieter and Ernst had ascertained the previous night. Lydia Schneider, a garment manufacturer from Vienna, divorced or widowed, raging and fuming at men, giving full rhetorical vent to her hatred, which old Perchtmann was unable to stop.

But everything was different from what Katharina had expected: She wasn't even aware of herself. If they had dragged her away or beaten her, she couldn't have resisted. She says she was deaf, inside and outside. Had she had her way, she could have played the fakir and certainly not even felt the bed of nails.

Now Mummi was in her room.

No, you cannot wear the fur, you can only drape it over your shoulders, otherwise you'll crumple your dress.

I'll freeze.

Kathi, don't be so stubborn.

Mummi was trembling from head to foot, fighting tears.

Katharina saw it and, although moved, found it ridiculous.

Why shouldn't the house collapse behind her when she left it, the walls simple topple like those of the cardboard house that she had folded up? She wanted nothing to remain.

She's smiling, Konrad Perchtmann said to his son, just look, what more do you want, she must feel wonderful.

Ferdinand ran over to her.

She walked down the stairs to the vestibule, almost tempted to slide down the bannister.

For God's sake, be careful with the train until the kids carry it, said Gutsi.

Don't worry.

Well? asked Georg Wüllner. Ferdinand shyly took her arm; the children grabbed at the train, pulling so hard that the seams cracked; the children were reprimanded, and the procession straightened out behind the bride and groom: Susanne Wüllner and Konrad Perchtmann, who elegantly concealed how difficult it was for him to walk; Lydia Schneider and Georg Wüllner; Uncle David, who had tenderly put his arm around Gutsi, his old Prince Albert coat making him look as if he'd come straight out of the tales of Hoffmann; Dieter and Ernst; the gardener and the cook, "who wouldn't hear of missing it." Friends and acquaintances would be waiting in the church.

How do you feel? asked Ferdinand.

And you? she asked him back.

She slid in her high-heeled shoes. Ferdinand held her a little bit tighter, but he too was insecure on the icy snow. She heard Father talking, joking. The children pulled at the train; she was afraid the coat might slip off her shoulders.

The street, which she knew by heart, stone for stone; then past the trolley stop, to the small church. The long, bright room, the two choirs on which she had been mischievous during the service for her confirmation. Father Emmel would perform the wedding; she had never been able to stand him, he reeled off divine words with the falsely fluttering eyelashes of a devotee.

Would Uncle David be singing? She hadn't managed to find out.

They heard the organ. The portal, the aisle, and curious faces on both sides. "I felt like pulling my skirt up to my knees and dancing all alone."

She says she can't remember a single sentence of the sermon; all she recalls is that when Emmel asked her to say "I do," the sweat beaded on his nose, and she was pleased that he couldn't pull out his handkerchief.

Ferdinand replied with am emphatic "I do."

She tried to say it nonchalantly.

She heard Mummi sob. At that instant, she could have wept too; annoyed about the stiff dress, she turned toward Mummi and saw Skodlerrak in one of the back rows. She couldn't tell whether he noticed her gaze; he was smiling, and his large face protectively blocked her memory.

Father Emmel made a few wiping motions with his hand; it took them a while to realize that they were supposed to sit down. So Uncle David *was* going to sing. As he explained later, he had had an awful fight with his darling sister about the choice of songs, and she had accused him of frivolity for the thousandth time. Had Katharina found the songs frivolous? She had taken him aside and asked: Do you know, Uncle David, I wouldn't have shed a single tear if you hadn't sung those very songs. But it felt good too.

Uncle David sang:

Do not sing in mournful tones
Of the loneliness of night.

No, the night, oh gracious beauties,
Is meant for togetherness.

Therefore, during the lengthy day,
Please remember, dearest breast:
Every day, it has its torment,
And the night, it has its joy.

During the pause between songs, there was the usual coughing and scraping and clearing of throats, plus a few giggles, which quickly faded when David, in an emotional and slightly uncertain voice, crooned Schubert's *Suleika*:

Tell him, oh but modestly:
That his love it is my life,
And his presence it will give me
Joyousness of love and life.

"While Uncle David sang, I wondered whether the sentiments weren't exaggerated. How much is demanded in that song? Is it this? Could Ferdinand mean that much to me, could I ever tell him that? Not yet, no, not yet. I was ashamed to think these thoughts."

David transcended the melancholy, the touches of sentimentality, by finishing his recital with one of his bravura pieces, Brahms's *The Maiden Speaks*, which she was very familiar with; she could have sung along in David's intonation:

Sparrow, tell me please,
Did you build your nest
With an old husband,
Or did you wed him
Only recently?
Tell me, what are you two chirping,
Tell me, what are you two whispering,
So intimately in the morning?
Isn't it true,
You're a newlywed too?

People cupped their mouths and laughed. David Eichlaub bowed to the bride and groom, the pastor blessed the congregation, they all filed out, and, Mummi told her afterwards, David hurried to the front, as if it were her christening; he kept looking back, an aging flibbertigibbet—

Katharina was grateful to him for his cheery informality, and she waved to him.

The men withdrew to the library, Susanne Wüllner attended Lydia Schneider, and Gutsi brought Katharina upstairs, telling her she had to change for the banquet and the trip.

Walking up the steps, she discovered several things for the first time: "There are so many things one doesn't see during half a lifetime; even though one uses them, one remains blind. I had often slid down the bannister, expecting Mummi to scold me, but I had never seen that it was held up by cast-iron roses. Had I ever truly noticed the gigantic carpet in the vestibule, its warm ochre? Or the Greek door frames? I drown and I see everything."

Hesitantly, she undressed. She wanted to undress in front of the mirror, but didn't—this wasn't the right time for it. Gutsi promised to mail her the wedding dress. She pulled the silk petticoat over her head. Watch your hairdo! said Gutsi. Katharina hugged her: You're a darling! And Gutsi murmuired: What am I gonna do without you?—Well, Gutsi, if that's a problem, Mummi and Father are getting more and more childish.—You never had any respect, said Gutsi, you weren't brought up right, and I couldn't do anything about it.

Skodlerrak had stood up when she passed him. She had sneaked a glance at Ferdinand to see whether he had noticed that man's eyes; but, either enjoying her presence or numbed by what was happening, he hadn't seen Skodlerrak. Standing next to Ferdinand, she recalled lying next to Skodlerrak, his tenderness, the way he had said goodbye to her. Perhaps it had been a warmth that she would never find again. When she looked back, Skodlerrak was gone.

Just think away, girl, said Gutsi.

I'm not thinking, she said.

You're dreaming.

Yes, sort of.

Your uncle sang marvelously.

Yes.

Only they weren't the right kind of songs.

They *were*, Gutsi, they were my songs. It couldn't have been any others.

He's just crazy.

He knows a lot.

And I tell you: he's crazy and thoroughly decent. Both things are true.

Gutsi embraced Katharina's waist: You have a lovely body, child.

Really?

A lovely shape. But you ought to wear a corset.

Why, Gutsi?

Because it's proper; and it shows off your figure.

I don't need one.

It's the fashion.

She slipped into the skirt of her travel suit and smoothed it out. Gutsi helped her into the blouse, into the jacket. Oh, and the coat, she said. Katharina had tried it many times, twisting, turning, the loveliest item for the honeymoon trip: a snug tube, sewn on the figure, made of soft lilac wool fabric, opening up to the knees when she walked. It closed off right above the ankles with a broad braiding of white fox; in lieu of a collar, a fox fur twisted around the neck. Plus the hat, a "sou'wester" with a narrow brim. Moving away from the mirror, she let Gutsi fuss with the hems and buttons, and found herself "utterly elegant."

Gutsi told her she had to appear downstairs. You can't stay here, girl. Gutsi said she'd make sure all the baggage got to the car; she was certain nothing had been forgotten. And she would give her the coat before they left for Loschwitz.

She resolved not to look back into the room, to discard it, forget it. They're all so odd, she heard Gutsi say.

The others were gathered at the fireplace in the vestibule, waiting for her. Kathi, c'mon, a glass of champagne before lunch! Wüllner shouted. They looked at her as she came.

Mummi was the first to reach her, not Ferdinand. Mummi hugged her, telling her she looked dazzling, a real woman. A glass was pressed into her hand. Father toasted her. Suddenly she thought of Elle, imagined her here, harsh, scorning the tinsel, "all these decadent customs," pictured her laughter—to think an entire world had gone under with Skodlerrak's rejection and Elle's death, passionate faces and a language she had been intimate with, a language that had promised her a future and had moved her; the language was gone, vanished, she would never again understand a single sentence in it.

Is it true that one lives several lives? she asked Dieter, who was standing next to her, holding her hand.

God, another typical Kathi question. You know, one life's enough for me.

She squeezed his hand, laughed, drank to him.

I thought of Elle.

Elle. He looked down at his patent-leather shoes, scraped the carpet, said: Elle would turn everything upside down here.

She let go of his hand, Gutsi brought the coat, helped her into it. She was admired; Ferdinand found her "simply beautiful"; she felt taller in the coat, or else she was growing next to Ferdinand.

They would drive to Loschwitz in three autos, everything was planned; the drivers would wait at the valley station of the cable car. She had always felt a bit scared in the cable car. Now Ernst was joking: "Don't fall too far!" The entire company burst out laughing. She was still at home, and she held on to it tightly.

"A few weeks later, I learned that Father was almost completely bankrupt. He had relied on the Dutch, on their good money; but to his surprise, they were insolvent. He had apparently taken too many risks, and the French partners shoved him out mercilessly. I would have done the same thing, he said, when Ferdinand condemned the whole of France with them; they're businessmen. That's the way it goes."

That vertigo, that soaring, and the landscape that lifted off with her in the swaying cable car, hovering, floating. That is what she remembers as the landscape, her landscape, even after the second war; different from here, on the Neckar—the Elbe cannot be compared to the Neckar, it draws light differently and reflects it differently, maybe not brighter, but, you know, it's more translucent, more physical—yes, it's a landscape like a perfect body, the leaping slopes with the terraces of the vineyards, the scattered cottages rusty red, dark brown, in a shimmering, almost yellow green, I could—but that's nonsense—I could write musical notes on such pictures.

The hands of the clock began to run. Even the glass of champagne had a disproportionate effect. It seemed to her as if the small company was scrambled and rescrambled several times before they sat down at the table in a lovely room. The waiters were zealous. She sat between Father and Ferdinand, both of them conversing with her; she heard nothing or everything at once, a chaos of sentences; Father was to speak, he was already standing; she looked up at him, he rocked again (she had known him, forgotten him, and knew him again at this moment), the short man placed his hand almost shyly on her shoulder, withdrew it, rustled the manuscript of the speech, and reinserted it in his pocket to universal surprise: My dear bride and groom, my dearest family, it would be all too theatrical of me to read a prepared speech, nor do I care to spout aphorisms to help you along the path of your life together—Pastor Emmel has strewn enough of them for you. I have never been granted large portions of wisdom, no; but I do have a little understanding of what life is all about, I know about finding happiness where one would least expect it—and that is what I wish for the two of you. You are traveling into a somber, agitated era. Do I know what looms ahead for you and your children? Do not let each other out of your hearts or your sight, and try to find words for each other. That is the only advice I can give you. To the health of the newlyweds!

They all stood up, raising their glasses. Mummi came over and hugged her. She smelled Father's tobacco breath. That was lovely of you, Father, she said. His voice had quavered during the toast. Oh, child, you know, now your mother, and I, and the goddamn factory are all alone. She laughed, she heard her own laughter, she kissed him on the cheek. You can count on us! He replied, intimate as always: You can't make such foolish promises, Kathi. First, you have to get to know your Ferdinand.

She was tipsy when they broke up. The entire company escorted them to the mountain station of the cable car. From there, she and Ferdinand would descend alone into the valley, where the automobile was waiting. That was the plan.

They waved at them. The cable car swayed, scaring her.

I'm really drunk, she told Ferdinand.

You're not getting sick, are you? Of course not.

She realized she was giggly and silly.

The auto brought them to Schandau early in the evening; a suite was reserved for them at the Hotel Quisisana. From there, the train would carry them off to Prague in two days.

"Ferdinand has really thought of everything," she wrote in her diary under the heading: Schandau, 14 February 1923. "He knows how much I love the Elbe and how often we visited Saxon Switzerland on weekends. Childhood Sundays are alive again; Ernst plunging into the Elbe in Postelwitz, one of the draymen leaping after him, both coming out of the water dripping wet, Father cursing away, promising Ernst the thrashing of his life, and handing a reward to the man who had saved him. Or the way I vomited under the table during lunch at the castle bastion: Mummi didn't notice; she criticized the unpleasant smell, and Father said drily: That smell was just produced by your youngest child. And we simply dashed out of the restaurant. The snow makes everything look more meager. But yesterday, the air was clear. The Elbe frozen along its banks, ice floes drifting—that was an image from my childhood, and it is haunting me."

They ate in their room. Katharina had never lived "in such baronial splendor"; she scurried in and out of the parlor, the bedroom, and the bath, while the chambermaid unpacked the suitcases.

We don't need all this for just two days.

It's appropriate, said Ferdinand.

He drew her over, lifted her up, kissed her. Well, you certainly won't grow any taller.

They drank another glass of champagne. Stepping out on the balcony for some fresh air, she relished the lights on the river: As if they were drifting away, very, very slowly, and then we too will have disappeared along with the hotel.

He told her she'd catch a chill. He took her back in.

I'm tired.

So am I. You can use the bathroom first.

Did someone take care of the flowers?

Yes, they're in the vases. They were very attentive.

I'm half dead, she said into the bathroom mirror. She undressed slowly, sat down naked on the edge of the bathtub, looked down at herself, stretched. "I was certain that my head had separated from my body; I no longer felt myself." She slipped into her lace nightgown and decided that the neckline was far too deep. Giving herself a poke, she walked into the bedroom. Ferdinand scarcely glanced at her; he said he'd finish up, and returned from the bathroom after a long time. She lay on the bed, uncovered, her hands folded under her head.

"I hope I don't get sick, I thought; I hope Ferdinand won't be rough; I hope I don't give myself away. I hope I don't think of Skodlerrak, much less Eberhard."

He stretched next to her and switched off the light. They lay side by side for a long time. Then he moved over to her and embraced her. He smelled of champagne. When he kissed her hand, she yielded and cuddled against him. He did not manage to make love with her that night. We're much too tired, she said. It would be better if we slept, tomorrow everything will look different.

She says she slept without dreams. The next day they strolled through the city and along the Elbe. She says it was bitter cold. They had lunch in the castle cellar. That afternoon, she says, they went back to the hotel: he undressed her, carried her to the bed, and made love with her very tenderly.

PART TWO

(Prague 1923–1925; Brno 1925–1945)

14
Guest in an Apartment

For weeks, the city made her forget everything else. Katharina wrote one letter after another. "Do you know, Mummi, the Hradčany is not a palace, or rather not only a palace, it is a city full of castles and churches and monasteries and the Cathedral of St. Vitus and little alleys, very tiny houses! I go up there a lot. Sometimes, I dream I'm a ghost, the spirit of a beautiful, desirable countess, for whom all doors open, all the secret rooms and all the centuries, so that I can travel through time—this is where I want to remain!

Ferdinand did not like her strolling through the city. She was out almost daily, neglecting the household, which, he said, she had to run for better or worse. He had registered her, he went on, at the Dvořák Housekeeping School, assuming she'd go along with it. He had done it even before going to Dresden for her: You see, I've thought of everything.

How could he act on her behalf without first consulting her?

He calmed her down. Prague is not Dresden, Kathi, the people here are different, so are the food and the weather. You'll have to learn, you'll have to be reeducated.

She did not intend to put up with it. Even the apartment had frightened her. Its location was wonderful; they had a view of a park filled with children. But the five rooms were darkened by heavy curtains, all-too-sumptuous rugs, and pompous, somber furniture, which intimidated her. Is that how people live here? she had asked the first time they walked

through the rooms. It wasn't his furniture, he said, but his parents' home
in Brno was appointed in the same manner. They had to show who they
were.

He did not introduce Božena, the maid. She brought a welcoming
gift: bread, salt, and brightly colored hollow eggs in a wooden bowl. He
barely noticed the delicate, inhibited girl. Katharina took the present
and asked her what her name was; she was glad to have someone else in
this gloom besides Ferdinand. He told her the maid was fresh from the
country, a bumpkin; she didn't speak a word of German but understood a
little. Servants are really not appropriate companions. This way she'd
learn Czech faster than she'd planned.

Ferdinand evidently expected her to enter a cocoon during the day
and then play the butterfly in the evening so long as he was at home and
not out of town. His factory absorbed him. He said little about his work
even though she asked him questions, curious, and occasionally wished
he would show her his place of work. Why should she be interested in
offices and factory halls? How and where did he work, she wanted to
know. Go on, that's men's business, Katinka. She hadn't expected his way
of life to be so alien to her. She realized he was very vulnerable, and
business problems left him taciturn and moody. German inflation had
made its impact here too, he would say. Things were in a miserable state.
She nodded at such sentences but did not pursue the topic, so the
conversations about his work soon died out. These five rooms: behind the
apartment door lay a gigantic, lavishly spacious "vestibule," characterized
if by nothing else than the four vast, walk-in closets along the wall next
to the door; they were large enough to live in, modestly, though without
light. A few random genre paintings hung on the walls. In the middle of
the somber room, which received some light from the courtyard through
two frosted-glass windows, there were five chairs and a table of black
stained wood, stiff and aloof, in "Old German Renaissance" style. From
the vestibule, two corridors and three doors led into the actual apartment. Behind the three doors were the dining-room and the study. One
corridor led past two toilets (one "for domestics and guests") to the
"salon" and the "noodle kitchen"; the latter in turn led to the real
kitchen, which was so enormous that from the very start Katharina
preferred staying in the noodle kitchen. You could only cook for whole
armies in that kitchen. Next to it, separated only by a narrow glass door,
was a tiny room, the "maid's room." The salon and the bedroom were
separated by a "dressing room," which she practically never used during
those two years, so it remained unreal; a worn carpet was its sole
decoration. The second corridor led to the library, the loveliest room in
the apartment; there were no books, of course. The library was triangular

with one circular side. This round part, one-third of the space, was the window wall, leading to a large balcony. The room was meagerly furnished, but it surprised you with two bellied china closets and a rust-brown Dutch stove covered with figures and ornaments; this would be a realm for children, if they came. The five rooms refused to welcome her.

They enclosed a past that hemmed her in. She was certain that even if the heavy drapes were removed, she would still have too little light. Ferdinand apparently was used to it. How light, how bright the house in Klotzsche had been. "It may, of course, be," she wrote to her mother, restrained so as not to sound whiney, "that this apartment responds to my vague, general anxieties. I feel menaced and trapped. I never knew that people could feel comfortable in such a dignified gloom. Ferdinand is a darling; he tries to talk my anxieties away—and we're going to get new bedroom furniture too. But when I wake up in this huge, high bed, it's twilight again. The bit of brightness is swallowed up by the dark-brown silk wallpaper. Ferdinand probably considered me more resolute. And I am. But this environment is not alive. Prague, in contrast, is a miracle! You know Prague. But I am going to be your guide when you pay us the visit you've announced! For some time now, I have been attending housekeeping school, the Dvořák Institute, where I have made a nice friend: a young Jewish woman in Prague society. Her name is Mirjam Hribasch, and she is the wife of a well-known jeweler. I am learning Czech from her and from dear Božena, our maid. Goodness, what a tongue-twisting language. Trchiatrschizettschemperle—whether you believe it or not, that means 'thirty-three doves.' If I did not know we would be leaving this apartment in two years and moving to Brno, I would get melancholy or rebellious. More likely melancholy with Ferdinand. . . ."

She changed little or nothing in the apartment, not wanting to be more than a guest. During the first year, she freed herself from the burden of this milieu. She made a few friends, whom Ferdinand did not especially care for but put up with for her sake. She and Ferdinand had also gotten into the habit of exploring the surroundings of the city on weekends, and Prague itself had become a playing field for her fantasies, her dreams.

Ferdinand felt she was overdoing it; he said she had a bee in her bonnet about Prague. She bought books on the history of the city, she gushed on about life at the court of Emperor Rudolph, and she spent long hours in the garden of the Valdštejn Palace, reviewing the heroes, conversing with them. She sometimes felt she was slightly whacky, and if she was talking to herself, she became embarrassed when passersby eyed her quizzically. But she forged ahead into the city, making it livable for herself.

At dinner in the dining room, she told Ferdinand about the day's experiences. They sat face to face at one end of the long table, lost in the huge room. After the heavy crystal chandelier had burned during the first few days, making her feel "like the last guest at an all-too-lengthy party," she brought a floor lamp from the study, and now they sat in its narrow beam.

Do you know the porter? she asked Ferdinand.

What porter did she mean?

The one on the Charles Bridge, the statue. She had looked it up; it was by a sculptor named Brockhoff. Seventeenth century.

You're getting more and more erudite, Kathi.

Did he remember the porter?

He said he wasn't sure. He did recall St. John Nepomuk and St. Luitgard in front of the crucified Christ.

The porter, she said, didn't really stand out that much, and he wasn't alone.

He asked her not to leave him on tenterhooks. What did she like about the statue?

You won't understand and you'll make fun of me.

Stop carrying on—when did I ever laugh at you?

It's the face. Do you remember? He's wearing a "scale helmet"—I'm not sure if that's the right term. He's carrying his porter's pole on his right shoulder. He's strong. He's carried a lot in his life. A serf, one who works silently. His face is turned away from his load. His chin is resting on his shoulder. It's a broad, heavy face, Slavic. The eyebrows are almost on the eyelids. You can barely see his eyes. The load's too heavy. He must feel it. He's used to it. And whenever I study the calm in that beautiful peasant face, I sense that the calm is hiding something—a power that touches me directly. An inveighing. I once said to him out loud: Throw those people down. I'm sorry, I'm being silly.

I like the way you tell me about it. But you're probably reading much too much into that face. I'll have a look at him the first chance I get—your porter.

"I've written about the porter figure on the Charles Bridge several times already. A few days ago, I spoke to Ferdinand about it. I did not tell him the whole truth. I could have told him why I feel so close to the stone man. He reminds me of Skodlerrak. He looks like him. Why, he could be his brother. When I stand in front of him, I practically caress him. I know what he's thinking. I know his anger and his grief. I speak to him often. Am I getting peculiar?"

In early summer, she stopped having her period. She said nothing to Ferdinand. Instead of going to the Dvořák Institute, she went to a doctor recommended by Mirjam. He told her she was pregnant. She said nothing to Ferdinand for three weeks. "I'm alone with the child. I am glad, and I have an unabating fear."

When Ferdinand heard the news, he said: He's going to be our son and heir. You're so beautiful. When women get even more beautiful during pregnancy, it means they're expecting a boy.

It's definitely going to be a girl, she replied, amazed at her own refractoriness.

15
A Conversation in Bed

She had expected the question. She had been uncertain what she would answer. She had prepared answers and then rejected them. She would reply on the spur of the moment. But a long time had gone by without his asking. So she assumed he was too shy to bring it up, too embarrassed.

In the evening, when they lay side by side in bed, they would talk . She liked that. She lay on her back, so did he; they didn't look at one another, they spoke toward the ceiling, waiting to hear what the other would say.

But then he did ask her. It took her a long time to reply.

Katinka?

Yes.

It's stupid of me to ask.

What? Ask me!

Was I your first man?

What do you mean?

You grew up rather freely. From what I know of your family.

Yes, Father and Mother are broadminded, they've never been hidebound. They understood us children.

What about your sister's life style?

Basically, Elle was chaste.

Hey, now listen.

Don't say "Hey," Ferdinand.
Sorry, you'll never break me of that habit.
I will.
You'll see. Eventually, you'll be saying it yourself.
Never.
You haven't answered my question.
You were talking about my parents and Elle.
Yes, but I had a reason.
You think we're all libertines or something of the sort.
Oh, that's nonsense.
You said something about Elle and her life style. . . .
What I was told.
Who told you what?
It doesn't matter, Kathi.
You're right, it doesn't matter.
What about you?
Of course I had boyfriends, Ferdinand.
Boyfriends?
Yes, I ran off with one. His name was Eberhard.
I know.
Who from?
Your mother told me.
Mummi? I'm surprised.
Your mother said it was a crazy story.
I was crazy.
Did you love him?
I don't know anymore. Maybe. Otherwise I wouldn't have run off
with him.
Where did you two want to go?
We wanted to start a new life. And be together.
You left him and returned home?
That's not quite true. He ran out on me.
You mean you would have stayed with him, Katinka?
Not for long probably. But I really liked him.
And nothing happened?
Happened? We squatted in an empty house and he dumped me.
I mean . . . you know—more?
More? Isn't it enough for you, Ferdinand, that I'm adventurous and I
can just take off at the drop of a hat?
You were a child, a teenager.
No I wasn't. Or else I haven't been since then.
So there was something more.

As much as there can be between children, if you wish to hear it. You did say I was a child.

And that was all?

What do you mean "all"?

You can drive a person crazy.

I don't mean to.

What about later?

Later, I never had another real boyfriend like Eberhard. Never.

You're not fooling me?

Why should I fool you?

You might be embarrassed.

Why? I didn't know I'd meet you and marry you.

That's a very unconventional view.

I don't care about conventions.

You're a little witch.

If you say so, then I am.

I'm sorry I was so insistent.

You can ask me, Ferdinand. I have nothing to hide from you.

Then everything's all right.

16
Mirjam or The Cat Game

It was a relapse, she felt, but it was pleasant. She was repeating her childhood with Mirjam. The teachers at the Dvořák Institute probably regarded them as silly geese, always huddling together and giggling. In the cooking courses, they outdid one another with extravagant dishes. But they learned quickly, becoming good cooks after six months, mastering "domestic bookkeeping" and the "rules of good society." They often cut classes and always together. Katharina soon met Herr Hribasch and took Ferdinand along. The two couples visited one another now and then. Katharina discovered a new world. Hribasch's store on the Moat was very elegant, a glass casket in which precious objects were mirrored. During her first few visits to the store, she tiptoed over the carpets—when she noticed it, she was annoyed. Hribasch was a corpulent man of thirty-five with short legs and an almost bald head. He acted self-confident, advising his clients without a trace of obsequiousness. And yet whenever Katharina was with him, she felt that he was timid and was merely hiding it skillfully. Tell me, is your husband shy? she asked Mirjam. Are you kidding? Mirjam was astonished. That would apply more to Ferdinand. Wasn't she projecting Ferdinand's character onto Emil? Hribasch was very interested in politics; he was always up on current events, an enlightened, distrustful citizen, who despised people like "Herr Hitler over in Munich"—those were dangerous symptoms of a national insanity; the fire could spread to the "fools in the Sudetenland";

it was enough here for the Germans to hate the Czechs, the Czechs the Germans, and for both of them to hate or persecute the Jews. He wasn't religious, but he did attend the Pinkas Synagogue regularly. Mirjam was devoted to him; she treated him like a father, which confused Katharina. Behind the store, where the showcases glittered, there were the offices with their baronial appointments. He often invited the two women in "for a sherry," sometimes opening the safe and showing them the best pieces: diamond rings and ruby diadems, waiting sublimely for a beautiful murderess, or pearl necklaces whose subdued glow expanded into an opal infinity if you absorbed yourself in it for a long time. His hands caressed the pieces; he was not just a connoisseur, he was obsessed, and his expertise was well known far beyond Prague.

Katharina said the schoolgirl Kathi was still inside her, which she enjoyed (a jitteriness that made it easy for her to still be curious and delight in secrecy and in running away). But the Hribasches treated her as an equal, a married woman in the best circles, "Frau Perchtmann." To be sure, Hribasch was reserved with Gentiles (Mirjam didn't care), and he relaxed only after Mirjam told him that Katharina's mother was Jewish and Uncle David, during a visit to Prague, called on him with Katharina, impressing Hribasch with his wit and education. Ferdinand remained on the periphery, never a nuisance for Katharina, for she had received only cool acceptance from his friends. Hribasch was quite well read. He told her about Franz Werfel's latest book of poems, discussed Thomas Mann's *Royal Highness* with her, and explained Sigmund Freud's discoveries in detail, often paraphrasing Freud's lucid statements, and thus falling victim to the very mechanisms exposed by Freud. He was, as this showed, a prude, marked by the conventions of stern parents—an only son, he had inherited his business from his father after his parents had died in a shipwreck.

Basically, he felt closer to objects, they were more precious to him than people, and he tenderly called Mirjam "my jewel." Katharina, irritated by such a love of objects, had tried to reform him. While presenting precious items that had just arrived, he had reached into a casket lined with dark-blue velvet and taken out a pearl necklace with an expensive clasp, a huge ruby mounted in platinum. Holding it against the light, he then cautiously pressed it against his cheek. It was an undisguised utterance of love. Katharina shuddered.

She said she found his relationship to objects exaggerated.

The necklace was in no way an object, he said, it was a living creature, and beautiful as well.

She said the necklace was indeed beautiful, but it *was* an object. You know, Herr Hribasch, I'm indifferent to objects, I often don't notice them, except in connection with people.

He had cautiously placed the necklace back in the box, locking it with a tiny key and returning it to the safe. He said he felt like having a cup of coffee: Could he invite the ladies to the Lloyd?

In the street he took their arms, proud of his attractive companions.

I don't wish to be insistent, said Katharina when they reached the café, you said the necklace was alive, didn't you?

It leads a life that I'm very familiar with, dear madam: It is altered by every light, by every skin it lies upon. It is never the same; it breathes and it slumbers.

She gazed at him, visibly amused, so he would see how surprised if not annoyed she felt, and again she liked the moist brown eyes behind the glasses, their sadness. Those eyes never joined in the laughter.

Well, then let's put the pearls aside, Herr Hribasch. She noticed how free and easy her language sounded in his presence. He chose his words meticulously, speaking in a kind of singsong, hesitating occasionally, thinking about his sentences.

"I really enjoy talking to Hribasch. He is very aware of language, almost a poet. And yet he is always very precise, very *akkurat* (ha! I am using a Prague word: *akkurat!*) A businessman who has to express himself precisely, who always has to think about his customers."

I can understand it in regard to pearls and diamonds, or any valuable and beautiful jewelry, even though it gets on my nerves a little, I must confess. I can't really understand this stuff. But what about other things? Let's say, furniture? Or your automobile, Herr Hribasch?

He ran his pale, stubby fingers across the marble table top: I could tell you stories about this table.

You mean "make up" stories, Herr Hribasch.

I can make them up only because I know this table.

Well, then you could also think up stories about me. But they wouldn't be true.

They would be accurate, dear madam. They might not be true, but they would be accurate, because I believe I know you sufficiently. The stories would be *for* you, not about you.

That's too convoluted for me.

For me, too, Mirjam broke in. Whenever Emil gets nutty like that, I could scream. It's fine for you to love this jewelry, it's your job. . . . But why tables too?

It's simple, said Hribasch, and his voice resumed the psalmodizing intonation as if he wanted to calm himself, make himself feel confident:

Because these things are made by us. All of them. Shouldn't the creators respect their creatures, appreciate them?

"The things Herr Hribasch says are exaggerated. I am certain of that. But there is something behind his words . . . a good heart or even piety—which I respect. If it were only the expensive glitter, I would not trust him. He is a serious and difficult man. If Mirjam did not act like his child, their marriage would not work. Ferdinand laughed when I told him about our conversation. He said he had already figured it out. Hribasch a philosopher! Like all Jews, he is cunning, says Ferdinand, and he is to be respected as a businessman. When I broke in, saying that my mother was Jewish, he replied: It vanishes in the course of time. At that moment, I hated him from the depth of my soul. I went to my room, and he did not even realize why."

Mirjam was her first friend. During her eight years at secondary school in Dresden, she had had "loyal companions," and "confidantes," but had never formed close friendships like most of the other students. She kept bringing home different girls. Susanne Wllner had given up noting their names. Gutsi could remember, she had a good memory for names and faces; and besides, she was happy when one of the girls came more than once: She could develop into a friend, Kathi. Katharina was busy with the house, with herself, with her brothers, with the ponies. And she preferred playing with boys.

Mirjam was two years older than Katharina, and she was obviously practiced in having girlfriends. Like her husband, she was an only child. Her father, a lumber wholesaler in Budějovice (Budweis), seemed to be filthy rich, for the family lived in a "chateau," and Mirjam had been raised by governesses and private tutors. Her "dearest girlfriends" had often lived with her for weeks; she knew all about whispering and secrecy, giggling and gossiping about men—everything that Katharina had once disliked now attracted her; she saw it as a relapse, but she enjoyed it; and when they strolled arm in arm, under a parasol, across Wenceslas Square or along the Moat, Katharina rediscovered herself: The little girl in her was an invaluable weapon against Ferdinand.

It does you good associating with Mirjam. She makes you cheerful, Kathi.

Mirjam was not always cheerful. She had unexpected crying spells; an innate melancholy would grab hold of her, making her impossible to talk to. She said she knew she would take her own life some day. A short time later, she had forgotten everything, and was acting playful and silly again, cracking up over Katharina's bewilderment and earnestness. Katharina said she did not find death threats a laughing matter.

But Kathi, it's all just a joke.

You didn't feel that way a few minutes ago.

Mirjam would terminate such conversations with a "forget about it." Katharina did not dare touch upon the "it."

The Hribasches lived above the shop. It was more of a *garconnière* than an apartment for a married couple. There was something Katharina had never seen before: separate bedrooms; and when Mirjam showed her the two rooms, Katharina asked: Aren't you ever together? Mirjam waved off the question with a few fluttering gestures: Of course. There were two servants in the house and an elderly man, "our Adamek," who could be both a butler and a messenger for the shop, he brought up coals from the cellar, and, when Mirjam was alone, he would occasionally regale her with endless tales about his youth in the Bohemian Forest: "When I remember what things were like back in Krumlov, well. . . ." Katharina liked the apartment. It was bright and modern, the dining-room was furnished in Chippendale. Ferdinand's reaction was different. After his first visit, he stated that the Hribasches were too worldly, which was reflected in their furnishings, and he had always found that Hribasch had a touch of the fop about him. She didn't contradict Ferdinand. She felt it was more sensible not to discuss the Hribasches with him.

She was visibly pregnant by now, although she wore a corset for the first time in her life.

She could no longer wear those light, snug frocks like Mirjam, and she envied her.

They had decided to go shopping that afternoon; they headed their separate ways after the Dvořák Institute. Katharina had strolled home, knowing Božena would have lunch ready. Ferdinand was a stickler for punctuality (although he often came home late, blaming work that couldn't be postponed). She changed for lunch, peeked into the pots, made sure the table was set correctly, and tried to converse with Božena.

Co je to, Božena?

Drůbky husí, paní Perchtmannová.

And both laughed.

Katharina said: I'll never remember that. I'd rather say "goose giblets." Say "goose giblets," Božena.

And Božena obediently fumbled: Goose giblets, ma'am.

Ferdinand assumed Katharina did most of the cooking herself. You know, he had told her, we do have a cook in Brno, but my mother was unsurpassable—my God, could she cook dumplings, and her noodles with diced ham! Božena enjoyed the conspiracy. She knew that "Herr Perchtmann" did not even trust her to prepare a tasty soup. They ate in silence. He gazed at her. Drew the watch from his pocket. Thoughtfully tapped his index finger on the edge of the plate.

You look dazzling.

I feel fine too.

Have you been to see Professor Maindl? Is everything all right?

He said I'm a model patient.

Just don't strain yourself.

Oh go on—I'm leading a marvelous life. And you're a darling.

He complained about the export laws: they were costing the firm considerable sums: the Švehla regime was awful.

But, she reminded him, he had agreed with the policies of the Agrarians. You misunderstood, Kathi. It's too complicated anyway. You weren't here at that time. I do respect Masaryk. And he did invent the Pětka—voting the five pre-war parties into the republic's parliament. Švehla *is* a beginning. There simply should be Germans in the government. If only the Czechs weren't such chauvinists.

What about the Sudeten Germans?

That's a national struggle, Kathi. It has nothing to do with minority politics.

I can't stand their politics. The things they write. Their language! And they're against the Jews.

So are the Czechs.

After lunch, he took a cat nap. She sat down in the small parlor, reading, dawdling, listening to Božena singing and clattering dishes in the kitchen.

"I am no longer a foreigner," she wrote in her diary in July 1923, "but perhaps one week from now I may write: I am a foreigner here. These are moods. What helps me is the daily rhythm. I am alone often enough. I really do not care."

Mirjam was expecting her. She said she was all alone. The two maids had the afternoon off, and Adamek was running an errand for the store. Miriam had opened all the curtains, all the doors; the rooms were flooded with light. She loved it like that, she said.

She said she had to change for the shopping trip.

I'll wait here, said Katharina, hurry.

No, come along. I can show you my new evening dress.

Katharina sat down eagerly on a small, rickety upholstered footstool, playing with the equilibrium, enjoying the brightness of the room, the delicate waves of perfume and powder scents.

Perhaps I'll set up my own bedroom in Brno.

Your husband won't like it.

Maybe he won't want to keep the baby in the same room.

Can you already feel the baby?

Sometimes, like paws in my belly.

You wear a corset, don't you.

Yes, it's horrible.

She watched Mirjam undress. To her astonishment, Mirjam stripped naked. She stood in front of the mirror and then turned to Katharina. Katharina was startled, their bodies were so much alike: the same light skin, the same solid high breasts, the same black triangle of pubic hair. Only their bellies were different.

It's incredible—as if you were my sister.

That's exactly what I was thinking.

Mirjam asked Katharina to help her pick out a dress.

She accompanied Katharina to the closet wall, yanked all the doors open, then paused, speaking hesitantly, pronouncing every word in isolation: I really want to see whether you could be my sister.

Then she ran through the room, laughing, raised her arms, pirouetted, and flopped on the bed, belly down.

You're a child, said Katharina.

Why not, asked Mirjam, squatting, with her arms around her knees. It's warm and this light makes me beautiful. You can hear the people from the Moat, male and female voices; you can imagine what they would say if the stone were made of glass. You walk up and down in front of them.

Katharina told her to hurry. They had wasted a lot of time. Her husband might show up.

He never does, said Mirjam.

C'mon, let's pick out a fabulous dress, Mirjam. You also wanted to show me the evening gown.

No, I want you to get undressed.

I can't in this state.

Mirjam hugged her, saying: Don't be a party-pooper.

She wasn't embarrassed, she just found it crazy. And the corset left marks on her skin. She wouldn't look as pretty as Mirjam.

Mirjam helped her. She unhooked the laces, cursing the corset, and when they stood naked in front of each other, Mirjam placed her hands on Katharina's shoulders. They were equally tall. They gazed sideways into the mirror. They stared at each other silently, for a long time. Katharina was glad to see she wasn't all that fat yet. When they stepped toward each other, their nipples touched, rubbed together: the sensation surprised them. Katharina drew back. Mirjam leaped toward her, hugged her, threw her down, they rolled across the carpet, Mirjam's skin was pleasant, it was softer, more familiar, "more sisterly" than Ferdinand's.

Careful, don't let anything happen to the baby, said Katharina.

Mirjam placed both hands on the bulging belly: You're lucky, Kathi.

You can have a baby too.

We haven't managed.

Just wait.

They caressed each other.

For a while, they lay close together. She wanted it to go on forever. Then she became worried that these more and more intense feelings might injure the baby. She sat up. Mirjam tugged on her arm to keep her down.

No, Katharina said, it was beautiful. You really are like my sister. But now we have to go. Otherwise we'll never get any shopping done.

Who cares.

But I want to. She leaned over Mirjam and kissed her on the forehead. You're crazy.

We're crazy, said Mirjam. Just don't tell anyone.

They got dressed, helping each other.

Katharina recorded almost everything in her diary, every important event; she pasted in letters, newspaper clippings. She did not mention that game with Mirjam until twenty years later, in 1945, after Ferdinand's death: "I have never stopped thinking about Mirjam. She could have escaped with her husband. What became of her? We were like cats. I still do not know whether it was love. If not, then it was a closeness that is achieved very seldom. We knew very little and yet a lot. We were lucky. We played. That one time only."

17
Wotruba's Rage or Curiosity Canceled

The man stood in the vestibule, his cap in his hands. Božena had let him in. He was probably confused by the vastness and unreality of the room, for when Katharina came, he had retreated into the penumbra of the closet wall. He was only slightly taller than she, but brawny. He bowed reluctantly or awkwardly, explaining that the Herr Direktor had sent him. I am Wotruba, Zdeněk. He spoke German with a Czech accent.

She wondered whether she should ask him to sit down, but did not have the nerve. So they remained standing.

His composure disconcerted her.

Do you have a message for me, Herr Wotruba?

No message, Ma'am. the chauffeur is sick. The Herr Direktor knows me, so he sent me. He says I should tell you there's some manila folders in the top drawer, it says "cash" on top , and you're supposed to give them to me.

She asked him to please wait a moment, she hoped to find the folders immediately.

Now she asked him to please have a seat.

When she returned with the folders, he was sitting erect on the edge of the chair, gazing at her. He stood up. She told him to please remain seated, she wanted to write a note for her husband.

This was the first time a worker from Ferdinand's factory had entered the apartment. She found Wotruba pleasant; he was sure of himself, not obsequious. While she wrote, he glanced away, to avoid looking at the paper.

Have you been at the factory a long time, Herr Wotruba?

Since the age of thirteen.

Are you a weaver?

No, I'm a machinist, I'm responsible for the machines.

You don't mind my curiosity, do you?

Certainly not, Ma'am.

Your German is very good.

My grandfather was German. And I deal with Germans.

Do you have children, Herr Wotruba?

Nine, Ma'am.

Gracious me! You have to support such a large family?

My wife works as a charwoman. Babička [Granny] takes care of the kids.

Isn't it hard?

We get along, Ma'am. People like us are not demanding.

Where do you live, Herr Wotruba?

In Vršovice, on Kodaňská ulice, not far from Luna Park.

I've never been there.

No, that's not a neighborhood where you might go ordinarily, Ma'am.

She finished the letter, folded it. Božena turned up; she saw Wotruba to the door.

Please wait, said Katharina, I'd like you to write down your address.

He stood in the doorway. Now, his stocky build looked slightly violent, she felt his resistance.

Why?

Perhaps (she cast about for some explanation for her vague wish), perhaps I could help your family.

We help ourselves, Ma'am. His tone was firm but not defiant.

I don't want to intrude. Just write your address down anyway.

He said he had nothing to write with.

She handed him her fountain pen and a slip of paper. He looked around for something to write on. He was about to go back to the table, but stayed put, placing the paper on the window sill, crouching down, and writing.

There you are, Ma'am. Na shledanou, paní Perchtmannová.

She said goodbye to him too in Czech, with the irony of his "Na shledanou" in her ears. He's not a good man, said Božena.

That evening, she asked Ferdinand about Wotruba.

He said he didn't know him especially well. He wouldn't have sent him if he hadn't happened to be in his office when he learned the chauffeur was ill.

You really don't know your workers?

Very casually.

Doesn't someone have to look after them?

That's up to the foremen.

I find that wrong.

Oh, you don't know people like that, said Ferdinand.

The remark offended her. Why did people prohibit each other from getting to know one another? She was sure Ferdinand would be angry if she told him about her plan to visit Wotruba and his family. Mirjam laughed at her. She said Kathi would confuse these poor people with her curiosity. She couldn't do much for them anyway. And they didn't care two hoots about fine words.

I have no reason to go to Vršovice. Should I stare at them like animals in the zoo? What connects me to Wotruba and his people? The fact that I think of Skodlerrak and Kasimir? A foolish charitable impulse? Fine, I could buy linen for their children, or maybe their babička needs medicine she can't afford. Or am I lured by the unknown? I will wait a few days, but I will not be talked out of visiting them.

At first, her agitation distorted every image, every impression. She had given the hack driver the address; he had eyed her sharply, and anything she saw during the drive contracted into a shaky gray strip of façades and faces. She did not know this area. Factories along the streets. She recalled similar streets in Dresden. Trucks and horse-drawn wagons occasionally blocked the road, and the driver yelled out in Czech. I'm in no hurry, she tried to calm him, but it sounded like a game; the others yelled back just as vehemently, and once the street was clear, the combatants tipped their caps to one another.

The hack halted at the entrance to a tenement.

Should I wait, Madam?

No, she said, she didn't know how long she'd be.

Confused, she handed him a large tip and walked toward the entrance. She was surrounded by children; her confusion turned into fear; her decision was wrong, useless. She stopped, and the children stopped too, waiting; she began to run along the building, talking to herself, turning back after a while. The afternoon hours fell long and hard on the street, the row of buildings opened up, sheds or small workshops stood isolated in the midst of scrubby fields, people pushed through bushes here and there, silently, like dolls, even though everything was surrounded by a din, an incessant snorting and panting, interrupted by a terrifying hiss from the chimneys of the nearby factories. She turned around and walked slowly to the entrance. The children trailed after her, whispering to each other; she could not understand their Czech.

Does the Wotruba family live here? she asked one of the girls. The girl answered in Czech, pointing through the entrance. Keeping their distance, the children followed her. She entered a narrow treeless courtyard lined with wooden booths. She looked up the six or seven stories; laundry hung from most of the windows, and flowerpots stood on most of the sills. Old women were leaning out most of the windows. The courtyard stank like a latrine; no one paid any attention to her. She looked quizzically at the little girl, who smiled for the first time and pointed at the opposite wing, at a door. Mucky gutters ran through the courtyard. She made her way gingerly, despising herself for her mincing walk. Now a couple of children laughed, running alongside her, aping her walk. She let it be. She didn't care whether she got dirty. An iron stairway consisting of six steps led to the door. The bannister had come out of the wall. She balanced her way up the steps, pushed the door open, and discovered a wall with slips or scraps of paper of various sizes, bearing names in diverse handwritings. The name WOTRUBA was followed by "ground floor." The dampness in the hallway drew smells of food, sweat, urine, rot. Five doors lined the corridor, the fourth belonged to the Wotrubas. She found no bell, no knocker. She knocked. As she did so, she felt like dashing off. She no longer knew what to say. The words she had mentally prepared were gone.

A girl of about ten opened the door a crack, scrutinized her, said nothing. The few Czech phrases that Katharina knew were all jumbled up now. The child waited motionless. After a while, Katharina asked: Je Pan Wotruba doma? The child nodded, shouted something into the room, and opened the door. Katharina saw a strangely picturesque arrangement of at least ten people in a not very large room. Yet she instantly noticed the overly rigorous order and cleanliness. The floor was shiny. After Katharina entered, an old woman came with a rag and wiped away her footsteps, the dirt from the courtyard. It was probably the babička whom Wotruba had mentioned.

Wotruba had been sitting on a sofa, he had gotten up and was standing in the midst of his family. He did not seem surprised. He was dressed for home, wearing only trousers and an undershirt. "When I saw him, in his gray undershirt, the naked muscular arms, I thought of the

Prague German word for undershirt, '*Leibl*,' and I could not get it out of my mind, I kept thinking '*Leibl, Leibl, Leibl.*'"

Good day, Frau Perchtmann. He did not say "Ma'am." Would you care to have a seat? Child, give the lady your chair, and all of you, keep still while we talk.

They kept still. They had to be still; otherwise they would have long since lost their minds in this confinement.

My wife will soon be here.

Katharina had sat down after saying hello to the babička. She sat opposite Wotruba at the table.

My wife is hanging the laundry.

You must be annoyed at my visit, Herr Wotruba. He did not respond, he asked: What brings you here, Frau Perchtmann?

She didn't know. She couldn't say: "Curiosity, or pity, or the memory of a few phrases spoken by Skodlerrak and Kasimir that have become vague in my memory." She said: Perhaps I can be of help in some way. She listened to her own words and was annoyed by her insecurity.

Well, he said. Standing up, he pulled out a drawer in the fragile sideboard, took out four glasses, distributed them on the table. Well, a person can help in all sorts of ways, but I don't know how. Would you care for some liqueur, homemade? It's good.

His wife came in. Katharina had expected a matron, a heavy woman, the mother of nine children, but she saw a girl—almost a child—skinny, with a blank face.

This is Frau Perchtmann, said Wotruba. Our director's wife.

Katharina stood up and shook Frau Wotruba's hand. The woman smelled strongly of cheap detergent; her rough palm rubbed against Katharina's hand.

Sit down with us, Wotruba told his wife, his sarcasm growing more and more aggressive with each word. Some liqueur will do you good. And help us figure out how Frau Perchtmann could help us.

He said it, and his wife began to laugh, clasping her hands and leaning over the arm of the chair; her face turned red, she was beside herself, screeching.

Katharina, terrified, asked Wotruba: What's wrong with her?

Well, Frau Perchtmann, he said, standing up and walking around the table, grabbing his wife's hair and shaking her almost tenderly, well, your helpfulness has made an impression on her.

Now Katharina wanted to be somewhere else, run away, even if they pursued her with laughter, with curses. Wotruba noticed that she was at the end of her tether.

One moment, he said, turning to her, his hands on his wife's shoulders, one moment, Ma'am. That was the first time he addressed her like that—with no derision, but with a sharpness that hit her, widening the gap between them. Since you've come to help us, which I would like to thank you for, you can't leave without hearing me out. His hands rubbed his wife's shoulders, she sat there calm and stiff, gazing at Katharina with no disquiet in her eyes. Believe me, I don't like giving speeches, believe me. When do I get a chance anyway? Usually, I'm the one who has to listen to speeches, as you can imagine. I hardly know your husband. He's upstairs, in the director's office. Do you think he goes through the factory a lot? He's got his nice office. I don't care. And he doesn't care that I've been working in the factory for seventeen years now; he doesn't care what I earn or how many kids I've got or what I'm supposed to live on or how or when. He goes home, he has his money. You must think Ma'am, that that's a law of nature. I was stupid enough to believe that and to adjust to it. No one gave me anything when I was born. No one showed me how to make my way up in the world. Or whether I can think at all, think more than the next man. Do you think that's possible? I didn't think it was possible. I'm sure you don't think it's possible either. Now you're visiting the menagerie of the poor people, and we can see how shaken you are. You've never seen anything like this. You live someplace else. In an elegant world. Life is beautiful there. We peer over at it, sometimes, and a few wise people among the rich say that poor people aren't even envious. They're wise and stupid. And we'll overcome them. You can believe Wotruba's a Communist, Ma'am, for all I care. Do I know whether I'm a Communist? I'm not in the Party because it's hard for me to enter the Party. But look, there's a big pot on the stove, and there's soup simmering in it, day and night, the soup never runs out in the pot. Ženka or Babička throw vegetables into the soup— barley, or groats, or a little meat. Whoever comes—they fill up, and anyone who's hungry can have soup from the pot, including visitors like yourself, as long as they're hungry, and you will never know what hunger is. That's what you don't know. And you don't know a bed with three bodies in it, rolling around, not letting one another sleep, until they finally get used to falling asleep a hundred times a night. My father worked for a farmer, near Kolin. My mother died when she bore her fifth child. My father got us through because the farmer allowed us to work for no pay, just a soup at the farmhands' table; the farmer called it the "farmhand stable." Yes indeed, Wotruba learned order. He learned where the farmer is and where Wotruba, Zdeněk is. I up and ran away to Prague. There a foster uncle brought me to the factory; I've been there ever since, and I started a family with Ženka, we've got a heap of kids; Ženka's mother, Babička, helps us, so we can work. Do you believe, paní Perchtmannová, that I ever learned how to read and write properly? Do you believe that anyone ever told me how to think? The only thing they said to me was: You're a good man, Wotruba, you're a fine worker, and you don't make any mistakes, none at all, and that's the way it should be; you submit, and everything has its order, Wotruba Zdeněk, so just keep working. Then I read about the workers in Vienna and their uprising and about the Commune in Paris. Now I know what people like us are deprived of, and what we do all day at the machine, and the director, who knows Wotruba at best by sight, and from saying three nice phrases at New Year's—the director gathers his money in the bank and he's got his factory, which is also valuable for him. Or maybe not? And does the manufacturer ever touch the machines? That would be stupid of him. After all, he learned how to think, he learned how to deal with money and debts, with checks, and Lord knows what else, and he got the factory from his father or from his wife at the wedding, maybe that's how he got it. He uses his head a little and a bit of skill and the hard-working workers, who mustn't get any ideas at the machine. So long as the worker can go to a tavern now and then, get a little drunk, not too drunk, because he's got to be sober for work the next morning. Do I know what justice is? But this isn't justice. The pot on the stove is justice. Our justice. And the future, paní Perchtmannová, will not be to your liking. Because other people are thinking now, and thinking a lot more. I don't want to take anything away from you, and the fact that you're bright and charming is already a distinction; that's something no worker can take away from you. And the fact that you see what helpfulness is, as you've imagined it. My father always got the farmer's worn-out shirts, without the collars, of course, and I hated him in that shabby shirt, which was better than his best shirt. Now you know, and if you like you can stay for supper and have a bowl of soup, a piece of bread, and a beer.

She stayed. There were thirteen other people crowded around the table; the youngest child was three years old. No one talked. Whenever one of the children wanted to break bread or get soup out of turn, Wotruba would look up briefly, and the movement halted. Katharina found the soup tasty, even though her stomach had balked at the sight of the overcooked vegetables, threads of meat, and billowing groats drifting on the surface. Wotruba toasted her with the beer. She took a long draught. Now she discovered the pictures on the wall, cut out from illustrated newspapers, with a reproduction of Delacroix's *Liberté* underneath.

She had underestimated Wotruba. He was not the factory messenger who had stood facing her in the vestibule, with his cap in his hand. Yet he was different from the phantom figures in Kasimir's and Skodlerrak's speeches. She feared him, but strangely enough, she also trusted him.

She no longer dared to ask whether she could help him.

She took her leave. The babička kissed her on the forehead. Ženka Wotruba said: When I laughed before, Ma'am, I was confused, please don't hold it against me.

All the children shook her hand. The oldest was one head taller than Wotruba, who said: Pavel is already at the factory too. And so is Tonek. Three Wotrubas are already in your factory. They say Tonek's becoming a good dyer.

He walked her to the trolley stop.

She told Ferdinand she had visited Wotruba and his family, which angered him. He told her to please never do it again, even though Wotruba was a decent sort and not a yahoo. What sort of an impression had his home made on her?

She said she had eaten with the family.

So they're not badly off, said Ferdinand.

It all depends, she said.

Well, you're not going to tell me the Wotrubas are starving to death? Should they be?

You're being argumentative, Kathi.

No. I liked the Wotrubas.

Well, he's not uppity, said Ferdinand. At least, I don't think he is.

No, he's not, she said, he's a serious and reflective man. A good worker, as you say.

She dreamed that Wotruba was pushing her through a crowd of people; all the men were wearing high hats, and every woman had one breast exposed. He kept pushing her higher and higher, up a rugged hill, until she stood at the edge of a gigantic barricade; a deserted city was burning down below, and Mrs. Wotruba started laughing behind her.

18
Conversation about Elvira

Decades later, she could repeat certain conversations word for word—a literalness she insisted on. Her children and her friends noticed that at most she altered a few phrases very slightly in the course of time. She could explain why it happened to be these conversations in particular: Either she had been in a state of tension that was a relief rather than a burden, or else the topics had never stopped haunting her throughout her life. Furthermore, her memory had always required an environment that helped determine the course of the conversations; or a dress that she remembered clearly because it had been festive or she had worn it for the first time.

She said she had often thought about Elvira, and whenever she saw *Don Giovanni* or heard it on records, the discussion was repeated in her mind, fragment by fragment. It had been a quarter hour of fluency and impudence, in which there had been no wavering, no uncertainty for her.

She was in her seventh month; the small irksome complaints had stopped, she no longer felt nauseated, and she could breathe efficiently again even though her belly was visible now. She no longer wore a corset. Heavily as she moved, she felt very light. She had taken over a silly phrase from Ferdinand, repeating it at the most absurd moments, much to everyone's surprise: I am free of any liability. It didn't matter to her what this actually meant. All she wanted to express was her sense of invulnerability.

She prepared for the evening at the opera. Ferdinand had invited her and the Hribasches to a performance of Mozart's *Don Giovanni* at the National Theater. Unfortunately, Ferdinand said, it was no longer being done at the Nostiz Theater, where it had had its premiere. The cast was ideal, he added. She did not trust Ferdinand, for she had gone with him to a *Bohème* that had suffered from all sorts of last-minute replacements and a *Tosca*, whose level she had called utterly provincial, thereby infuriating him.

They were to meet the Hribasches in the lobby.

She had seen *Don Giovanni* twice in Dresden. There was no work of art she felt closer to, and she sometimes used it to explain herself, if unintentionally. The first time she saw it, at sixteen, she remarked, to her father's amazement: Nowhere was human freedom more obvious than in the tremendous forms of bondage presented here in a music that was absolutely free.

She began dressing early in the afternoon, trying to recall the arias, trilling and humming, playing Zerlina and Elvira. She had bathed briefly in lukewarm water; the doctor had told her not to take long or hot baths. She had powdered her face, dabbed on some perfume, and held her belly in the mirror. She had sat on the carpet, her legs stretched out, her hands on her abdomen, feeling the baby's movements. One month earlier, taking Ferdinand's advice, she had ordered a concealing evening gown of light-gray tulle, with a strass trim along the hem and the scarf collar; she had complained she would have little chance to wear it. Božena had sewn the gown. Katharina took it and held it against her body; the fine material tickled her. She enjoyed it very much.

When Ferdinand came home in the late afternoon, she was still undressed. A child, with a foolish, introspective look on her face. The tiny bowls, the vials of scents from her father's factory were scattered in front of her on the carpet: toys. Ferdinand wanted to scold her, but he was moved by the scene. He sat down next to her, placed his arm around her shoulder, and murmured: Are you all right?

They sat for a while, then he pulled her up: We have to hurry, Kathi, or we'll miss the performance.

She was startled when he pointed at the clock.

She dressed hurriedly, she enjoyed her haste again. She murmured to herself: In a flying hurry, in a flying hurry.

Mirjam ran toward her holding her arms out excitedly. She said they had already assumed something had come up. The first bell had already rung, she said.

The footman opened the box for them.

The two ladies sat down in front of the gentlemen. Mirjam realized she had forgotten her opera glasses, and Katharina offered Mirjam her own, saying she didn't need them, she was looking forward to the music more than anything else.

Ferdinand's prediction was correct: the cast was fine. Don Giovanni was agile in his voice and gestures.

He's handsome, Mirjam whispered.

Yes, said Katharina, but he's always handsome, even when he's fat— the music makes him beautiful, he can't be anything else.

They were conversing during intermission.

Her good mood infected the others. I have to say something very stupid, she said as they strolled into the restaurant (Hribasch had invited them to a glass of champagne, "it fits in with the theme, doesn't it?"), beginning the conversation: I'm so happy that it hurts.

You're a bit overexcited, said Ferdinand.

At every step, the wide skirt nestled against her legs; she toyed with the scarf collar.

They found a table, somewhat away from the throng. A waiter brought the champagne in an ice bucket, and Hribasch toasted the beauty of the ladies. Although I do not care to heed Don Juan's advice, I prefer the morality of the final chorus, which we will soon hear.

But Mozart doesn't make it that easy for us, said Katharina.

Shouldn't morality have the last word? asked Ferdinand.

To be perfectly honest, I don't much care about morality.

What *do* you care about? Mirjam may have suspected what Katharina was driving at. But in the conversation, she would realize her mistake.

No character in art gets me as angry as Elvira does—can't you understand? I'm a woman.

As we can see; Hribasch tilted his head, smiled, raised his glass.

How lovely, she said, a pantomime of politeness. A few minutes of Mozart's music, and we move to his beat.

Don't exaggerate, said Perchtmann.

She felt pains under her breast ribs. She stood up, saying she needed fresh air, she had to breathe. She told them not to think her capricious if she stood behind the chair and leaned on the back.

Ferdinand jumped up to help her.

Stay seated.

He sat down again, eyeing her sharply.

It's nothing. It'll pass quickly. It's just a normal condition.

And why not? said Mirjam. It lends great emphasis to the scene, since we're in the theater anyway.

What annoys you about Elvira? asked Hribasch. You mustn't conceal that from us.

Not at all, that's the whole point.

Just Elvira, asked Mirjam, and not Don Juan too?

He too, he too certainly and always.

She leaned forward, noticing that the rhythmic motions of her upper body softened the pains.

Are you going to give a speech? laughed Ferdinand.

She's not getting a chance, said Mirjam.

Dear lady, you must not hold back your opinion of Elvira any longer, said Hribasch.

It's basically a very simple matter. And that's why it makes me so angry, because it *is* so simple. Why, I ask, does Elvira humiliate herself constantly, why doesn't she turn the tables, why doesn't she let Don Juan leave after those ominous three days, so she can look about for another man? Why is she so attached to that womanizer, why does she whimper after him, letting herself be taken in by him and his servant, why does she allow her rage and thoughts of vengeance to eat her up? That's her role. It's our role. Don Juan wouldn't be Don Juan if Elvira weren't Elvira. It's like an equation, isn't it? If the equation were different, Don Juan would be omitted. But the equation was made dully and stolidly by a culture that doesn't expect a woman to act as freely as she could. I want to—if only I knew how to put it—I'll put it like this: I want to make up for it.

Hribasch had leaned back and was playing with his feet. He tried to affect an expression of irony, while his eyes, which she liked, remained sad. Ferdinand had not put down his glass, he gazed at it. Only Mirjam giggled, but she had grasped nothing.

Katharina now stood upright behind the chair, no longer holding its back; her hands were crossed over her chest. She felt the looks of passersby. It was easy for her to speak, she had thought about it often enough.

Haven't any of you noticed that none of the characters who dominate the stage are free? Elvira is tied to Don Giovanni; so is Anna, and she's also tied to her revenge; and Ottavio is Anna's creature, her servant, just as Leporello is Giovanni's servant. Zerlina, as light and darling as she may appear, can be in everyone else's power, she doesn't know what freedom is, while Masetto recognizes his bondage, and Don Giovanni, who plays with other people's freedoms, he, I think, is especially unfree: Since he's given up all bonds, he can no longer know what freedom is. That's one of his forms of bondage. And a person who won't accept his death is equally bound. Don Giovanni is wretched. Since we are even less free, but he plays with freedoms, we find him wonderful. Don't we?

She had confused all three of them.

Hribasch was the first to regain his composure: You must have thought about that for a long time.

Not about that, about me.

I can't go along with you, said Ferdinand. It would turn the world upside down.

Just because Elvira could make up her own mind like Don Juan?

You know, said Mirjam, who was only just beginning to see the light, men never want us to deprive them of their privileges.

But these aren't privileges, Mirjam, these are conventions, to which women simply submit.

The bell drove the audience out of the restaurant and the lobby. Hribasch took Katharina's arm: These laws, dear lady, are the trick of our culture, and (he turned his head back, so that Perchtmann and Mirjam could hear him too) when men are challenged to act, don't they always lie at the feet of women? Don Giovanni strikes me as being the hubris of this stance, the exception.

She laughed. You are expressing the fear that we could rewrite your laws, that Elvira, whom I meant after all, could make a fool of Don Giovanni. And that would be simple. All she has to do is court Don Carlos.

No, Katharina, cried Ferdinand. He was loud and upset, and a few people halted and looked at him.

She tried to keep talking in the box, but Ferdinand reacted angrily: The curtain's about to go up, Kathi.

Just let me add this. Doesn't Elvira sing the following in the trio with Don Giovanni: "My heart, why are you frightened? Now stop for him your beating." The melody had come to her as if by itself: she could sing it.

Yes, yes, Ferdinand broke in.

And then Elvira says she mustn't forgive him. She loses the freedom she has almost gained. Her hatred binds her to Don Giovanni.

That's true, said Hribasch, go on. . . .

That's how one person steals the other's freedom.

She pressed her feet against the floor and sat up straight in the chair.

Perchtmann noticed it: Are you all right, Katinka?

The curtain opened, they looked at Don Giovanni and Leporello, who were arguing with one another. Shush, she said, Leporello wants his freedom too.

> *Eh via, buffone, non mi seccar.*
> *No, no, padrone, non vó restar.*

19
The Twins

The water bag burst. She was standing next to the bed. The water spurted between her legs, sloshing upon the floor. She forgot everything she had known and read. The contractions hadn't been all that strong; she had decided to wait a bit longer before waking Ferdinand. The midwife lived only five minutes away, and the doctor could come quickly. She hadn't expected to be so helpless. She writhed, yammering, stood in the puddle. Ferdinand slept on. The contractions came in rapid succession. If they were ten or fifteen minutes apart, she was to call the midwife, the doctor had advised her. She went into the bathroom, noticing that she could walk without difficulty. Everything she did was suddenly new, different, and she was afraid of every movement. She wanted to get a rag to wipe up the amniotic fluid. Then she thought of Božena. She opened the kitchen door and called to her. Božena reacted immediately. She was wearing a peasant nightgown of linen. It hung to her ankles, and her hair was up in curlers. Is it time, Ma'am? Katharina told her to hurry and get the midwife. Right away, said Božena, right away. Mrs. Růžička will wait. She was gone instantly. This calmed Katharina down. She knelt by the puddle and wiped it away.

Ferdinand was awakened by the noise. She heard his hand pass across the empty pillow. She told him not to worry, she was here in the room. What's wrong, Kathi. He had sat up, she saw his shadow against the curtains. It was growing light.

The contractions have started. She didn't tell him what had happened.

What are you doing?

I'm walking back and forth.

Lie down.

Please let me do what I want.

He stood up. I have to get Mrs. Růžička and call the professor.

Božena is getting her. The midwife will call the doctor.

Do you need anything?

No, I'm going to lie down again. She went into the bathroom, hiding the rag from him.

Should I get up?

That would be better. Božena will fix your breakfast. You can't stay in the room.

She lay down again, watching him dress.

Are the pains bad?

So so. They're coming faster now. She tried not to groan or moan, and she realized that the strain made her rigid.

Go on, she said, leave me alone, and bring Mrs. Růžička in as soon as she gets here.

Oddly enough, the contractions shot into her head, filling it up, virtually numbing it.

She relaxed, yielding to the pains.

At some point, the midwife arrived, the voices were mingled—Božena's, the midwife's, and later the professor's. Katharina confused everything.

Sometimes a face would emerge, very sharp, only to dissolve into smiling or speaking lips, into eyes.

Katharina asked them to open the curtains.

That's unusual, said the midwife.

Why shouldn't there be light.

The contractions came in rapid succession. The pains annulled one another.

I'm a bundle, simply a bundle.

The midwife pushed pillows under the small of her back.

The doctor pressed her legs apart.

It's all right, she said, I'm fine.

Then she felt the child coming.

She heard her own gasps as if they were someone else's.

The voices were concentrated, there was a slap, the professor yelled at the midwife, Božena cried "ey, ey," Katharina heard the baby crying. But the contractions got more intense.

For God's sake, the doctor said, I suspected as much, the heartbeat was so strange—there are two. You've got twins, Frau Perchtmann, you've got twins.

She didn't care.

The second time, she ripped apart.

I'll have to sew her up, said the doctor.

She was no longer here, she reeled between waking and sleeping.

The pains had become a condition, she was hovering.

The babies cried.

Would you like to see them?

She nodded.

She saw two tiny bodies. They belonged to her; they were her children.

Two at once, she said.

She heard Ferdinand's excited voice. He leaned over her, trying to kiss her on the forehead; his smell disgusted her, and she turned her head away.

She's exhausted, she'll have to get some sleep. Mrs. Ružička is staying here, said the professor. Everything's all right.

She hears water. The babies are being bathed.

Twins, says Ferdinand.

He sits on the edge of the bed.

They changed the sheet before he came, removing the blood, the filth. At some point, they also washed her carefully.

The professor sewed her up.

It won't hurt, he said.

Nothing could hurt anymore.

We wanted to name him Georg, said Ferdinand. Should we name one of them Georg, Kathi? And again, he bent over her, though more cautiously.

No. No.

What? But that's not so important now.

It is, Ferdinand.

Well?

Peter and Paul.

Why those names?

Just because.

She was asleep, in her sleep she heard soft noises in the room.

It was October 14, 1923.

20
Birdseed or Wüllner Adjusts

Georg Wüllner acted like Peter Schlemihl, the man who lost his shadow. He had no shadows now and he forbade others from speaking about shadows. Katharina had received mail from Dresden at least once a week, mostly letters from Mummi, and a few from Gutsi. Only Gutsi's letters hinted at the debacle, but they were from an outsider who happened to pick up bad news but could not explain it. Strangely enough, the news barely touched Katharina. She trusted in the good fortunes of the family. She had casually asked Ferdinand whether the Combella Works were faring badly; Ferdinand had come up with all sorts of excuses: no one was doing well at this time and maybe her father's plans had been on too large a scale and he now had to tighten his belt a little.

Her parents had repeatedly promised to visit them. She heard that Father had been in Franzensbad. Dieter had passed through Prague, he had dropped out of the university; he was so agitated that he took off again after two hours of jittery chitchat, claiming he had something to do in Vienna. She did not find out what it was. He did not even want to see Ferdinand. Ernst wrote from Leipzig. He had set up a law office there. "If it doesn't embarrass you, just go ahead and address your letters to Back-Stair-Shyster Dr. Wüllner."

The twins made a visit from the grandparents necessary. They had wired their "tremendous joy" and "pride," and Gutsi, "after mature reflection," had offered her services as a nanny. "I may be fifty-six, but I'm still strong enough to raise a whole flock of kids." Katharina had thought that Gutsi was over sixty. The offer came in the nick of time. Mrs. Růžička had recommended a girl whom she personally guaranteed, but Katharina still had a hard time with Czech, and it sufficed for her to twist her tongue with Božena, who now knew as much German as Czech.

She telegraphed Gutsi: If it wasn't too much of a surprise and not too much trouble, could she possibly come with Katharina's parents.

Katharina knew that the milieu she was living in was breaking apart; there were bloody conflicts, old and new were challenging one another— but she did not participate. During one of her walks, on a street in the Old City, she had watched a young man chased by a group of other young men; they had caught up with him in a building entrance and beaten him. No one shouted or screamed. Everything took place in harried soundlessness. She couldn't tell whether the young men were Czechs going after a German, Communists ganging up on one of their opponents, or Nationalists persecuting a Socialist. She had halted and then, after a split second of terror, dashed away. She didn't know why the collapse did not reach her. She expected an uproar: they would suddenly be out in the street, Ferdinand without work or property. When she pictured it, she had no fear. Sometimes she wished that the course of days would change. But it didn't.

Ferdinand and she were at the station waiting for her parents and Gutsi. She hadn't wanted to take the twins along because of the cold. It was snowing; at the end of the platform the snow blew about like a skimpy curtain. The train was late, no one could tell them how long it would be. Ferdinand put his arm around her, they walked up and down the plat-form. They bought a hot bouillon at one of the moving stands. The waiting became a game. In the snow flurries, the locomotive first became visible as a powerful shadow. Tears came to her eyes. "I realized I had not yet gotten away from my childhood home, I had been tied to it by girlish memories throughout my time in Prague. I had not really begun a life of my own. I was embarrassed when it all became clear to me; I felt unfit for life."

The train brought noise into the station, the noise was rhythmically broken by the shouts of the porters: Nosič zavazadel! Nosič zavazadel! Ferdinand had waved over one of the men as they scurried along the train. Gutsi waved from a window in one of the very last cars. Katharina ran, laughed, waved. Susanne Wüllner stood in the middle of a mountain of baggage, which Wüllner tried to put in order.

Katharina hugged one after the other.

Ferdinand came with the porter, who scrutinized the baggage, shaking his head: he couldn't handle it alone, a *kolega* would have to help him.

Like princes, said Katharina, you're all crazy.

You know, we want to get out a bit too, said Wüllner. Besides, we've brought along all of Gutsi's belongings.

We'll have to take two cabs. Ferdinand led the caravan.

Father hadn't changed. He was dressed as elegantly as Mummi, who was wearing her black sealskin coat. "In my memory, she was older. Now she looked young, enterprising, and Father was the experienced companion."

The cabs separated in front of the Imperial. Wüllner had asked for "an hour's recess" or "even two." He didn't want to upset their plans. Besides, they had to introduce Gutsi to her new work. Ferdinand went to the factory for "at least two hours."

They had managed to rent two rooms for Gutsi in the attic of their apartment house so she wouldn't have to sleep with the twins, she could withdraw if Božena took over her chores. The rooms had been furnished without pomp, and Gutsi liked them on the spot.

Listen, she asked as the elevator took them down to the apartment, do all the people here speak Czech, Kathi? Do I have to learn Czech too? Gutsi had grown smaller, or else Katharina's memory had made her larger.

Not at all—there are a lot of Germans here,—a lot of Czechs speak German, and Božena will understand you. While unpacking, Katharina had prepared Gutsi for the vast gloom of the apartment; nevertheless, Gutsi was startled when Božena opened the door and they entered the vestibule together. "Why, this is a gruesome palace," said Gutsi.

She liked Božena.

Were the babies sleeping?

They walked down the corridor to the nursery. Gutsi said she had to orient herself. "How beautiful our villa is compared with this." Katharina softly opened the door and the three women tiptoed over to the two cribs, which stood side by side not far from the dutch stove.

Gutsi crouched clumsily at the crib bearing a small sign that said PAUL. She said she hadn't seen such teensy-weensy tots for a long time, but she wasn't out of practice. "That's one thing you can't forget."

When did Katharina nurse them?

I've weaned them, Gutsi.

Gutsi pulled herself up along the crib; the baby began to squall; she stopped whispering: That's horrible, Kathi, or are you sick?

No.

Then I can't understand it.

Why should my breasts get ugly?

Oh, c'mon. Gutsi went to the cupboards, reached into the baby linen, then said after an annoyed silence: But otherwise everything is all right. You can go about your duties.

The parents came with Perchtmann, Sr., who had waited for them at the Imperial. Ferdinand wasn't back yet. The conversation went arduously until the men withdrew to the study, and Susanne Wüllner remained alone with Katharina.

You look fabulous, Mummi.

Yes. What's Gutsi doing?

Grumbling a little.

Well, this apartment is a nightmare.

Ferdinand feels that it's stately.

Don't be unfair, child.

No, no, that's what he said. How do I look? Be honest.

Very pretty, you've filled out a bit, it's becoming.

How's Father?

Oh well, he'll talk to you.

Do things look bad at the factory?

I promised him I wouldn't say anything to you, I'd leave everything to him.

All right.

December 14

I have to catch up on my entries, I did not get a chance to keep my diary during my parents' visit. We were out a great deal. Father especially was insatiable. We had to go to the theater, introduce him to our friends. He flirted uninhibitedly with Mirjam. He still isn't quite the most tactful man in the world. During an intermission, he said: Jewish girls are really quite appealing, aren't they? I should know. Mother blushed, Mirjam was annoyed. He didn't notice the embarrassment of the others. Strange, I used to laugh at his remarks, I found them unconventional, free. I never dreamt they could offend people. Nevertheless, we had a wonderful time. Even old Perchtmann was not quite as stiff as usual, and he likes my parents. I do not know what kind of trouble Father is in. Whenever things go badly for him, he always manages to come out on top. He did not have his talk with me until after a week, two days before their departure. (*Talk* is the wrong word: he explained the situation to me.) Mummi and Ferdinand were also present, Ferdinand did not say a word. Later on, in our bedroom, Ferdinand said he had always considered Father a gambler as long as he had known him. We argued; I forbade him to talk that way.

Wüllner got right to the point. We're broke, my child. We may end up in the poorhouse. If we didn't have a bit of real estate, which is also heavily mortgaged, we'd have to go begging.

What about the house? Why did she think first about the house, not her parents, not Father's factory ("I was never concerned about it, I only cared about Father's alchemical work at home, his mixtures with their daring smells")?

We still have the house, Wüllner said drily.

It's gotten too large for us. Susanne Wüllner wanted to comfort her daughter. Now that Gutsi's gone too, and we can barely get the gardener to keep the garden from going to seed altogether, it makes no sense for us anymore. A small apartment would be enough.

And we've thought ahead (Wüllner tried to camouflage his emotions casually). You know that lovely apartment in the factory—I've got lifetime use of it in the contract with the new associates.

But it's much too small.

We're not getting any bigger.

His conduct, his appearance (he wore an impeccably tailored navy-blue flannel suit) seemed to belie his words. He was a good loser. Susanne Wüllner, however, was on the verge of tears. Every so often, manipulating her lace hankie, she eyed her husband reproachfully.

Katharina could barely get the words out: so you've lost everything?

Almost everything, Wüllner replied. As I've said, we still have some property worth a tidy sum, and I'm paid for every new perfume creation. The factory's down the drain but they're dependent on me.

Katharina had forgotten that she was the hostess; Ferdinand had gone out, telling Božena to serve tea. Wüllner asked for a cognac, "if it won't cost you a fortune."

Why does he always make things so hard on us and so easy on himself?

What about your French partners?

For them my perfumes are sheer war profits, they're carrying on alone.

Can't you sue?

Did I win the war, my child?

Ferdinand, who had returned, burst out laughing, slapping his hands on the arms of his chair: You're one of a kind, Father-in-Law.

Don't I know it, Son-in-Law.

And where do you go from here?

The currency will be reformed sooner or later, Kathi. A lot of people will be caught empty-handed. We'll have gone through that already. If worst comes to worst, we'll sell the house for the new money. In January, a currency adventurer is moving in. We'll see.

You could get a lot for the house.

There's a mortgage on it.

Why?

How do you think I financed everything, especially at the start—my experiments—and what do you think you all lived on? All your little extras!

And yours, said Susanne Wüllner. That could have terminated the painful conversation, which was especially tormenting for Ferdinand, but Susanne was provoked by her husband's devil-may-care attitude. You've got plans for the future too, you shouldn't conceal them from the children.

Her irony made him unsure of himself. This is really unnecessary.

No, Georg, after all I'm part of it.

You, Mummi? Katharina felt queasy about these hints.

When Father makes plans, they're always long-range.

Don't keep us on tenterhooks.

The fact is—this time, Wüllner could not gloss over the disaster. He asked for another cognac, stood up, looked through his jacket pockets, found nothing, sat down again, and said he had misplaced his cigarettes. Ferdinand offered him a cigar.

You're making us all nervous, said Susanne Wüllner, should I tell them?

Very well, we are starting a birdseed company.

What? cried Katharina. Her mother began to laugh. Yes, a birdseed company, Susanne Wüllner confirmed.

This is no laughing matter, said Wüllner. You all keep forgetting the situation we're in. It won't be an expensive undertaking. What, I ask you, does a decent man keep alive even in poverty? His pets. Men have to eat. Birds have to eat. We can almost certainly avoid disaster. I've got suppliers, the contracts are signed, the pouches are already being manufactured: Wüllner's Superior Birdseed Blend. Two salesmen are under contract. Mother, together with a couple of ladies will weigh out the portions and bag them.

And you, Father?

Oh, I'll be running the business.

Wüllner left the room, Ferdinand followed him. Katharina comforted her mother.

Do you think he's still normal, dear?

He hasn't changed one iota, but the era doesn't fit him.

They went to visit Peter and Paul. Gutsi, holding the two babies in her arms like a heraldic figure, bald-headed Peter on the right, Paul with his black furry head on the left, gave them the bottle alternately.

Wüllner the birdseed dealer! I could not believe my ears. I was so flabbergasted that I could not react. Mother weighing out portions! It did not sink in until that evening. Ferdinand could not help me. He maintained a stubborn silence, finally saying: Not another word about your father, Kathi, for you will reproach me forever. Then, a few hours before Father and Mother left, the row between him and Ferdinand. They are basically so alien to one another—or must I be taught how to live? That is a silly and intrinsically illogical statement. Such is my present frame of mind.

They had gone to the Café Majestic after their final stroll through the city. They were sitting at one of the huge windows, watching the activity on Wenceslas Square. Beautiful, said Susanne Wüllner as if there had never been a war and everyone were well off. The muffled din penetrated the café.

Appearances are deceiving, we are going to have one cataclysm after another. Katharina was surprised by the resignation in Ferdinand's voice. The nation has licked blood. The rabble will not give in unless someone establishes a new and credible order.

Wüllner apparently had no interest in responding to this eruption. With his head on his hand, he gazed through the window, pretending to be absorbed.

Don't *you* find the revolution scary, Father-in-Law?

Wüllner shook his head: It's not all that new, Ferdinand. For you perhaps. And besides, one side views order per se as justice, the other doesn't. That's too primitive.

Susanne Wüllner asked her husband to escort her to the pastry buffet.

Oh, stop carrying on, Susanne, you can get your cookies alone.

She remained seated.

Have you lost your appetite?

Don't be so sneaky, Georg.

He gazed out the window again.

Ferdinand didn't realize they were talking about him. He obstinately stuck to his guns: If that Hitler fellow and General Ludendorff gain a large following, couldn't they create order? After all, last year, Mussolini marched to Rome, he took an enormous risk and he won everything.

Wüllner turned to him: You are a chauvinist, a nationalist, Son-in-Law.

Ferdinand disagreed: The issue was not a political view but the foreseeable decline of European culture.

Wüllner feigned surprise. My honored son-in-law sees Western Civilization going under. And he has chosen the savior, Hitler, who marched not through Rome but straight through Munich and ran away when the bullets started whizzing.

What's at stake here is not the individual person, but the principle: How are we to find our way out of total confusion and uncertainty?

Why not uncertainty, Son-in-Law, why not doubt? What if we made up our minds to reject the older orders—and they were good for us, weren't they?—and left them behind? How about it?

You're talking like a Communist.

Perhaps I'm becoming one in my old age. A Communist!

Wüllner's voice had gotten loud, and Ferdinand looked around.

Are you afraid I might be thrown out, I, a bankrupt perfume-maker and possibly a Communist?

Georg, calm down, Susanne Wüllner begged him.

"If Ferdinand had suspected that I was proud of Father when he said those things! He was showing his strength. He wasn't just a charlatan. He had simulated a character that was easy to love yet could be escaped effortlessly. But now, he would not give in, he expressed what was on his mind, and Skodlerrak would no longer have despised 'your clan.'"

Do you know what I'm losing, Son-in-Law? A pile of crap. It's all the same to me. Granted, Susanne will have a hard time adjusting—but so much for that. Perhaps my imagination is inflationary. That wouldn't hurt me. What I possessed is all in my head anyway. Perhaps your Herr Hitler will have my head chopped off when he comes to power.

Georg, please stop it. Susanne Wüllner stood up, saying she and Katharina would wait in front of the café.

These are only vague opinions, Susanne, that's all.

You're a cynic. She drew on her gloves and left. Katharina remained seated. Wüllner ignored her and Ferdinand.

We have to go, said Wüllner. The train leaves in four hours. You can call me a dreamer, he said; perhaps I was a dreamer all my life, and other people probably found me comical—isn't that so, Katharina?—but I was always interested in people, no doubt too superficially. Now, all at once, I see them.

Katharina brought her parents to the station. Ferdinand had excused himself. There was a thaw, the day was wet and unfriendly. No conversation developed. Susanne Wüllner was busy with the baggage, counting the pieces.

Don't take me seriously, Kathi, said Wüllner, leaning out the train window. Your mother's right, I'm unbearable. But never let anyone else tell you what to think.

"I did not wave. Father stood at the window, swaying, making himself look tall. I loved him."

21
Once Again Elvira or
Ferdinand Cheats on Katharina

She learned about it in installments. In one of Ferdinand's suits, which she gave to Božena to have dry-cleaned, she found a love letter written in an intelligent hand. She read it and crumpled it up; she had not been prepared for such a discovery, she had not—as she owned up to herself—"regarded Ferdinand as at all capable of an escapade"—and this in the second year of their marriage. She was at a loss. She lay down on the unmade bed, rubbing the letter to bits between her fingers. It took her a while to realize how offended she was.

Ferdinand had "betrayed" her.

For her, "betrayed" meant something incomprehensibly coarse.

"He can only have forgotten who I am, my skin, my love, my thoughts. Everything. Everything people say when they love each other."

Gradually, her mental numbness subsided, and she tried to figure out how Ferdinand had gotten together with the other woman. She pictured her as resembling Mirjam, with Mirjam's body, and Ferdinand gazing at her. She had both of them naked, touching each other, caressing, sleeping with one another. Oddly enough, these fantasies relieved her pain and she wanted to keep playing with the images.

She recalled that he had asked her whether she had loved any man before him but that she had never asked him about other women. She hadn't weighed the possibility, had assumed that he had come to her without amorous memories, that "I had been his first love."

She began hunting for "clues" to this other woman in his other suits, she sniffed them for the smell of some strange perfume, she rummaged through his desk, looked through the last books he had read. She found nothing, she went to the kitchen and asked Božena whether she had a boyfriend.

Of course, the girl replied.

Was he older than she?

She was still young, after all, said Božena, so the man had to be older, didn't he?

Is he married?

Are you joking! said Božena.

It could be.

Again she felt the resistance of the apartment, she ran through the twilit vestibule, switching on all the lights, helped Gutsi diaper the twins, grabbed hold of them so vehemently—much to Gutsi's annoyance—that they began to cry. Gutsi asked: What ever's wrong with you, Kathi?

Nothing, she said, except that Ferdinand has a mistress.

Gutsi said he was starting early.

Now, Katharina could weep. She bawled together with the babies, Gutsi took them from her, finished diapering them, and placed them in the cribs.

It's like that almost everywhere, said Gutsi.

That's not true.

I don't know of any other way, girl, when I think of your father.

Katharina didn't want to hear anymore, she locked herself in her room. Ferdinand had said he wouldn't be home for lunch. Katharina got dressed to go downtown; she told Božena she would not return until evening. She wanted to visit Mirjam, changed her mind, wandered along the narrow streets up to the Hradčany, doubled back, sat down in the park of Valdštejn Palace. She was afraid everyone could tell just by looking at her that her husband was unfaithful.

She remembered the hours she had spent in this park when she had first come to Prague; she recalled conversations with Ferdinand and Mirjam. Hadn't she awarded Elvira a new freedom? How easily she could have countered Don Juan. She had meant it seriously after her experiences with Eberhard and Skodlerrak, and her resoluteness had annoyed Ferdinand. Now, cornered, she gave up the "new Elvira," behaving just like the "unfree" woman she had denigrated. It was easier breaking out of Elvira's captivity with her own concealed experiences than remaining, after being betrayed in the freedom she had won.

Should she find a lover merely to get even? But as she thought about it, she knew she couldn't. The children were too close to her.

Thinking about Elvira had calmed her down, she was sure of herself again.

Early in the afternoon, she went home after buying pastries for tea with Gutsi, and when Gutsi tried to talk about Ferdinand, Katharina rebuked her, saying the matter had been taken care of, it was her business alone. Gutsi should not take occasional surges of emotion so seriously. Katharina was amazed that Ferdinand had not changed in any way. He noticed her scrutiny. He asked whether there was something wrong with his suit. She said she was just glad to see him. He hugged her quickly, kissing her on the forehead. "At that moment, I wished more intensely than ever before to sleep with him."

Božena served dinner. Gutsi had excused herself: Paul had hiccups, and she wanted to remain with the babies. Ferdinand talked about the "fantastic gifts" of an indigo dyer. He planned to hire him for his factory in Brno even if it caused resentment.

Her question had barely any weight: Are you cheating on me, Ferdinand? Yet it hit him hard. He peered into her eyes and said after a while: You're crazy, Katharina. How can you ask something like that?

When a woman's alone, stupid thoughts come to her.

He said he would work in the study for an hour.

She went to bed, waiting for him. He came in less than an hour. They made love. He was bewildered by her intensity. That evening, she conceived her third child, Camilla.

22
The Breathing of a Spring Day

During her second pregnancy, Katharina was less stable, more susceptible to fantasies, more sickly. In the first two months, she felt so awful
that she asked Ferdinand to entertain less at home and to go out without
her. Mirjam would drop by, but her shallow chitchat enervated Katharina, and Mirjam complained about Katharina's whininess; so they got
together very seldom. She and Gutsi exchanged memories of Klotzsche,
she could delight in frequently repeated anecdotes. She had discovered
that Ferdinand, as she put it, had no metaphysics whatsoever; his sense of
reality oppressed her. She had never leaned toward realism, she said,
overstating the matter; she leaned far more toward activism or nihilism;
that was why, she said, she had been attracted to anarchists, who, after
all, should have been foreign to her, what with her background and all.

She thought a great deal about Uncle David, who seldom wrote, but
he had promised to visit her after they moved to Brno. He might have
understood her perhaps and he could have cheered her up.

Meanwhile, the sun had risen higher. After taking the trolley to
Wenceslas Square, she planned to visit her seamstress. Suddenly, she felt
the air. She inhaled, stopped short, looked at the sky, which was
cloudless—a pale, agitated blue. She sensed almost physical warmth and
felt as if she were floating in the air. The city had changed; the heavy
stone dissolved in light, the Hradčany hovered over the hill, a thoroughly
perforated filigree.

She didn't talk much with the seamstress, who gave up her efforts to start a conversation with pins and needles between her lips.

She didn't want to return home right away, she strolled aimlessly. At Masaryk Station, she waited for the trolley, although not actually wanting to board one; she let several go by without getting in. Swinging her purse like a child, she stood among the people, inhaling the air, which made her breath palpable. Someone was watching her. To her left, just two paces away, stood a young man, obviously also waiting for a streetcar; he was scrutinizing her. He wore a lightweight beige suit, his shirtcollar was open; with his hands playing in his jacket pockets and his left foot forward as if he were about to leap, he peered, unabashed, impudent. His gaze held her tight; she dared not move lest she escape it. His eyes resembled Hribasch's eyes, but they were more belligerent, more insolent. Their gazes began to play with each other. The boy's impertinence irritated her. Couldn't he tell she was pregnant? Shouldn't her condition discourage him from flirting with her? She placed her left hand on her throat. She knew she might go off with him. But he didn't take a single step toward her. She could no longer control her smile. Now, he smiled back, a bit too coarsely, too blatantly. She *would* be able to escape him. She convinced herself that it was this air, which was all too intimate with her body.

Now she felt hostility, a desire to hurt the man, to mortify him publicly. She could scream, accuse him of harrassment. He read her eyes and became serious again. Was he speaking to her? Did he already dominate her so thoroughly that he could read her mind and influence her? This was too much for her. She avoided his gaze. At that instant, she saw a fat, elderly woman with a market hamper jump in front of an approaching streetcar; the woman shrieked as the motor car knocked her down and dragged her along. The brake squealed, the driver pressed his face against the window pane. Instantly, a cluster of people gathered. Katharina was jostled back and forth; she felt sick, she was afraid she would have a dizzy spell; the baby moved in her womb. He was suddenly with her, placing his arm around her shoulder briefly, then letting her go. His hand clutched her arm. His closeness confused her utterly; she felt his palm on her skin. She didn't look at him. He spoke Czech, she didn't understand. Then he spoke German flawlessly.

Can I help you? It is obvious you are not feeling well, dear madam.

She concentrated on the pressure of his hand, on the sensation triggered by his touch.

Now he stood next to her calmly. They looked as if they had been waiting together for the trolley for a long time.

The scene had become turbulent—the police came, an ambulance arrived.

It would be better to walk to the next stop. May I escort you there?

He did not wait for her answer, instead he nudged her in that direction. He adjusted his pace to hers, sometimes his hip bumped hers; she enjoyed the rhythm, which she could interrupt whenever she wished.

They soon reached the next stop, which she secretly regretted. She did not hesitate to get into the next trolley, although it wasn't her line; he followed her, sitting down next to her, again placing his hand on her arm, with light emphasis. Katharina tried to escape his touch by simply omitting the place on her arm from her sensation. She trembled, felt goosepimples.

She got off at the next stop, she didn't care where she was. When he stood up to accompany her, she said very definitely: Thank you, I don't need your help anymore.

She quickly found a cab, and the instant she came home, she changed clothes, then pulled a chair to the parlor window; she sat there until twilight, when Ferdinand called for her and they went to dinner.

She had not only been touched by a strange man, she had allowed it to happen, without resisting; that was why she was certain that the handsome young man had been a messenger.

I can swear that he did not arouse me sexually. Granted, during both pregnancies I have experienced phases of desire, yearning for love at the oddest times, yearning for skin, physicality; but that was not the case yesterday. Basically, the boy repelled me. Some vague kind of magnetism—I have no other explanation. And the day, that splendid day with an air one could taste on one's tongue! I am probably exaggerating. I am in a bad mood, and my imagination is overwrought. But only he could have inspired all these thoughts. What will happen if I die? I can picture my own funeral, the company of mourners. I can picture that final flash, that last moment. Nothing existing anymore. Can one truly imagine it? We have created heaven only because we want to see further. The world is in my head and it will end with me. Why did he inspire such thoughts? I do not know. He behaved so impudently—he played a role, for me alone, because that was how I wished him to be on that spring day. He will never come back again in that guise.

Ferdinand, who was extraordinarily attentive during this period, telling her that she was growing more beautiful from day to day, surprised her with the news that he had bought a house in Brno, in the Black Fields, so they wouldn't have to live with his father. She was delighted and felt fewer qualms about moving.

23
Moving or How Uncle David Lost His Voice

Several days after they moved, only a few rooms in the new house were inhabitable—Gutsi had adamantly made sure that the three children had a place to live and peace and quiet; Peter and Paul were making their first attempts at walking—two robust, well-developing boys—Camilla, in contrast, was delicate, "she's simply a child of despair." Božena left the kitchen, unable to put it back in order.

A few days after they moved, Uncle David showed up unannounced. He knew his visit was inconvenient, but, megalomaniac that he was (his words), he wanted to make sure of a proper housewarming. She was startled; he looked like a skeleton held together by old-fashioned clothes.

The peace of old age is emaciating me, my child. He reacted to her fright as ironically as ever; his bearing was likewise unchanged, elegant and slightly exaggerated.

One vanishes—isn't that an apt way of putting it? No, he didn't want to see the house for another week. She mustn't invite him in. He said it made a stately impact on the outside, and he liked the newly designed garden. Everything thoroughly modern. Your Ferdinand is on the peak of the era; I have trouble breathing up here.

You of all people. What are you doing in Brno?

He said an old friend had invited him to his estate in Třebová; he was supposed to go hunting there, but didn't feel like it really, and he was also supposed to take care of artistic entertainment on the side.

One more week, she said, by then the guest room will be furnished. Very good.

Could she get him a cab?

He said he knew the way. A short stroll wouldn't hurt him. He kissed her on the forehead and vanished behind the fence, waving.

As trivial as the conversation may have been, it had a tone that she had forgotten and that made her feel freer the instant she heard it.

However, she didn't realize she needed it. She had been incapable of resolving to be an adult or what the more capable people, like Ferdinand, meant by "adult." Ferdinand, to her surprise, had taken her along to the factory on one of the first few days, showing her through the weaving and the dyeing sections—she was the new owner's wife. Old Perchtmann had welcomed her in his office, a large room with wooden paneling, which tastefully emphasized his dignity. Offering them a sherry, he said little, but treated her amiably, almost solicitously. So far, she had not gotten to know the city, she had seen the fortress on the Spielberg, the cathedral from afar. Now, they had driven along an ugly factory street, the Gröna, which nevertheless struck her as peculiarly familiar. Sometimes, when seeing houses or streets for the first time, she imagined they might be important to her later on. That was how she felt about the Gröna.

The house was practical, it became homey. A young Viennese architect, a friend of the famous Adolf Loos, had built it for a hotel owner, who, upon moving into the villa, had immediately committed suicide with his mistress. The disavowed widow tried to sell the house as fast as possible, but had to wait a year until Ferdinand came along. Katharina's complaints about their Prague apartment had impelled him to look for "something modern." The financial terms were feasible.

Gutsi and Božena were likewise satisfied with the new surroundings. The children adjusted quickly. However, Camilla's delicate health still caused anxiety, and Gutsi immediately contacted a pediatrician who lived in the neighborhood.

Two evenings a week Ferdinand did not come home; he met with friends in a club that admitted only Germans. Suspicious but unprotesting, Katharina noted that his political statements were colored more and more by German chauvinism.

She missed Mirjam, whose letters were peculiarly insipid.

Her room was not yet completely decorated, though she had already selected the furniture. It was on the second story, facing the garden, and lit by two windows that, reaching almost from the floor to the ceiling, were cut like strips into the wall. The nursery and Gutsi's and Božena's rooms were on the third story. Only the split-level living room on the ground floor was uncomfortable in its vastness. It gradually filled up, and eventually the carpet in front of the fireplace became the twins' favorite spot, which they vigorously defended against the other children.

Looking forward to Uncle David's visit, Katharina drudged away. She drove the workers; new items were delivered all the time; furniture, carpets, lamps. She and Božena pushed furniture around until late at night. She was afraid that the grand piano, which was to stand in front of the windows facing the garden, might not come in time—but it did come, one day before Uncle David's promised arrival.

He would be able to tell her about her parents, who always asked about the grandchildren in their letters, while revealing little about themselves. Father was evidently traveling a lot again; the birdseed company seemed to be flourishing. A sentence written by Susanne Wüllner ("the days are long, I only look up when our bagging room gets dark") made her wonder.

Ferdinand had invited several of his old friends, former schoolmates, and friends from the tennis club to a "housewarming" and "a small concert."

Should we wait for him much longer? she asked. Irritated and slightly tipsy after being in the club, Ferdinand rebuked her: That's up to you. I don't know your Uncle David.

Well, she said, since I do know him, I advise you to go to bed and I advise myself to stay up a while longer.

It was after midnight.

Ferdinand left her; now, I despise him again, she said to herself; then, spelling it out many times in a row: David Eichlaub, David Eichlaub—there are names that are tender to their bearers. She heard the car arrive. She wanted to stand up and run to the front door—but remained seated; she didn't want to be disappointed, it might be one of the neighbors, not David.

The doorbell rang. Now she hurried, shouted, heedless of the sleepers in the house: I'm coming! One moment, Uncle David!

She had forgotten to switch on the light over the portal, so he stood there in the twilight, again like a creature from the Tales of Hoffmann, clutching his hat and his traveling-bag, he could whoosh away again, she told herself. She said: Stay there!

He took a step back, almost vanishing again. Only his shock of white hair was visible, so were his eyes; he took up her fear, teasing her: I'm not certain I can. My brother Ahasuerus, you know, Heinrich Heine's cousin, is waiting around the corner, and he does not wish me to find a hospitable house.

He disguised his voice, mumbling, clearing his throat.

She leaped upon him, embracing him, holding him tight, smelling an old man's skin, tobacco, and sour sweat. She took the bag out of his hand, asked him in, and told him he couldn't always remain outside the door, promising to visit.

She led the way; he said: You no longer walk like a child. He stood in the living room, turned around several times and nodded, saying a jocular architect had had a fling here. He discovered the piano, stationed himself inside the curve, posing, wandered around the instrument while running his hand across the polished black surface, opened it. Ah, a Blüthner, our colleague Steinway is going to have a fit. He played a few measures; she stood behind him, propping her arms on his shoulders; he cringed, saying she was too heavy for a frail old man.

Did he feel tired?

He didn't but he assumed that she did.

No, I'm delighted you've come after all. She told him he hadn't apologized for arriving terribly late: I missed the train in Třebová.

Was he hungry, did he care for something to drink?

A glass of red wine would be nice.

He refused to sit down in the deep armchair at the fireplace, he preferred sitting next to her on the piano stool.

Was the hunt exciting?

Oh, child.

Is that a stupid question?

No, it's not stupid, that's how people break the ice.

Well then. . . .

I was in Berlin, during a street fight, I saw a man get shot, he probably wasn't involved, just a passerby like me. When the shooting began, we dashed across the street, headlong, looking for a building entrance. He stopped when I reached the entrance and I looked back at the street; he was just a few yards away from me, with a face in which life had paused—can you imagine it? He was hit. You couldn't see any wound. The bullet must have gone into his back. He stood there, dead, until he slowly collapsed, like a puppet whose strings have loosened.

Uncle David's left hand lay on the back of her chair, an old hand. Katharina could not come up with a response to his story.

Are they friends, your people in Třebová?

Yes. I mean after an experience like that, it's hard to go hunting. I provided the indoor entertainment.

You'll have to do that here too. Ferdinand has invited people to an evening of lieder.

Goodness, you must be hard up. Is your Ferdinand asleep?

For some time now.

How are the children?

The twins are so funny, you'll enjoy them. And our little girl is so-
so; she gets sick a lot.

Does she worry you?

Not really.

She brought him to his room; he found it "grand." Should I settle in
here permanently, dear?

Why not?

Your Ferdinand would smoke me out.

She stole into the bedroom, avoided making any noise so as not to
wake Ferdinand; she slipped cautiously under the blanket.

She took over the preparations for the soiree, getting more and more
excited, refusing to let Uncle David "abduct her to the city." Besides, she
was nervous; she was meeting Ferdinand's circle for the first time, and
there were hints that some of the people were German nationalists who
might say things that would offend Uncle David.

The evening began well. She dressed early, and then sat with Gutsi
and Uncle David in the living room. Ferdinand wasn't ready yet, they
made fun of him for taking as much time as a woman.

Uncle David described Mummi's work day, which she spent with
three women, next to the apartment, in the "Wüllner Factory," a ware-
house of the old factory; amid sacks of seed and grain, they sat at a long
table covered with scales and pouches. While Father was on his feet
again.

"I was not really listening. I was not there. The tension of the day
had absolutely twisted me. I realized I was taking a leap at that moment. I
anticipated old age for several seconds in order to grow older."

Ferdinand came, drew his watch from his vest: the guests were due
any moment.

You'll make the introductions, won't you? she said.

Of course. Are you scared, Kathi?

A little, I don't know anyone.

People are looking forward to meeting you.

An hour later, she knew everyone and no one. She knew about an
extraordinarily elegant married couple who owned the largest department store in Brno, their name was Netzkarz. The husband, in his fifties,
seemed aware of his effect on women, while she, a buxom, tempestuous
blonde, attracted men. Katharina had been introduced to an elderly lady,
who impressed her, a very large, corpulent woman, with innate grace,
dignity, and a great deal of wit; her name was Dorothee Neumeister and,
like the Perchtmanns, she owned a dyeworks. Franzjosef and Eva Nagel

were the same age as Katharina—he, a partner in a printing press, so shy that he stuttered; she, imitating him, evidently out of sheer affection.

All in all, there were a good dozen guests to whom she had to be attentive. With the help of Gutsi and Božena, she succeeded with bravura, as Ferdinand admiringly put it afterward.

For Katharina, the evening was characterized by the language, the melodious German dialect of Brno, with its drawling umlauts.

Well, what can I tell you?

Well, I just sort of simply turned my baaack on him.

Well, should I saaaay anything?

Uncle David's songs were applauded, he was accompanied by a young musician from the opera.

She did not recall a single conversation—only a few sharp, silly utterances about Teutonism, about the chauvinism of the Czechs, about Masaryk's weakness, about Jews. She did, however like Dorothee Neumeister; she wanted to stay in touch with her.

It wasn't until everyone had gone and Gutsi and Božena had cleaned up that Uncle David thawed out; he had been unable to display his full range of wit. He sat down at the piano and improvised, Katharina said she hadn't realized he could play so marvelously.

When a music-lover loses his voice, he has to find some way to compensate for it.

But you have a wonderful voice.

What I recall was long ago.

You couldn't sing anymore, Uncle David?

Not a peep. He stood next to the piano, opening his mouth and playing a voiceless man in a painfully funny pantomime.

It wasn't all that bad, he added.

Gutsi stood in the door, watching the scene, and Katharina said: Why don't you join us a bit, Gutsi, or are you too tired?

Camilla wakes up early.

Gutsi said she had heard that Herr Eichlaub had once lost his voice. She didn't want to miss the story.

A young man who wants to be a singer but has to become a pharmacist is in a quandary. Mummi can tell you the whole sad story, Kathi, she had to put up with all my despair, she was practically still a child. So I studied pharmacy at the University of Leipzig and, unbeknownst to my parents, I took voice lessons from a renowned singer. He was very encouraging. He said I could make pills any time, but my voice was a gift that I mustn't reject. My pharmaceutical studies dragged on, much to my parents' annoyance. Art, in contrast, thrived. During one phase, when I was absolutely sick from lack of self-confidence, I made up my mind to tell my parents the truth—but then I fell in love with a delightful and frivolous creature whom I had met through my singing coach. Her mother was a mediocre soprano at the opera house; the daughter was more promising. She enchanted me; I was crazy about her. Women still wore corsets in those days, and her waist was practically a public attraction. The bust above it, the backside below, each was a sight to behold—ah, I'm carrying on after such a long time. I should have realized what a slut she was right off the bat. She toyed with me. She was obviously experienced at it, we met frequently. I swore my love to her, she acted accommodating, and I was on the verge of proposing, I didn't give a damn about the scandal it would cause my parents. My ardor must have been too risky for her, for she dropped me overnight, rejected me completely. I found her with another man. Her scorn poisoned me and— here it comes—it took away my voice. I couldn't sing anymore—I croaked, gasped, coughed. My venerable teacher was beside himself, he sent me to great medical authorities. They were at a loss. Only one of them, a thoroughly progressive man, analyzed the loss of my voice as a dreadful case of hysteria, which had previously been diagnosed only in females. The pill-makers got me back. My parents welcomed me lovingly, and then helped me buy a pharmacy, they overlooked my peculiar ways, which got worse. For a while I avoided all women. Until I fell into the hands of an efficient housekeeper, who wasted no time luring me into her bed, where I loved the Leipzig girl right out of my body. And—whether you believe it or not—when I leaped out of that bed, I could sing again. What good was it now—I had the pharmacy, and opera remained a youthful dream.

Katharina took his hands, they were light; she wondered what she could say, but he fended her off:

Not a word, otherwise I'll never again lure guests here with my singing.

24
The Czech

He had been waiting in Ferdinand's room for two hours. Božena had served him tea and then liqueur, but Ferdinand did not arrive as scheduled. Katharina knew that he was a Czech manufacturer from Přerov, "a pompous chauvinist," who wanted to work with Moravian Knitwear because of his financial dilemma. Ferdinand had put him down in unusually harsh terms. She asked Božena how the man was behaving, was he impatient? Božena said he was waiting very patiently, reading a newspaper and constantly smiling to himself.

Katharina was embarrassed. She decided to talk to the stranger a little. When she entered the room, the man jumped up and bowed. He said his name was Čermák, he was waiting for her husband. She apologized for Ferdinand's delay. The man replied that it didn't matter, he had time. His German was impeccable. She said her husband should arrive any moment, but would he care to make do with her company during the brief wait? He said he would be delighted but did not wish to impose. Even though he was exceedingly polite, his words as well as his gestures came from a depth of hostility. Not that she was afraid of him; but she remained alert, focusing on every word she spoke.

His hands had no patience, they contradicted his outward calm. She looked in astonishment at his hopping, tapping, scratching fingers. Although he noticed her glances, he did not relax his hands. He apparently did not wish to camouflage the dialectics of his character.

He was not tall, and he was plain in a way that stuck in your mind. He was very skinny, his movements were wooden. He had the sensitive, freckled skin of blonde people; his forehead was high since the front half of his head was bald.

She couldn't get past cordial phrases.

Do you know why I am visiting your husband? His question sounded ominous.

She said she had heard he was having financial problems.

He replied that this was true. He smiled again, and now she realized that his smile covered up his shyness.

You are not from Prague, dear lady?

No, I come from Dresden.

Oh, yes, so I was told. From Germany, the *Reich.* He stressed the word *Reich* in such a way that it sounded like an insult. But she ignored it.

His hands kept talking while he remained silent.

She waited for him to go on.

I know Dresden, he said, I spent some time there before the war. It's a wonderful city. Are you homesick?

Not really. But there are reasons why I am not.

Nearly all of Čermák's questions wounded me. I do not know why, for they all remained within the limits of convention. He was certainly not presumptuous or overly inquisitive. I must have seemed naive, if not childlike, and that goaded him on: I'll show this little goose. Or am I too easily offended? I am exaggerating again. But then: Are you homesick? Should I not have spontaneously answered: Yes, yes, I am homesick. His question made it clear to me that I had lost my childhood homeland. The loss of the house in Klotzsche snuffed out my desire to go back. Even worse, I was all the more frightened by the thought that I was now wholly dependent on Ferdinand. There is no emergency exit left, none. So now I am here, only here, in this house in Brno, with my husband and children. I could write: This is my homeland. Why do I not dare? Does a person have only one home in his lifetime? That is nonsense. But why cannot even the children impel me to say to myself: I am at home with you children. I owe all these strange broodings and insights to Čermák.

Is Dresden—please excuse my indiscretion—no longer your homeland?

I don't know, Herr Čermák, I must confess that you have made me uncertain.

Really? But it is quite simple. If not Dresden, then Brno.

It is not that simple.

Homeland, he said, does not just mean houses, towns, landscapes, or people one is close to. It can be a lot more. Listen, I know Brno very well. I studied here before the war, in the monarchy, in the "multi-national state," as the term went, and there were actually people who considered the situation good, viable, just as it was. I was a student, a Czech in his own country, without many rights.

But you had the same rights as the Germans, I know you did, Herr Čermák.

You know. I did not know. And what do the "same rights" mean, dear lady? A Czech among Czechs in the land of Czechs? Did the Austrians or the Germans invent us?

I am trying to understand you.

Do not try! She felt like leaving the room, but he would take it as an affront, and she could not tell whether such an action might make it difficult for Ferdinand to converse with him.

Do not try! No one wanted to admit it. And why, I ask you, in a Czech city like *Brno* (he made a point of using the Czech name instead of the German *Brünn*) do Germans own businesses, hotels, factories, and such beautiful houses as this one?

She murmured very softly: You are going too far, Herr Čermák.

He put his smile forward ("Oddly enough, he did not seem sordid for even an instant, I liked his solidity"), then he bowed apologetically without getting up: I have let myself go, dear lady, it is a centuries-old bitterness, and people like us cannot wash it out of our mouths.

I barely know the history of this country.

That is a mistake, it is a panorama of rebellion and humiliation, with little security or control. We certainly had our princes, our kings, Slavic rulers, before the Germans came, but they fell out with one another; they were melancholy or powerless, and Europe's center kept getting divided, Moravia alone was cut up three or four times. The Luxemburgers came, they ruled us, the Hapsburgs, the goodness-knows-what crowned nobodies. Our nobility betrayed us to Vienna, the Czernys, the Lichnowskys—

But wasn't the nobility simply international, Herr Čermák?

That too. It took refuge in internationalism. What was a Czech, what is a Czech? Nothing! How long did it take us to produce a national literature, and I am amazed that the Germans do not claim the great Antonín Dvořák for themselves.

Why have you come here, Herr Čermák? Do you wish my husband to help you?

She did not want to deal with his despair any longer. What a miserable background this man used to justify himself, and how little he had to counter with.

In your language, "Slav" and "slave" are synonymous. We are inferior people. Whenever someone comes along and talks about Slavic civilization, then Pan-Slavism is decried as the horde thinking of semi-humans. How disgusting! And now we have Masaryk, we have our state, our patriotism is no longer insulted—nevertheless, we are still second-class people. Are we not?

The Germans have their rights as a minority confirmed.

Now just tell me, dear lady, that Masaryk loves Goethe.

People claim he does.

It is true. But his love of Goethe helps you, paní Perchtmannová, more than it does us.

Isn't he the center of the Czech republic?

I greatly respect him.

Then I do not understand you.

We are merely *talking* about a dichotomy, paní Perchtmannová, and that is basically impossible. It has to be experienced.

Do you, as a Czech in the Czech republic, see yourself really as a Slav?

Yes.

You are making things hard on yourself, Herr Čermák.

Yes, I have come to ask your husband for support, a Czech turning to a German.

Is that bad?!

Yes. Not because Perchtmann is a German and Čermák a Czech, but because the power is distributed in this way.

Are you turning private matters into a general condition?

The Austrians kept us down, you know, the process is very simple, the German firms were given preference. And because they are big and powerful, they are also given preference in the republic.

That is not true.

Am I not an example, paní Perchtmannová?

I cannot verify what you say, I do not know very much about economics.

Don't you trust me?

His fingers were drumming on the arm of his chair.

A Czech director has joined my husband's company.

They had to hire him. They needed a token Czech. I am afraid he is a fool.

My husband says he is an excellent businessman.

He says so in order to justify employing a moron. The man does not get in his way.

You are becoming nasty, Herr Čermák, your anger blinds you.

We have been raised blind. We have been told a thousand times: Play blind, see nothing; and so we have become blind. We are gradually learning to see again, see ourselves, and we are overcome by nausea, we see the others and we see too late that the people who brought us up are still in power, the power that we have attained, too late.

That is too complicated for me, said Katharina.

I was describing a process.

I have completely neglected to pour you some more tea.

Please do not go to any great trouble, paní Perchtmannová.

I am embarrassed that my husband has made you wait for such a long time.

Haven't I also told you about patience?

Patience? She noticed the outrageous allusion too late: You keep putting me in the wrong.

("Why did familiarity develop despite all the hostility? Why did I not put Čermák in his place? He was downright insolent. Was I not up to him? Or would he have gotten close to me in his way?")

That is the peculiarity of all people without rights.

She stood up, so did he, she shook his hand. My husband will come very soon. I have to take care of my children.

He held her hand: You have children?

Three. Twins and a tiny little girl.

I have eight.

Eight children!

His hand clutched hers, dry and cool.

He said he was very happy with his family.

The change in tone embarrassed her. She hurriedly left both the room and Čermák, who had suddenly relaxed.

Ferdinand arrived a bit later.

Had he forgotten about Čermák?

Some business had come up. He had to go to Vienna the next day. Is the guy still waiting?

She had been unable to get rid of him.

He's pushy, and he's a loser. He also gets on people's nerves with his crazy nationalism.

I found him very intelligent. She contradicted her feelings and the tormenting dialogue. "I could not understand why I yielded to my impulse to protect him from Ferdinand and his arrogance. It was one of those moments when I separated myself from Ferdinand, not for some cause or person, but only to avoid getting lost in a world that Ferdinand represented and that I found incomprehensible."

The conversation was over in just half an hour. Božena saw Čermák out, and Katharina did not see him again before he left.

She asked Ferdinand what the upshot of their meeting was.

I'm going to help him.

So then he's not as incapable as you say.

You're mistaken, Kathi, he's an ignoramus. But if I support a Czech enterprise, I'll gain some prestige with the authorities and also with a few banks.

25
Perchtmann & Son

The "old house" was a phrase that aroused Katharina's discomfort if not resistance. But she held back so as not to annoy Ferdinand. His father kept away from the Black Fields, the "wilderness"; at best, he "poked his head in," the chauffeur kept the engine running, Perchtmann, Sr., waited at the garden gate, surveyed the children, handed out candy, let the boys kiss him, breathed on Katharina's forehead, and drove off. Grandfather's visits were sensations for the twins, and they could somehow sense when one was in the offing.

The "old house" referred to an eight-room apartment in an elegant building on Franzensberg, near the cathedral. The windows of the smoking-room, the salon, and the dining-room looked out upon a small park, which Katharina loved, and she often went there without ringing her father-in-law's bell. To her and, later, the children's delight, the park gate was locked by a uniformed guard every evening. When darkness gathered, the guard would shout into the park three times, at intervals, and then push the two gigantic wings of the iron gate together. One of the most adventurous wishes of the twins was to get locked in the park and then climb over the gate in the darkness.

Katharina could not and would not break into the relationship between the father and the son. The early death of Ferdinand's mother had brought the two men very close together. Their resemblance, despite a considerable difference in age, was basically laughable. They were completely alike in certain gestures and figures of speech.

Konrad Perchtmann eventually began to trust Gutsi, if only because he felt Katharina did not spend enough time with the children and imposed too much on the old woman. Gutsi could report on his merriment, his tenderness, his funny playfulness. The old man could fool around wonderfully with the children, said Gutsi, and when she went down with them into the park, he would sit at the window, delighting in every minor event, which he then repeated to her: Paul sliding along the gravel walk on the seat of his pants, Peter unable to comprehend that he could make his wooden horse stand up again, Camilla's funny habit of stretching her two little arms into the sun over and over. This was a side of the old man that Katharina did not know. When she visited him with Ferdinand, he would shut her out of the conversation. She could not tell whether he was shy with her or perhaps disliked her. In any case, she had taken away his son, who had been his constant companion for years. If the old man did address her, then it was usually indirectly, through Ferdinand.

But she liked him. His frailty aroused her tenderness. He resisted her. He had never offered to let her address him in the familiar form. She had gotten into the habit of calling him "Father Perchtmann"; he called her Katherina, and they used the polite form with one another: she was grateful for this distance between them.

Every morning, until his death, he had his chauffeur drive him to "his factory," his "bureau," where Ferdinand had to welcome him; his father would brook no tardiness. For all his love, he distrusted Ferdinand professionally. He had set up a small, unsightly office for him next to his own, discrediting the son's demands and railing against him in temper tantrums, calling him "weak, soft, incapable of running a company." Ferdinand endured such reproaches unprotestingly, which offended Katharina. The only person who stood up for Ferdinand against the old man was the Czech director, Prchala, a fat man, who looked like a peasant and had surprisingly agile movements. He greatly esteemed the younger Perchtmann. Ferdinand, however, suspected Prchala of planning to "Czechify" the firm after his father's death and pushing Ferdinand out. Katharina failed to talk him out of his suspicion. Moreover, she annoyed Ferdinand because she always invited Prchala to "her Circle," and because she liked his matter-of-fact intelligence. It was all the more surprising to hear the old man's wish that, "since she wasn't taking care of the children anyway," she ought to come to the office as much as possible and help Ferdinand. And at the office, he spoke directly to her, rather than through Ferdinand; he even grew to trust her in business, but never came to trust her in private life. Now and again, he would invite her to his office for a sherry (Ferdinand made fun of it) and explain business procedures to her. He told her that if she felt like it, she could go into exports under Ferdinand's aegis. Ferdinand regarded this as one of the old man's many eccentricities. But Katharina insisted that Ferdinand at least get her involved a little. Reluctantly, he allowed her to sit in his front room from 9 A.M. to 1 P.M., with the senior clerk and three women, and to learn about exports to Poland, Austria, Hungary, Romania, and Bulgaria. She worked her way in quickly and well, dealing with currencies, formulating terms of payment without help. Prchala jokingly called her "Frau Boss."

> Ferdinand and I are fighting more and more. He is annoyed, we leave the house at different times and reach the factory at different times. He acts frosty toward me. Others notice it too. I am certain that people are saying our marriage is in trouble. And is it not true? Was that Father Perchtmann's intention when he asked me to work at the firm? Yet he does not know Ferdinand all that well. Could not Ferdinand have also been glad I was near him, glad about my interest in his work? It appears to me that an incursion into his sphere spells a loss of prestige for him. That notion is sheer nonsense, but I am unable to speak to him. Once I began, but he broke in: Leave work in its place. I don't want to hear anything about it at home. Like his father, he has gotten it into his head that I am an awful mother. Yet he knows I spend every afternoon with the children and I put them to bed every night without Gutsi's help. He would prefer my remaining at home all the time; he makes fun of my friends, my interests, thereby closing himself off. Our only shared pleasures are theater and opera. Perhaps he has a mistress again. He hardly ever touches me, although I have not become uglier—indeed I am prettier, as Gutsi keeps telling me. Odd that I am almost indifferent to him, almost indifferent,

she wrote in her diary on April 18, 1927.

After a time, they allowed her to take part in the board meetings. Konrad Perchtmann got her involved in negotiations. She understood why he had become so successful, how he had gotten so far with his father's small beginnings. She accepted his authority. He had a knack for analyzing situations, then quickly making up his mind. Numbers, which remained numbers for her, led a life of their own for him. And his misanthropy had not dimmed his knowledge of human beings. He could do almost anything. Although he couldn't stand Prchala, he nevertheless respected his proficiency. Konrad Perchtmann also spoke Czech fluently, but seldom used it. He did not like walking through the factory. He remained beyond reach for the workers, most of whom were Czech.

If Konrad Perchtmann talked politics, she held back. When she tried to make her antipathy clear to Ferdinand, he rebuked her: In his long life, Father has accumulated experiences that we do not have.

She said he always offended her whenever he talked politics.

Ah, Katharina, I keep forgetting that Jewish blood flows in your veins, he would occasionally say, which did not prevent him from vituperating, in her presence, against the "Jewish pack."

Prchala was the only person to disagree with him at such times, albeit mildly. One day in one of the strange conversations that took place during business or terminated a conference, the old man attacked Katharina directly.

Have you gotten a reply from Löwenstein in Warsaw?

It arrived this morning.

Well?

He's ordered fifty bales.

Jesus Christ! What an order!

His joy brought out her unabashed candor: Herr Löwenstein apparently got to like me during his last visit—and this is the result.

Ferdinand laughed: If that's the case. . . .

Prchala sensed what was coming. Walking over to the filing cabinet, he pulled out a folder and leafed through it, turning his back to the others.

Sort of Jew to Jew, said the old man, that makes it easy, doesn't it, Katharina?

She was speechless.

Please, said Ferdinand.

Is something wrong, my son?

I think you're exaggerating.

In what way?

Now she could finally speak, Ferdinand's hesitancy helped her: Perhaps you are right, Father Perchtmann. My success does confirm your opinion. Jews among themselves, right? Business is in our blood. And old Löwenstein probably thought that this poor little half-breed among all these goyim should have something to gladden her heart. For the sake of Perchtmann & Son, right?

I sensed that you would feel attacked, Katharina.

Yes, you *have* attacked me, Father Perchtmann.

Is it not in the blood?

That's silly, it's a business deal you can be satisfied with. And Herr Löwenstein is a man of honor.

Have I denied that?

No. You called him a Jew.

Isn't he a Jew?

Yes. But for you a Jew is not a human being.

Who says so?

Didn't you once say that the Jews are vermin ruining the world?

Come, come.

Prchala turned back to them, the file in his hand, and said: A good half of our clients are Jews, Herr Perchtmann.

What does that prove? snapped Perchtmann. He broke off, asked Ferdinand to see him out and to call the chauffeur.

Ferdinand defended him afterward even though she hadn't said anything: He's a good German. The Germans used to have privileges, Ferdinand went on, which they lost in 1914. Hadn't she noticed that his father had pictures of the last two German monarchs on his desk? Now he saw Germans and German culture being pushed back. He could not resign himself to the new situation. Granted, many Jews had stuck by the Germans, and German was their language too. But in general they were pitting the Czechs and Germans against one another.

That's nonsense, Ferdinand, and you know it.

Why won't you listen to reason? You'd have an easier time with Father if you made some effort to understand him.

With you too, she said.

I don't care, he said. I know you.

I'm not so sure.

Do you want to argue with me?

What happened, asked Gutsi, did Ferdinand hurt you?

No, they merely explained to me that I am messing up the world.

You? Why you of all people?

I and the Jews.

Gutsi didn't really understand; she said she found everything topsy-turvy anyway in Czechoslovakia.

Now you're talking like Father Perchtmann, said Katharina.

Konrad Perchtmann died in winter 1927. He died in the car while driving between the factory and his apartment.

Ferdinand just about ignored the factory, the children, and her. For a while, she ran the company together with Prchala, and Ferdinand did not get involved. He sat in the Opera Café, pretending to read news-papers, not conversing with anyone. The children couldn't cheer him up. He decided to sleep in his study. Božena made sure the change went smoothly. She and Gutsi did not dare to say anything about the unpleas-ant situation.

Katharina tried to win him back. She made herself beautiful, changed her hair style, dressed attractively. But he didn't notice.

I'm useless, he had said the night after the funeral, I'm a daddy's boy, and now I'm nothing.

She had tried to embrace him, but he had pushed her away, saying she couldn't help him.

The house is asleep. She cautiously opens the door to his room, she is naked and shivering. She wants to sleep with him. She is starving and sometimes she has wild dreams, mostly about Kasimir, who bends over her, presses her down on a felled tree, and rapes her. Ferdinand is sound asleep, he doesn't notice her gliding under the cover. She caresses him, and he hugs her, half-asleep. She pulls off his pajamas, he helps her and, suddenly awake, pounces on her. Then he tells her about his mother, whom he barely knew: She was like you—she talked back to Father and then she wasn't there anymore, it was just Father and me.

26
The Trip Back

When cities are taken up by memory, no longer experienced, only imagined, they do not stop changing: they proliferate or contract into details.

She took the twins to Dresden. The preparations agitated the family. Gutsi was constantly on the verge of tears. Katharina would have liked to take her along, but Camilla would have been without supervision, and Katharina trusted no one but Gutsi. Ferdinand cursed the "travel fever trinity," railed at every half-packed suitcase, and avoided the twins, who jabbered on about the Orient Express. Gutsi had taken the boys, who were almost five, to the railroad station several times, and locomotives had then become their favorite topic of conversation. Whenever possible, they turned into steaming, hissing monsters, and only Peter, the more submissive twin, would occasionally agree to play the tender, but only on condition that he could load more coal at every corner, which made Paul, the locomotive, lose his composure after just two stops. They fought often and passionately, and Paul, whose hair was brunette, not black like Peter's, was better coordinated and more skillful. On the other hand, Peter led the way when it came to inventing games.

Camilla, who gleaned a few things hazily, became nervous. She badgered Gutsi, hung on to Katharina.

It was time to leave. They intended to stay for two weeks.

The factory chauffeur called for them. Ferdinand had said goodbye that morning, explaining she'd be so busy with the kids she wouldn't have time to wave goodbye to him. Besides, he added, he couldn't stand railroad station scenes.

She had once hoped she'd be traveling this road frequently, but this was the first time in five years, and she saw herself as a "different person" en route, no longer a girl, but a married woman, the mother of three children. Their first-class seats were reserved. No other passengers entered the compartment.

The twins instantly took over the space. Gutsi had made sure they'd have enough toys; she had filled a small red valise.

They would be traveling all day, until late at night. Katharina was afraid the children might become cranky after a while, which they did. They kept yanking the compartment door open and shut and bothering the other passengers. Katharina, at first apologetic, was so irked by the hostility of the adults that she eventually let the children be. They seldom looked out the window; the changing landscape didn't interest them. But when they entered Prague, they just had to see the fortress, which they had heard so much about. The view of the Hradčany in the noonday light did not disappoint them; in their travel stories, a tangle of truth and fiction, the Hradčany actually gained a mythical grandeur, becoming an unattainable Castle of the Holy Grail.

During supper in the dining-car, the twins, much to Katharina's amazement, lost all patience. She hadn't come here with them for lunch, she had brought along enough food, and she had planned to take the tired children to the dining-car that evening, partly as a reward. This was a mistake. The twins were already tired by the afternoon, they felt cooped up in the compartment, and they were also train-sick. Both were about to throw up. She took the wailing boys to the toilet several times, without success; they choked and whined, but nothing came up. Meanwhile, she felt nauseated herself. She despaired of calming them down, she told them to lie on the upholstered seats; they fell asleep that same instant. She leaned back and peered out the window. The train would reach the border in two hours. After the waiter with the gong had passed their compartment, she had cautiously wakened the children. Drowsy, shaken by the train, they reeled ahead of her. She hoped that in this half-numb state they would cause no trouble. But the new environment, the people in the dining-car, excited the boys. No sooner were they at the table than they wanted to play. The silverware became cars. She kept admonishing them, taking the knives and forks out of their hands; she felt silly, like a governess. Paul, more active than ever, yanked on the table cloth, grabbed a small marmalade jar, and hurled it violently at the nape of a man sitting at the next table. The man screamed. The maître d' turned up immediately, talking away at Katharina, threatening the boys. The passengers split into two camps and launched into a heated debate. You really couldn't blame children, such a long trip. . . . They were simply badly reared brats. You could see how far you got with modern upbringing, there was no discipline. Katharina stood up, grabbed Peter and Paul, yanked them along, and left the dining-car. The walk back to the compartment became too long for her.

She pushed the children on the seats and sat down across from them. The twins had obviously not yet understood. They watched their mother cry and, after a while, they began sobbing too.

She now regarded the days in Dresden as an appendage to the trip; she could not get over her exhaustion, or else she talked herself into it.

Her parents said that she had changed a lot, she had grown more mature, yet strangely withdrawn—was she happy?

They had been looking forward to seeing her; the turbulence of the welcome was familiar to her. The children enjoyed it.

They took a cab to the factory (although she knew better, she expected the car to head north, toward Klotzsche). It halted in front of the rusty iron sliding gate, and they got out.

When Wüllner, standing between two valises, greeted them, she saw how frail he had become; he did not protest when she took one of the valises. They had to cross the courtyard. A few men who were working did not greet them. Everything astonished her, driving out the past. The apartment was not large, but the ceilings were exceedingly high; she recognized most of the furniture; the sideboard was still marked by Elle's cigarette stubs. She had had the terrible habit of leaving cigarettes there while she talked, and the stubs had slowly burned down, scorching the wood. The furnishings came from the house, but they were much too large, and crammed together as in an attic.

The children were put to bed; to their delight, they were allowed to sleep together in a "grown-up's bed."

The tea was already prepared. The two white-haired old people plied her with questions. She knew all the questions in advance. They talked.

Ernst was doing fine as a lawyer.

But why had Dieter decided to become an army officer?

It fitted him; she ought to see him in his dashing uniform. People said he would go far.

She slept in a storeroom, which had been straightened up. She was unfamiliar with all the nocturnal sounds. In the morning, when she walked into the combination kitchen/living-room, the table was set for her and there was a cozy on the coffee pot, but Mummi and the twins

were gone. She sat down, waiting for something to happen. In the
courtyard, men were loading crates; she watched.

Then she wandered through the apartment, gazing at the pictures
on the walls, all of which she could reconstruct for herself. At the end of
the corridor, she discovered an iron door with a yellow sign above it:
"Keep locked! Factory rooms!" She opened the door and saw Mummi,
several women, and the twins sitting at a long table. Each woman had a
scale in front of her, a tub of birdseed, and a pile of colorful pouches. The
twins were playing with pouches. Mummi looked as if she were wearing a
disguise. She had a kerchief tied deep down on her forehead, and she
wore a gray apron like the other women. Katharina recalled photographs
of workers in old-fashioned domestic industry. Mummi introduced her to
the other women. No one expected her to say anything about the work.
Susanne Wüllner fairly pushed her daughter out of the room with words.
She told Katharina she didn't have to worry about the twins, they'd be
kept busy here. Where was Father? In his "bureau," right next door.
When Katharina heard the lofty word *bureau*, she laughed; the women
laughed too. Susanne Wüllner took her there. He sat at a small, empty
desk, his hands flat on a sheet of paper; he gazed toward her.

She said she only wanted to say good morning.

He stood up and kissed her on the forehead: she ought to have a look
at the city.

She said she would, yes.

Elle's grave was overgrown, ivy rankly covered the flat stone, devour-
ing the inscription.

I stroll among graves, she said aloud to herself and was afraid
someone might have heard her.

She took the streetcar to Hellerau. The settlement had spread out.
She walked to and fro under the arcades, peering into the shop windows.
She looked for the building in which she had found refuge with
Eberhard. She chanced upon the apartment house where Skodlerrak had
lived; she read the nameplates, none of which bore his name. If he
turned up now, she thought to herself, she would sleep with him on the
spot, not giving it a second thought.

She took the number nine streetcar to Klotzsche. The distance from
the trolley stop to the house was shorter, the hedges had grown higher.
She stood at the gate. A woman lay on a chaise longue in front of the
terrace, she raised her upper body and peered at Katharina, a summer
scene urging itself on her memory. Thus, she forgot the house.

She invited her parents to the Café Kreuzkamm, and the children
were surprisingly well-mannered. Paul rode the dolphin in the Zwinger:

You are Arion, she said, but he didn't ask who Arion was. She would have liked to tell him.

They played tag on Brühlsche Terrace.

On Sunday, they went on an outing to Moritzburg, and the children were allowed to ride a steamer.

Although they talked a lot, and Wüllner was very optimistic about the future of the birdseed company, she felt as if her parents were mute. She visited Uncle David several times; he had a varicose vein and was not supposed to take walks. A female admirer had given him a gramophone, and he played Caruso, singing along.

She herded the children along the platform, exchanged kisses with her parents, waved. It was early in the morning; Mummi was not wearing a kerchief, she had an elegant, broad-brimmed hat on, Katharina asked, and was embarrassed, if she could help them, she said she meant financially, but Wüllner rebuked her. She leaned out the window, holding up Peter and Paul alternately until the train chugged off, and she said, Look at the city once again, boys, and wave to Granny and Grampa, hurry, hurry, I once lived here, that was a long time ago.

Ferdinand asked Katharina how her parents were.

She said they had managed to adjust, in every respect; they didn't need help.

27
Katharina's Circle or Why a Salon?

A salon? she had replied to Dorothee Neumeister, a salon? That's not for me, I couldn't, I'm not very educated, and I don't much enjoy amateur wits. During the very first party in her house, Katharina had instantly trusted Dorothee even though they had barely conversed; a few days later, she had visited the "dyer," as she was generally called. Dorothee had been living alone with a chambermaid ever since her husband had fallen to his death while mountain-climbing eight years earlier; and one noticed very quickly that, despite her sociable ways, she was very good at solitude. She said she had never really needed men; they belonged to mythology, and that was quite sufficient. Yet her curiosity, her sense of justice, and her provocative character made her popular among men too. She said she had hit it off with Katharina right away because, from the very start, Katharina had not feared her "trumpet blasts." And now it was Dorothee Neumeister, of all people, who tried to talk her into having a salon. She told Katharina to pay no attention to Ferdinand: if he went along with it, fine; if not, then that was his problem, and he could make do with the factory stench. Men were not to be consulted in such matters.

But he's head of the house.

And you're mistress of the house.

That's not the same.

Very true, he lets you run the house and also demands that you work at the firm every morning.

He doesn't demand it. I want to do it.

All the better.

But can I start a salon in spite of him?

Not in spite of him; perhaps without him; possibly with him.

They discussed the guest list for the first evening; the Circle could change as time went by. Katharina knew so few people, said Dorothee.

That's just it, replied Katharina.

Dorothee Neumeister named names and described people, sometimes very frivolously; and after a lot of pros and cons, and the decision that they would leave out German chauvinists as well as super-Czechs, they had drawn up a list which, with Dorothee Neumeister's itemized characterizations, was quite appealing. It was headed by Jaromír Gawliček, the director of the music conservatory, a famous composer who, Katharina assumed, would not accept the invitation.

She was mistaken, Dorothee replied. Gawliček was a bachelor and would be delighted to socialize. He had to deal with musicians every day.

Katharina had never even heard of Jan Waldhans. Despite his name, Dorothee Neumeister explained, he was not German, he was resolutely Czech, a good journalist. His only child, a daughter, had been living with him ever since his wife's death. The girl was a renowned beauty, but she was less well-known as an artist, or rather a miniaturist. However, she would embellish the party. She's an enlightened hysteric, I tell you, very lively.

Now we need some Germans.

I know, to keep your husband happy.

Katharina felt uneasy whenever Dorothee laughed at Ferdinand; Dorothee sensed it, and tried to make up for it by offering to use the familiar form, *Du:* Conspirators cannot talk at a distance.

Now for the Germans.

There are already three of us—you, your husband, and I. I think the Wagners would fit in nicely.

Katharina had heard about Wagner, who owned the huge bakery. Božena usually shopped there. Wagner liked art, he promoted young musicians, bought works by unknown artists, and had a legendary collection of Impressionist paintings.

You know about him?

Yes, said Katharina, but she knew nothing about Frau Wagner.

To discreetly understate her style: she has relationships. Or, to put it more crassly, she's a nyphomaniac—although she's intelligent, she's got a sharp tongue, and, as you can imagine, she's attractive. Wagner has evidently resigned himself to her escapades and he nurses his wounded soul by looking at perfect pictures.

Acting on an impulse that she subsequently interpreted as her response to Ferdinand's criticism, she suggested Prchala; Dorothee concurred, saying he was smart, and a good business sense was no defect.

Katharina felt stirred by putting together a list of people most of whom she didn't know: it stimulated her imagination.

The Jewish component is lacking, said Dorothee.

If not I—

I know, Katharina was interrupted, Mirjam Hribasch told me.

You know the Hribasches?

For ages. He's one of the best jewelers in the country, and I have a weakness for precious stones.

The Hribasches could sometimes come as guests.

He doesn't travel much.

He knows how fond I am of Mirjam.

She's a little slut.

Katharina rebuked Dorothee Neumeister, telling her she greatly underestimated Mirjam, she had found very few people as understanding as this woman, who seemed so superficial at first glance.

The two traits are not mutually exclusive.

You're opinionated.

You'll discover other faults in me. I'm thinking of the Gottgetreus. They might fit in. Leo Gottgetreu is head physician of the pediatric clinic, a good doctor and a gem of a human being. He thaws out slowly, but he can be a fascinating conversationalist. His wife, Cora, loves literature and occasionally writes about Czech poets in German newspapers. She's an expert on Němcová.

Since Katharina had only just recently read Němcová's *Babička,* this information helped her.

If Ferdinand did not stay away, said Dorothee, there would be eleven people, and that was enough for a good conversation. Besides, occasionally, illustrious guests would be the star attraction, *nicht wahr?*

Whenever Dorothee Neumeister grew excited, her diction became elevated.

Katharina said she would invite people the first Friday of every month.

Katharina was a good hostess. Her grace, her natural curiosity about people helped her to deal with the difficulties of such invitations. She could set the tone without appearing pushy, and she was equally deft in going along with someone else's tone; she had a knack for intelligent insights and witty remarks, and moreover, she clearly remembered the dynamic evenings in Hellerau. There had been warmth and closeness, which she yearned for now. Why not look for friends again?

However, there was a great deal of tension before each evening. Ferdinand had had his qualms and made nasty comments about some of the guests: Wagner was a moron and a jellyfish. But finally he gave in: How would it look if he left her alone, people would gossip. The tension nearly made her dizzy. Nevertheless, she always put the children to bed, cuddled Camilla, who couldn't fall asleep without a lot of "kissies," and she told the boys stories about highwaymen in Klotzsche. Before the first soiree, she pictured herself becoming a Rahel Varnhagen or George Sand in Brno, teaching Ferdinand a lesson, and showing society a new style: instead of going along with the dismal, anxiety-ridden time, they would be witty and always on the trail of something new. She looked forward to everything, tried to play Chopin's Nocturne in D flat Major, which she especially loved; Ferdinand listened to it too. She enjoyed the silk of the long, severely tailored gown she had ordered (with a low-cut back, which Gutsi called overdone); she moved the material back and forth on her skin and, while playing the piano, she saw arrangements of people, as if under a very bright limelight, couples standing here and there, four guests sitting around the small table, a young man flirting with an exotic-looking girl at the window. Once, she had (secretly) read *Conversations of Courtesans*: that may have been the reason for these risqué fantasies. When Božena brought Dorothee Neumeister into the living room, Katharina was already stimulated, even without company, and she was certain that this evening at least would succeed, and the salon would continue.

She was the center, without any help. Whenever a pause ensued, barely perceptible, Dorothee stepped in, and her topics (her gossip spared nobody) were never exhausted. But the guests all concentrated on Katharina, so that Ferdinand, who had intended to stay aloof, was drawn in.

There were certainly side conversations, but the guests kept regathering, as though intentionally, to discuss a "major theme"—a habit that Katharina later learned how to direct.

And the intensity of the conversations inspired her to capture them in her diary; it also flattered her to render "secret feelings," intimate reactions to the conversations, which she then omitted, despite her emotional involvement.

Conversation about Love

August 1927

I do not know who began, it was probably Swetlana Wagner, whom Dorothee had described as a nymphomaniac; and she lived up to her reputation, flouting all conventions by flirting shamelessly with Gawliček. I must say, I was amused by her attacks, nor did I feel

sorry for Wagner, but Dr. Gottgetreu expressed his dismay. She is a
striking woman, her agitation is catching. Ferdinand was annoyed
by her dyed red hair and her raw silk frock, which was slit up the
sides; she played with her dress constantly, and sometimes you could
see her legs all the way up to her hips. Ferdinand told me later that
Wagner had brought her to Brno four years ago; she supposedly
comes from Budějovice, but Ferdinand speculates that she used to
earn her living as a prostitute in Prague. I do not believe him. She is
certainly extraordinarily lascivious, and has nothing on her mind
but men; yet she takes part in all conversations intelligently and
attentively, and she is remarkably well educated. I enjoy knowing
her.

I do not recall every detail of the conversation. It began with a
statement by Ana Waldhans. Everything about her is too fine, too
translucent, the fully curving lips look like painted glass. She
irritates me, and I would not care to get too close to her.

I remember that one thing she said to herself, as if she had
forgotten the presence of the others, made us all perk up our ears:

Basically, love is unnatural. It hurts. And would nature want
something like that? Why do we talk about the pain of love, the
sorrow of love, and very seldom about the joy of love? Why are
people interested in unhappy romances, why do they write books
about them, poetry, but never about a happy romance? Is there an
anti-Madame Bovary, an anti-Effi Briest? Isn't it nonsense, consider-
ing that all the people trying to improve the world are demanding a
right to happiness?

Gottgetreu had been ready to break in after her first sentence,
but he let her speak her mind.

We physicians, he said, know that pain is helpful. It often
indicates when something has gone wrong. Might there not be a
comparable pain in love, and does it not stop in the course of a
relationship?

At that point, love ends too, said Ana, so opiniated as to brook
no contradiction.

But Swetlana Wagner did not care: You're exaggerating! Beautiful art. Yes, yes, love can be painful. If you're deceived, if you're
deserted. But you get over it. I simply cannot imagine that a human
being can get along with only one love. After all, love lives chiefly
on curiosity. What's he like? What's she like? And once your
curiosity is satisfied, then love grows dull. Besides, dear Fräulein
Ana, you have forgotten that love seeks the body, needs it, wants it.

I don't know how to put it. And that pain, that very physical pain is part of the happiness for me, even if the happiness is not lasting.

Wagner said that these were truly sophisticated opinions.

They strike *me* as demonic. Gawliček pronounced these words in such a dry tone that we all had to laugh, as if at a joke. If only I could describe that man. His face, his voice. After all, he went on, paní Wagnerova is referring to what we usually conceal in lofty conversations about love: the drive. The fact that we can be blind with lust, that the killer in us is aroused, or the uninhibited visionary. Art knows it. Love is often numbing, it becomes a hunger that must be sated in the teeth of all reason, a sickness that is actually accepted as a gift.

That is not wrong, said Swetlana Wagner.

It is too extreme for me, said Jan Waldhans. We are speaking about love as if it existed only on heights or in depths. The fact that it can be pedestrian between two people who know one another well and have been together for a long time, the fact that it can be renewed, can ebb, can change, and become new again—all that strikes us as too banal. Does it not? Expecting Ferdinand to disagree with me, I added: That's true. And in such an everyday love, one often doesn't realize that one is still in love. Or else one realizes it again when one is lying with the other person.

Ferdinand held his tongue. Gottgetreu nodded at me.

Perhaps most people are simply vegetating in a loveless existence, and they resent those who love, said Cora Gottgetreu.

We continued debating for a while.

Conversation about Versailles

February 1928

Prchala, who is frequently silent all evening long, can startle the others with sudden cynicism. Yesterday it was he who dropped the catchword "Versailles."

Granted, the exorbitant reparations are political madness, but basically the Diktat of Versailles was necessary in order to expose some of the bad characteristics of the Germans. For instance, their self-pity or their tendency to keep blaming others, or, if nothing else helps, the faith in dark forces. Isn't the invention of the stab-in-the-back legend typically German?

Strangely enough, Dr. Gottgetreu was the first to respond, and quite sharply at that: And what is typically Czech, Herr Prchala?

Forgive me, Herr Doktor, I let myself get carried away. But

aren't you, as a Jew, one of the people who stabbed Germany in the back? If I am to believe Hitler and other nationalists.

That's just a lot of hot air. The gutter can open anyplace.

Excuse me, are we talking about politics now or not? asked Jan Waldhans.

Versailles was demonstrably a major disaster, said Ferdinand, a political folly. Erzberg had to pay the price, and others will follow. One cannot exhaust a nation like that, it is bound to trigger extreme reactions. And now they are here. Just look at how the Communists are getting stronger.

Or Hitler, said Wagner.

Ferdinand did not like to talk about Hitler. Oh, well, Hitler. But I wouldn't compare him with the Communists. Hitler's goals are national, which is something one can't say about the Bolshevists. After all, he does want a new Germany.

Which Germany? asked Prchala. Such conversations always make the tension between Prchala and Ferdinand palpable. They cannot stand one another. I regret it.

A national regeneration, can't you understand that, Prchala? Is there nothing comparable in Czech history, in the national strivings of the nineteenth century?

Those are two different things, said Prchala. We were living under foreign control.

And the Germans aren't?

I was afraid Ferdinand would go overboard with his German chauvinism, so I broke in: We all know that the French are occupying the Ruhr.

There you are.

Still and all, said Gawliček, we profited from Versailles. In 1918, we proclaimed our republic. And what did you lose, dear Perchtmann, what? Ferdinand was not prepared for this cunning question. I? Nothing.

You are German.

I am. And I am a citizen of the republic.

If you will, you have even gained something, dear boy.

It is difficult to answer you.

Gawliček is a sophist—Wagner was delighted at the drift of the conversation.

Or, Gawliček continued, do I write Czech music, German, Hungarian, Austrian?

Ana Waldhans, who admires Gawliček's art, said resolutely: It is Czech music.

That too, dear Fräulein, but, needless to say, it should be understood just as readily by an American—or at least so I wish.

Not as readily as by us, said Prchala.

What does all that have to do with Versailles? asked Dorothee. Observing the rules of the salon, she wanted us to stick to the topic.

Nothing, said Waldhans. But I would rather talk about Gawliček's music than about some morons in Liberec who are soon going to be claiming that the Neanderthals already felt German. Do you think this is what Woodrow Wilson had in mind? Politics usually takes a different course from what the politicians assume.

Conversation about Children

November 1928

I learned from Dorothee that Ana Waldhans is pregnant and refuses to reveal the man's name to anyone, including her father. Dorothee says that Ana had an affair with a younger painter two years ago, but soon left him. Since then, she has occasionally been seen with other men. I tried to picture Ana naked in a man's arms— is she not much too frail, and does not her beauty frighten men? Or is she, on the contrary, very attractive—might a man not wish to torment her, destroy her? Perhaps she needs passion, she may want to suffer. I am revolted by all those rumors that link her to goodness knows whom, all the gossip-mongers who are trying to figure out the father's identity. And I am annoyed by Ferdinand's stupid, off-color remark that he always had second thoughts about that still water.

The problem was marvelously resolved tonight by Jan Waldhans, probably after he discussed it with Ana. (I am setting this conversation down right away, the guests have just barely left. Camilla is softly clearing her throat next door. She still has the light, fitful sleep of children. I have to take her back to Dr. Gottgetreu. Ferdinand has gone to bed. I am too tense to go to sleep, perhaps writing will make me drowsy.) Waldhans said: You probably know that Ana is expecting a baby.

To which Swetlana Wagner feigned surprise with a "goodness gracious me."

Ana smiled amiably at everyone, then placed her arm around her father's shoulders.

Cora Gottgetreu said: You must be very happy, Ana.

Yes, she said, I like children.

I expected someone to say: But the child will need a father. Instead, everyone remained silent, casting about for words. Dr. Gottgetreu was nonchalant enough to end the embarrassment: You are going to bring the child up alone, aren't you?

Yes, she said, unless I find a father.

You won't have an easy time of it, said Prchala thoughtfully.

I know. It won't be so bad as long as I can protect the child against other people's stupidity. Besides, my father will help me.

The gossip had obviously not reached Gawliček. He was surprised by the news, and his joy was undisguised. He went over to Ana, and kissed her hand. Children are miracles for me. How quickly they are ruined. Why do we forget that we were free during our first few years, untroubled by restraints, by considerations, by foolish hopes or memories? Why don't we take a remnant of that happiness along with us on our path?

One can hear it in your compositions, said Dorothee.

Perhaps.

You're being arch, said Waldhans.

When I think of Jossel, our eldest child, said Cora Gottgetreu. She often talked about her five children. Jossel needed protection even in his adolescence. He suffered from terrible fantasies, which we couldn't explain. He was what they call a mama's boy. Now, he's been putting a gap between himself and us since he was seventeen. We're the oldsters, as far as he's concerned. He feels he doesn't need us anymore—isn't that a claiming of freedom, Herr Gawliček?

It is a different freedom, my dear lady. Isn't this type of freedom constantly challenged, sometimes by oneself?

It's odd, said Dorothee, no one has commented that a child needs his father.

And yet three fathers are sitting here, said Wagner.

(Whenever the conversation turns to children, Swetlana usually tells everyone she hates the little brats and doesn't want one for anything in the world. Why else is there such a thing as condoms?)

If no father is available, then the other fathers evidently prefer not to talk about obligations, I said, and I found myself rather impudent.

I admit, replied Ferdinand, that the situation is delicate. But why shouldn't I say that children need a father? He is the authority and he has to make sure that children recognize authority.

Gottgetreu and Waldhans concurred.

Gawliček wiped away that wise statement: Authority is just a figment.

Yes, said Ana, and how many people arrogate it to themselves. Authority is a combination of love, knowledge, self-understanding, inner confidence, freedom, and many other things, and if authority puffs up its chest, then it is not authority.

When she left, I promised I would visit her in her studio when I was in town, but she politely begged off, saying she liked being alone.

The group, "Kathi's Circle," as it was later dubbed, continued meeting until January 1945 with changes and also with a small solid core that included Wagner, Prchala, Ana Waldhans, and Dorothee Neumeister.

28
Black Friday

It was not unexpected. She was immediately involved for the first time, she saw the events coming toward her; she could decipher parts of the messages, grasping, to the extent that she could, politics or what was called politics: economics, decay, turmoil, rhetoric, helplessness. Every morning, she and Ferdinand and Prchala studied the Wall Street rates. The price drops were tremendous. The firm had invested some money in America, on the advice of old Perchtmann, and their business friends in Prague, Łodz, and Vienna had encouraged them to do so until May 1929. Katharina was extremely tense; she had to put up with Gutsi's calling her a virago; but she had caught the men's fever and also their fear. Now she recognized Ferdinand's qualities, his abilities. They grew closer during these weeks, although they suffered from daily friction, and they couldn't talk to one another at night, they were too worn out by the debates, the hectic negotiations of the day. Moreover, she was pregnant again.

Prchala had advised buying as much raw material as possible. Now, not a day later; even go into debt if necessary. No credit could be expected from the banks, including their house bank. Ferdinand did not delay. Katharina, who had often been critical, decided to second all his decisions unhesitatingly. He needed support. Sometimes, during work, she felt a violent longing for him. If she had not been afraid Prchala or someone else might pop in, she would have tried to seduce Ferdinand. She noticed that extreme tension had an erotic effect on her.

Black Friday, the day the American stock market collapsed, para-lyzed their hustle and bustle at one stroke. They stopped; "we stopped, we were stopped, and we realized the world had come to a halt, it might be Doomsday." In this stillness, they became sleepwalkers, congratulating one another for ideas that were long since null and void and forgetting why they had been toiling for such a long time. Moravian Knitwear had become an abstraction, until a few days later, when Prchala called himself and the others back and began to sum up the situation: Their warehouses in Břeclav, Znojmo, and Prostejov were filled to the rafters with wool. Orders, however, were rapidly dropping off, a development that was far from over. A few major clients had been forced to close shop. The firm's agencies in Poland and France were working at semi-capacity; the one in Germany had stopped altogether.

The firm's reputation was intact. Moravian Knitwear was greatly trusted—and by the workers, too, as Katharina could glean from a number of conversations: They said the firm had proved it could hold out, it had been well managed. She reported this to Ferdinand and Prchala. Both advised showing great pessimism in front of the workers too. Otherwise there might be misunderstandings, disappointments.

By mid-1930, the time had come; the first workers had to be laid off. Katharina reviewed each case with the head of personnel, she was ashamed of her helplessness. Only Prchala still walked through the factory; she was no longer capable of doing so. Ferdinand usually avoided it anyway. And Prchala also expressed the first resistance. He asked to have a meeting, together with the two department heads, but he did not wish to indicate the topic in advance. Ferdinand, finding the whole thing mysterious, wanted to refuse, but Katharina urged him not to have conflicts with Prchala that went beyond the three of them; he probably wanted to talk about the dismissals. And indeed he did. After a few tentative remarks, Prchala, who was very agitated, informed Ferdinand that ninety percent of the dismissed workers were Czechs, and this was taking place in the Czechoslovakian Republic. He said that Ferdinand was obviously trying to protect the German workers in any way possible. (Katharina had pointed this out to Ferdinand at the very start, but he had ignored her.) Reaching into his pocket, Ferdinand pulled out a sheet of paper, from which he read aloud. He was visibly offended and angry; the department heads held back. Prchala was no less furious, he seemed to be deliberately steering toward a clash with Ferdinand. Of the four hundred seventy-six workers at Moravian Knitwear, Ferdinand read, three hundred sixteen, that is, far more than half, were Czech. Granted, among the foremen and supervisors, the number of Czechs was very small, at best fifteen percent. But dismissing any of these employees would be very damaging to the firm. They were experts, some of them were first-class dyers. So the dismissals had to begin with the ordinary workers, and they were mainly Czechs.

The ethnic makeup of the staff was unjust, Prchala retorted vehemently. For years now, Germans had been given preference for the most important positions.

Ferdinand, who had sat down behind his desk while the others remained at the conference table, replied very emphatically: No one was hired without your knowledge, Herr Prchala.

Oh yes they were! Who hired the two dyers from Fürth, presenting us with a *fait accompli?* You or I, Herr Perchtmann? If you'll recall, Prchala, both you and I had been looking for almost six months. Then I was given a tip. I was afraid you'd stab me in the back with your chauvinistic hiring policies. And after all, I do own the majority of shares.

I was expecting that, Herr Perchtmann.

What can we do? asked Katharina. We will have to fire more workers—I'm very pessimistic, given the low number of incoming orders.

We could make sure that things were handled more justly, Frau Perchtmann.

Prchala's national long-division! cried Ferdinand.

Katharina didn't care for his tone of voice, but she didn't want to rebuke him in front of the others.

The workers we dismissed were the least secure, they earned the least, they are the poorest. Do you wish to deny that, Herr Perchtmann?

No, but the firm needs them least of all, Prchala, and you know that as well as I.

Shouldn't we think humanely, Perchtmann? Prchala deliberately omitted the "*Herr,*" trying to disparage Ferdinand, which induced Katharina to step in: I looked at the papers prior to the layoffs. I must confess, I didn't notice the nationality, I didn't look to see whether they were Czech or German, but they were assuredly workers who did not earn very much, they were mostly unskilled laborers or women.

The weakest—said Prchala—Czechs!

Do you have any solution, Prchala?

Yes, go through the foremen and see if they are all absolutely necessary.

You're crazy, we'd be robbing ourselves of the best people.

Do we really know whether they're all as good as you claim?

Katharina suggested adjourning the meeting and making more of an effort to figure out what they could do.

It's too late, said Prchala, do you think these people are imbeciles? One week later, a large number of the Czech workers walked out.

Camilla was sick again, Annamaria still tiny, and Katharina had waited for Dr. Gottgetreu rather than leave Gutsi alone with her problems. As a result, she didn't get to the factory until around ten-thirty. Workers were standing at the gate, involved in a discussion. She paused on the stairway to the "director's wing" and leaned against the bannister, gazing at the workers. At first, the men hadn't noticed her, then one of them saw her; they greeted her, but did not stop debating. She knew two or three of them, they were from the dyeing section. She wondered whether she ought to go over to them; what these men had done was certainly uncommon: they had left their jobs. Ferdinand was bound to order her not to talk to them.

"At that moment, I thought of my experience in Prague. Visiting the worker at home, with his family. The way he jeered at me, and how helpless I was. I cannot remember his name. He made it unequivocally clear to me that I do not belong with them. I am on the other side, I belong with the plutocrats who exploit them. We know nothing about one another. It drives me crazy."

She made up her mind to speak to the men. Stunned, they moved several paces apart as she came toward them. She addressed the man whom she thought she knew best; she tried unsuccessfully to recall his name. He was older, slightly bowed. He had the face of a cunning father (which inspired her confidence).

Do you know me? she asked and felt silly.

Of course I do, Frau Perchtmann, the man replied, introducing himself: I am Kostka, Zdeněk.

She could never get used to the peculiar custom of making a first name a last name.

Oh, yes, Herr Kostka, she said, not knowing what to ask. Kostka helped her: We've walked out, as you can see. We're not striking, no. And all of us are Czechs. The Germans are working. So are a couple of Czechs. But why should us Czechs keep working if we're gonna be laid off anyway soon? Only us Czechs, not the Germans? That's what we wanna show you.

I know, she said. Germans have been laid off too.

Only a few.

The men moved closer together.

I'll try to help you.

You can't.

I'll do my best.

Injustice will run its course, said Kostka. But we'll defend ourselves.

Are you the leader, Herr Kostka? she asked.

If you're looking for a ringleader to punish, then I'm the one, paní Perchtmannová.

No, I only want to know who can speak for the Czech workers.

There are smarter guys than me.

Don't you want to go back to work? Every word she spoke sounded false; she knew it.

In ten minutes, Frau Perchtmann, not one second earlier. That's our deadline.

She nodded, turning away from the men. As she left, she wondered whether she shouldn't have shaken hands with Kostka, and she realized that even her thoughts were becoming uncertain and false.

Ferdinand had learned about the mutiny long ago. He said their insolence would absolve him of showing any consideration.

That would be the wrong reaction. They're going back to work, Ferdinand.

She sent for Prchala, asking him to be present at this conversation, since he knew the Czech workers better than she and Ferdinand did.

They're working again, said Prchala. He spoke as if he were one of the rebels and had to apologize.

It won't help them. That was a lesson for me, said Ferdinand.

I doubt whether you have learned anything, Perchtmann. The Czech workers only want to point out unjust things. They have no other way of doing it.

One of them could have come to me.

Are you serious, Ferdinand?

He didn't answer her.

She told them about her conversation at the gate. Ferdinand asked her whether she knew one of the workers, and she said Kostka.

He's a Commie.

What makes you think so?

I know it. Many of the Czech workers are Commies.

Well if that's the case, then I'd rather be red than black.

That wouldn't surprise me at all, with your past.

Ferdinand, please.

Prchala broke in: There must be no punitive actions of any kind, the consequences would be hard to predict.

Ferdinand insisted that they fire Kostka.

If you do, Katharina snapped at him, then I won't work here anymore.

So you *are* a Commie, said Ferdinand.
Do we really have to act so childish with one another?
Prchala left the room.
Please, Ferdinand, think it over.

(Perhaps I would rather be on the other side. I know it is a romantic notion, although I am more familiar with conditions now than during the Hellerau period. I am the daughter of a factory-owner, the wife of a factory-owner. I live in an elegant villa, and a nanny takes care of my four children. I do have problems, but they cannot be compared with Kostka's. Would I wish to be poor and live in a basement apartment? I am pigeonholed. But I can learn.)

Over a hundred more workers had to be laid off, this time more Germans than before. Kostka kept his job. The hoarded raw material helped the factory through the worst, and in 1934, when they were working at top capacity again, Ferdinand triumphed, for Prchala could not manage to dig up a Czech master dyer, as Katharina had advised him to do.

29
Katharina's Fairy Tale or The Way Time Gets Lost

Mami, tell us a story, the twins asked, a request that had become a refrain over the years, and that she sometimes was grouchy about fulfilling, for whenever she repeated a story, however vaguely, the children, even patient Camilla, would protest. So Katharina would think up stories during the day; or else Gutsi would read to the children.

ever since the twins, and then recently Camilla, had started school, Gutsi had been complaining that she didn't have enough to do; at sixty-six she didn't belong on the scrap heap, and she would not take charity.

Katharina pointed out that Gutsi was busy every afternoon helping the kids with their homework, playing with them.

that wasn't enough for her, said Gutsi, and she didn't want to encroach on Božena's territory. so she wrote a long letter every morning, but wouldn't reveal to whom. Katharina guessed she was writing to Uncle David and Mummi, and she encouraged the old woman's whim.

c'mon, tell us a story. . . .

I'm thinking about a little girl, she was, let's say, as old as Camilla, six or seven, and she lived in a big, white mansion with her parents and her brothers, and the mansion was surrounded by a magic garden—

as big as our garden?

Paul's question confused her. the garden around the house had been overgrown for a long time; the trees, including the gingko, had shot up high, and the family often spent summer days and evenings on the

170

terrace: but Katharina had never "seen" the Brno garden, had never regarded it as her own. whenever she imagined a garden, it was the one in Klotzsche, which was like a picture covering the present garden. whenever she walked through this garden, she was really walking through a different one. . . .

bigger, a lot bigger, she said intensely, a real park—

a park's boring, said Peter.

no, not really a park, that's wrong. a big garden with lots of magic nooks, a pond with fat carps swimming in it, a gazebo and a paddock with a herd of ponies grazing there. . . .

there's no such thing, the twins cried.

there is. it existed and it still exists, I swear. I knew the garden, believe me.

and Gutsi supported her: I know the garden too, yes. . . .

and what happened to the little girl? . . .

it's not a simple story, it's not a real fairy tale.

but it shouldn't be boring, said Peter.

I don't know. If you don't want to hear anymore, then say so.

let Paul say so, Camilla ordered.

I'm talking about a summer day, such a beautiful day, a very rare kind of day—

but what about the little girl, Camilla broke in.

she comes out of the house, she jumps down the broad, flat stone steps, she whirls around, spreading her arms. I believe she is very happy, the little girl. . . .

what's her name? asks Peter.

let's call her. . . .

she paused, wondering whether she should call the fairy-tale creature Katharina or Kathi. but that would confuse the children: how can a fairy-tale girl have the same name as their mother? she couldn't hit on any other name, she kept saying "Katharina" to herself. . . .

what's her name, Mami?. . . .

her name, she says, is Annamaria. . . .

and she was surprised at the completely alien name. that's her name now. . . .

I like that, said Camilla.

fine then. Annamaria ran out into the garden. first she dashed across the lawn, then to the pond. she fed dry bread to the carps. then she dashed over to the ponies, she had sugar in her pocket for them. and now she's waiting for her friend, Kate. they're going to play Going on a Long Trip.

you can't play that, said Paul resolutely.

of course you can. they could in that garden, even though you may not believe it. . . .

she pulled the single-axled pony cart out of the stable and called Max, the strongest pony, who obeyed her blindly. he trotted out, she opened the lattice gate and put the harness on the pony. she saw Kate from afar, running across the meadow, and she waved. . . .

that's no fairy tale, said Paul. . . .

yes it is. Kate and Annamaria loaded up the wagon, putting in their dolls and their dolls' belongings, flowers, also cakes that they had stored for the trip. they sat down on the bench in front. Annamaria tugged on the reins, clicked her tongue, and shouted, Giddyap. and the trip began. . . .

that's bull. you can't go on a trip in a garden. . . .

she had spoken herself back into her garden, and she didn't care what they said. she told "her fairy tale". . . .

let Mami talk, Gutsi ordered. . . .

first, Annamaria suggested, we'll travel to the Wolf Forest. it hasn't been explored very much, and we'll only look at it from outside. hundreds of wolves live in it, and you can hear them howling at night. a bad, bumpy road led to the Wolf Forest. They stopped at the thicket, and they were scared even to breathe. they heard the thicket crackling and growling, and so they decided to leave that dreadful area right away. let's go straight to the sea, said Kate, and Annamaria thought it was a good idea, even though the trip would take a long time, many days and nights. it doesn't matter, said Kate, we have time.

don't the girls have any parents? asked Peter thoughtfully.

they do, but the parents allowed them to go on the trip.

for so many days?

in a fairy tale, days and nights go by in a single day.

I've never heard anything like that. Paul was skeptical.

yes, they traveled endlessly. they froze at night, they sweated in the daytime. they crossed thick forests and deserts swept by sandstorms. they were thirsty, hungry. the natives gave them rare fruits filled with a delicious juice. and suddenly, after traveling through five deserts and seven jungles, they saw the ocean. they were jubilant. Max began to trot, his mane fluttered in the wind. they gazed at the ocean, and it became immense. they could see steamers and sailboats, and flying fish soared out of the water.

there are no such oceans, said Peter.

next year, we'll go to the seashore. you don't know such oceans yet, but they do exist. . . .

with flying fish?

oh yes. they're the brothers of the stone dolphin at the Zwinger. the real ones are a lot more beautiful. they danced in the sun in front of the two girls, until Annamaria and Kate fell asleep and took the dolphins along into their dreams. the next day, they set off for the Witches' Temple, a small house in the bushland. at midnight, that's where all the supreme witches gather from all over the world.

did they see the witches?

the girls haven't arrived yet, and they won't see the witches, no, because they're scared. they know that if a little girl is touched by a supreme witch, she turns into a witch herself. that's why they don't remain in the area until midnight. they're content to discover lots of footsteps left by witches.

everything she said came to her on the spur of the moment. she was astonished at herself and at the power that the old garden still exerted on her and her imagination. . . .

what are witches' footsteps? asked Camilla.

wherever a witch treads with her big feet, she scorches the grass, and she leaves the mark of her tremendous foot.

none of that's true.

it's as true as the garden. . . .

go on. . . .

at the end of their journey, they came to the land of wild horses. those horses live in the steppes. they can never be captured and they can't be ridden by any human beings except those who know the language of the horses.

horses can't talk, Mami.

we don't understand them today. the little girls didn't understand them either. but Max tore away from the wagon and galloped over to the herd. he was free again. Annamaria could heard her mother calling from far away, telling her it was late and she had to come to supper. she said goodbye to Kate and ran across the meadow to the house. she was worn out from the long journey.

now the story's over.

no.

but what else can happen?

nothing that takes place in a fairy tale.

then it's boring.

maybe. . . .

let Mami tell it.

the next day, Annamaria hurried back to the garden. she wanted to go on another journey, but the world shrank before her very eyes. the garden was small again, the land of horses was a narrow paddock, the sea

was a pond, the Wolf Forest was the small wood, the Witches' Temple
was the pavilion. and no matter how hard she strained herself and her
imagination, she couldn't repeat the happiness of the previous day. she
realized she had lost something that was gone forever; it couldn't be
summoned again. she understood that there is such a thing as time, and
that time cannot be abolished.

can people understand that? asked Peter.

people don't wish to understand it, my child, perhaps because time
is faster than our experience, and because we're afraid of being lost by
time.

what happens then?

nothing more.

In late 1929, Annamaria, the latecomer, was born. She was given
this name because when the midwife asked Katharina what the girl would
be called, the mother suddenly remembered searching for a name for the
garden girl, the fairy-tale child. Annamaria. It was very pretty, a very
Catholic name, Mummi commented, and Ferdinand said it sounded
pretentious.

30
Ferdinand Breaks Out

It was Uncle David's letter that first made the change in Germany clear to her. Even the "Circle" had stopped talking about politics after an agitated debate about the Folk Proclamations: Wagner had called Konrad Henlein, the Sudeten German leader of the Gymnastics Alliance, a cretin, and had then, much to everyone's amazement, been attacked by Dorothee Neumeister. She accused Wagner of sullying the Germanic spirit—which was finally growing strong again—and denigrating the border Germans, who had always suffered. Katharina had never seen Waldhans get this angry: The republic's minority policies were exemplary! Didn't the Germans even have a minister in the cabinet? But now the Germans had become troublemakers, and they shouldn't be surprised that the republic was defending itself! The survival of the democracy was at stake!

Katharina was stunned by Uncle David's letter, which woke her up. She was entangled in her day-to-day life—in her work with Ferdinand and Prchala, the "factory problems," as she put it, bringing up the children, her troubles with Ferdinand, and such little pleasures as the theater, the opera, the "Circle."

Thus [he had written on August 4, 1932], I am preparing for hell, experienced as I am in dealing with the devil and Beelzebub. Contrary to my expectations, Hitler has triumphantly won the

175

Reichstag election. The National Socialists make up the largest
faction. You can't imagine how jubilant even the most rational
people are. They think that this Messiah will lead them out of the
mess they're in. If not a Bismarck, then at least a Hitler. Hindenburg has gone down in ruins, people don't trust the Communists
because of their internationalism, and the Social Democrats are
more like a club than a party (I voted for them, grinding my teeth:
After all, they *are* democrats, aren't they?). And Hugenberg, that
scheming death-bird! God, what ghosts are attracting hopes. I'm
scared, girl. We Jews have an ingrained sense of danger. Nothing
can stop what's coming. Reason has abdicated, leaving all control to
madness. I can only hope that you people in faraway Czechoslovakia
won't be touched, but my suspicions are aroused by the things I hear
about Henlein and his fellow gymnasts, who have sworn their
allegiance to Hitlerism. I'm scared that Herr Hitler will stage a
putsch and grab the power; or else, and this is quite conceivable, the
stupid nation will frivolously hand him the power and quite legally
at that.

Your father is not so well, girl. He is ill. Also, and no one wants
to admit it, he has lost his faith in the world. You needn't be
alarmed. We are all quite alarmed as it is.

She did something unusual for her: she showed the letter to Ferdinand. He called it utter pessimism in every respect, and would not discuss
it any further. One could not put Henlein down like that, Ferdinand had
already protested repeatedly, and his indifference in conversations had
horrified her. Waldhans had characterized Ferdinand as one of those
people who are slow to notice something, who take a long time making
up their minds.

After his nights in the study became uncomfortable, Ferdinand had
one of the guest rooms fixed up for him. They still shared the bathroom.
He seldom came to her, and he was absent-minded in his lovemaking.
She had to admit to herself that she didn't desire him either. Sometimes
she dreamt about other men, about Prchala or Wagner, and she kept
recognizing a shadowy figure as Skodlerrak. She reproached herself for
permitting a long-past love to remain so deep inside her and still dictate
her dreams. If she were to run into Skodlerrak now, he would certainly be
a stranger to her. She blamed it on Ferdinand. He had never managed to
free her from Skodlerrak.

She knew she was attractive and had an effect on many men. But
she wasn't interested in having an affair. The children were too close, the
house too present, a circle that she had to protect. She assumed that

Ferdinand had a mistress, but she didn't care, nor did she look for any signs of one. He frequently came home late at night, but never blamed it on his work. He would say he had met friends. She never asked him for details.

He's cheating on me, she occasionally said to herself, an observation with which she gradually freed herself from him or at least tried to do so. The closeness based on their working together had lasted only briefly. She was aware of her wretched situation, and she was bound by her duties.

We should pay more attention to each other, he had said.

She was playing piano, Chopin or Schumann; it had become an evening relaxation for her.

Yes, she said, it's a pleasant rhetoric.

Why are you so sarcastic?

I?

It's hard to talk to you.

Then try. And what do you mean: Pay more attention to each other.

For the children's sake, Kathi.

You hardly ever see them.

You're exaggerating.

Ask the children whether I'm exaggerating.

It would probably be better if we split up.

This statement came so suddenly that she couldn't reply.

I'm exaggerating again, he added after a long pause.

No, not this time.

We don't belong together anymore.

That's easy to say after almost ten years.

It's hard for me, Kathi.

It's easy to talk if you've got a second home.

What do you mean?

I mean your concubine, to put it more precisely.

For heaven's sake, must you always suspect I'm having an affair?

If you knew how little it mattered to me.

There you are.

Why are you lying, Ferdinand?

I'm not lying.

Why should I keep provoking you? Just hide behind your fibs.

Yes, there *is* someone.

Do you want a divorce?

I don't think so, Kati. I don't know what I want. But we should be clear about how things stand.

You're making it clear to me. And I knew it.

Then it's all right.

On the contrary. We're lying to each other, and I'm a party to it. I don't want to leave here, and I wouldn't know what would happen to the children.

Then what should we do?

Let's keep things as they are.

That's probably best, Katinka.

31

The Second Mirror Image or
The Lady's Not for Burning Yet

Naked, stepping out of the bathtub, she sees herself, in profile, passing the mirror.

She hasn't stood at the mirror for a long time. She pauses, turns to her own image, steps up to the glass so that she feels its coldness.

She wishes someone could see her like this, not a voyeur, but someone who would share the mirror with her.

Her nipples touch the nipples in the mirror; the cold makes her solid. She doesn't move.

She finds she hasn't changed, but she knows a woman has an image of herself that no mirror can refute.

She still looks like Nefertiti, especially when her hair is pulled tightly across her narrow head. But her eyes are dimmer; she wonders whether that's a vestige of disappointment.

She stretches, stands on tiptoe.

Her belly is smooth, the skin hasn't grown slack even after four babies. The breasts, which she is proud of, are full and firm.

She pulls over a footstool, sits down in front of the mirror. She slowly opens her thighs.

You can't see time yourself, she says into the mirror. Only other people see time.

The mirror mutely repeats the sentences and her grimaces. It shows her a young woman, whom she likes, a woman with an attractive, slightly voluptuous body; she leans forward so that the breasts swing and she gradually draws her lips apart.

While the skin shivers with cold, but is warmed by increasing pleasure, she thinks up a mirror image, a big, muscular man, naked too, growing into the field of vision from the edge, leaning lightly against the seated woman.

She puts her hand between her legs, sits on and on, until she thinks she could pull out the mirror image if she wanted to, liberate it from the glass.

32
Georg Wüllner's Death

Uncle David had sent the telegram: "Your father died last night. Funeral tomorrow, 2 February. We expect you. Uncle David."

Hitler had been Reich Chancellor for two days.

She wished the entire family could come along: Gutsi insisted on attending the funeral. Ferdinand made some vague attempts at comforting Katharina; the bustle of the quick departure prevented her from thinking about Father or Mummi. The children, especially Camilla and Annamaria, had known their Dresden Grandpa little or not at all, and they were sad only because Mami no longer had a Papa now.

Ferdinand's chauffeur had bought the train tickets: rooms were reserved for three days at the Europäischer Hof. Ferdinand had insisted on the hotel: After all, Mummi would certainly be very busy, Dieter and Ernst would be staying with her, and Gutsi had already said she would not leave poor Frau Wüllner's side even if she had to sleep on the floor.

Under pressure from three adults, the children were quiet during the trip. They occasionally rebelled against the boredom and because no one wanted to play with them; but when Ferdinand turned out the light, they soon fell asleep on their seats, curled up like cats.

Katharina had promised to wake them before the border, they wanted to show their I.D. cards themselves and open their suitcases "if the soldiers want to sniff around." Ferdinand corrected them: They weren't soldiers, they were customs officials. But they did wear uniforms,

181

the boys said, and the Czech uniforms were nicer than the German ones. The boys pretended to be sophisticated travelers.

"Father is gone. He will exist no more. Children think their parents are immortal." They had not yet revised their faith. Odd how unfatherly her father had been; more like an older friend, who sometimes withdraws, who makes himself popular with surprises, and whose affection never wears out but is felt as a gift. Short as he was (she recalled the way he had balanced on tiptoe in order to look taller), she had never considered him small; and even during the final years, his presence had never changed his image of an almost youthful gambler.

The cordiality of the Czech customs officials struck her as melancholy. Border clashes had occurred during the past few weeks. The children, to their great regret, did not have to present their valises. Crossing a border after a night of traveling stimulated Katharina's imagination, moved her—as if she were crossing from one continent into another, leaving the nightland and entering the dayland; except that, according to Uncle David's presentiments, it was really the other way round. One of the German customs men said, "Guten Morgen," the other yelled out, "Heil!", angering Gutsi. She told him to stop terrifying the children with his roar, they had been traveling all night. Katharina leaned out the window, now they would be riding along the Elbe through Saxon Switzerland; if she hadn't been so despondent, she could have told the children: That hotel there, that's where Papa and I stayed after our wedding; there, by that bridge, that's where Uncle Ernst tumbled into the water—or was it Uncle Dieter?

It is as cold as it was back then. This is an area where the ice grows out of the soil. All at once, her memory takes a tremendous plunge: far below, in a focal point that gathers all brightness, there is what she was. "One grows older in leaps and bounds," she wrote to Uncle David after the trip.

He was waiting for her at the station, swinging his umbrella, dressed all in black, with his bowler over his forehead—he looked like Charlie Chaplin.

He smelled of mothballs. Camilla said so too, whereupon Uncle David explained to her that he sometimes covered himself up with mothballs and remained inside the big closet for a whole month, they had taken him out just a few days ago.

He said he had asked Mummi to stay home, she needed some rest.

Gutsi left them—she wanted to go to Frau Wüllner right away, and Uncle David supported her decision, saying they were waiting for her eagerly. The others drove to the hotel with him.

Outside the terminal, Katharina had noticed so many people wearing uniforms. This was the first time she consciously saw storm troopers. And everything struck her as fresh, spic and span, a sort of brutal cleanliness. The children enjoyed living at the hotel, they often had to be looked for. On the other hand, they acted humble with Mummi in the "birdseed apartment." They sneaked around so stealthily that Susanne Wüllner told them to make some noise for goodness sake.

The weather was clear and icy. The procession of mourners following the coffin was long. They had to be careful on the smoothly trodden snow, and the many small, slippery footsteps made a funny scraping noise. Katharina walked behind Mummi, who was led along by Uncle David. She held the hands of the twins and Annamaria, Ferdinand walked behind her with Gutsi and Camilla.

Mummi, without tears, had told her about Father's death: He had gone to bed in a good mood, taking along a small glass of cognac as a nightcap, and when she came in, he was no longer breathing. He had been ill for a long time. He simply up and died on us, Mummi said, and the sentence dug itself into Katharina's memory.

A young pastor gave the graveside sermon. He spoke of a "fulfilled life." Katharina thought of how it had been fulfilled, and she saw the small, nimble man in the garden at Klotzsche, in exceedingly elegant clothes, surrounded by a group of women.

When the four gravediggers were about to lower the coffin into the hole, one of them accidentally dropped the rope. The coffin tipped forward and slid down steeply. The mourners held their breath. Camilla began to laugh, Katharina pressed the girl's small face into her coat and felt like laughing too. Even here, Father had broken out.

Katharina recognized a few faces among the people expressing their condolences. Some of the men wore uniforms and clicked their heels together when they offered their sympathy to Mummi. Katharina was startled by every click.

Gutsi said it had been an "absolutely crazy" funeral, but Herr Wüllner would definitely not have wanted anything else. Susanne Wüllner excused herself at the cemetery gate, telling her daughter she would join them in the hotel later on, the apartment was getting on her nerves—but she had promised a coffee hour to the "birdseeders" (Wüllner's term for the women who filled the pouches with her). They had been her companions during the past few years, she said, and she couldn't turn them down.

They already had their corner in the hotel lobby, "next to the two palm trees." David Eichlaub had taken Ferdinand aside, and Katharina couldn't hear what they were discussing. Ferdinand nodded in agreement several times.

David, as Ferdinand explained to her afterward, had advised them
to have Mummi move to Brno with them. Ferdinand found it a sensible
idea. After all, the old woman, who was Jewish to boot, could not be left
on her own in this city.

Uncle David then started in without further ado after Susanne
Wüllner arrived: We are now going to tackle the Jewish problem, he said
so loudly that nearly all the guests in the lobby turned towards him
curiously.

Please don't act silly, David, Susanne Wüllner admonished him.

He lowered his voice again, and went on: We have decided to move
you to Brno for your old age Susanne.

Susanne Wüllner peered at him speechless and said, after a long
silence: Why not? I'll only miss my Dresden. And you'll have to take care
of Georg's grave.

Dieter and Ernst, oddly enough, had seen Katharina all the while
and spoken to her, yet not "noticed" her (Ernst had gone to fat and acted
like a slapstick comedian; Dieter wore his captain's uniform like a tux-
edo). The two brothers considered Uncle David's fears exaggerated, but
felt that Katharina's presence would give Mummi something else to think
about.

Is this still our Dresden or is it Gauleiter Mutschmann's? David
asked angrily.

Ernst tried to calm him.

You're political idiots, said David.

Please don't fight now, Mummi pleaded.

When? asked Katharina.

As soon as possible, said Gutsi.

She fully agreed, Susanne Wüllner added.

Now the city is cooling off for good. Even the fantasy garden will dry
out, the white mansion will no longer exist.

And what's to become of you, Uncle David?

He drew a tea rose from a vase standing on the table and handed it
to her: I'm staying on for a while. I'll be protected by my old age and my
foolishness.

Susanne Wüllner followed them three weeks later. They had found
her an apartment near the house: Gutsi moved in with her. The two
women came over on most afternoons; they helped with the children's
homework, the garden, the house. Božena disrespectfully referred to
them as the "old girls."

33
The Dawn of a New Era or
Gutsi Has a New Name

She seeks, searches, hears, she's frightened. Fear comes toward her, spic and span, with a flat sky for airplanes, with straight streets for parades, with squares for flags, with faces into which an omnipotent Führer has polished freshness, with men who have swallowed the Fatherland and now stand smartly, with women who have sworn to bear children for the Führer's weapons.

She reels through a flurry of news and rumors, picks up a few items, sees photos, reads about the abstract Reich, the happiness prescribed for everyone; even Ferdinand cannot resist, he has gone to Reichenbach, he has participated in the founding assembly of the Sudeten German Party under Henlein, in a telegram it joins forces with the National Socialists, offering the Führer the Sudetenland on a silver platter. Ferdinand comes home; warding off all sarcasm, he has drummed mottoes into the boys' heads—one Nation / one Reich / one Führer—and he threatens to fire Prchala for poking fun at him.

What are you going to do with a half-Jewish wife and a Jewish mother-in-law in your Nordic pantheon? Katharina asked.

Those are private matters.

He actually believed he could still keep politics separate from his private life, an Aryan who slept with a half-breed, at least occasionally.

"They are being raised as murderers," wrote Uncle David, "and they do not realize it."

Gutsi, who was rejuvenated by Annamaria's birth and now took care of the baby together with Susanne Wüllner, camouflaged her fear behind martial utterances, which terrified even the twins, who would have started wearing uniforms long ago, if at all possible: Come war, we'll manage. If people are dead, there'll be no bread, she shouted, driving the would-be soldiers along: Your Führer will get you soon enough, you'll have to pay with both Peter and Paul. Her fury intimidated the adolescents, who would rather have been with their teachers, now all German chauvinists, to celebrate the victory of Hermann the Cheruscan over the Roman rabble.

Dorothee Neumeister, proud of her education, was devoted to Rosenberg, *The Myth of the Twentieth Century;* she irritated the Circle with her mystical gibberish, a heroic woman gone haywire: Come now, what's all this jabbering about democracy and freedom, as if we didn't know that a society finding its strength can be shaped only by rigorous law and order.

When the synagogues were burning in Germany, Mummi said, First it was books, now it's houses of worship, next it will be human beings; and very few letters came from Uncle David:

> Whenever the Supreme Being speaks, I sit by the radio and listen to his visions. He has kindled the fire, girl. An entire nation has been scorched. And people like us are marked, we get a star in our ID cards and on our jackets. I'm a doddering old man, and I'm prohibited from using park benches and streetcars, restaurants and pissoirs, since my Jewish urine could discolor the Aryan urine. I'm a leper, someone who's been declared sick by the Almighty.

But he did not accept Katharina's invitations, and Ferdinand breathed a sigh of relief: Where did she want to put the old man up anyway, and besides, Božena couldn't be his nurse.

Politicians became caricatures, satirical verses were pinned to their backs, they were publicly displayed and went to wrack and ruin in schoolyards, Chamberlain with the umbrella and Daladier with the hat: That was how they hopped through Katharina's dreams.

Munich, said Dorothee Neumeister, silencing Waldhans and Gawliček, Munich is the beginning of an international politics that will be determined by the Reich, the Sudeten Mountains have been German since time immemorial; it was an aberration making them Czech territory. They all held their tongues, even Gottgetreu, who wanted to flee to Palestine with his wife and children.

But don't you have any faith in the future?

The Nazis, said Wagner, are also German. It will all settle down.

Gawliček, who did not have to take his own life—he was world-famous, a Czech showpiece—poisoned himself, and his funeral became a demonstration. Beneš attended it, numerous cabinet members followed the coffin, singers, a few musicians, some from the Reich, and his Mass was then performed at the Národní dům; Waldhans wrote in his obituary: "As peaceful as he was, his music was restless, spirits broke out from his dark soul and danced a Slavic round," whereupon Dorothee Neumeister crowed: If he could talk about Slavic music, then she could just as well talk about Germanic art.

Prchala put on the uniform, came to the factory to say goodbye; the mobilization included him as a reserve officer. The Czech workers bowed to him.

She could have fallen in love with him, years ago; she told herself, she could have fallen in love with several men, for the turmoil had made her susceptible: she wanted to be embraced and forget herself, she wanted to pounce on somebody, but Ferdinand was away.

When it became known that the Wehrmacht was about to march in, I was at Jan Waldhans's house, to visit his daughter, but she was out. He offered me coffee. The radio was on, announcing the latest news. Prague will soon be occupied. Waldhans pressed his fists against his temples, sobbing unrestrainedly. I took him in my arms, pulled his head to my breasts; we then kissed, endlessly, forgetting everything during that time. He wanted to sleep with me. I left. I should have stayed.

She was standing in the marketplace, with Gutsi, Ferdinand, and the children, among thousands of people. Swastika flags were being waved. Gutsi stood gloomy. She had brought along Annamaria and kept cuddling her. When the first cars, the first German soldiers, emerged, the people roared: Heil! Heil! Ferdinand was beside himself, his arm kept zooming up; the twins howled in their men's voices, which always disconcerted Katharina. Very few people kept silent.

We have come home, said Ferdinand. What home? He told her she was unbearable. She was. She thought of Prchala, who was probably a prisoner of war; she thought of the Gottgetreus, who had left for Warsaw four days ago. She didn't know why, but she thought of the 1934 street battles in Vienna, workers against Fascists, and she wished Skodlerrak were here, she wished for his fury. He must be dead, she said aloud. Who? asked Gutsi. Someone I loved.

Exhausted, they went home on foot. The trolleys weren't running, some streets were closed. The twins yelled; they walked arm in arm with Ferdinand. Mummi was waiting for them with Božena in the living room. She had listened to the welcome on the radio.

Now you'll have to wall me in, said Mummi.

Everything will turn out all right, Gutsi spoke her old pacification sentence.

Yes, yes.

Several days earlier, in her presence, Wagner had addressed Gutsi with her real name: Frau Schönfeldt. She said her name was Eleonore Schönfeldt. Funny, isn't it.

She had to be Gutsi again, simply Gutsi.

34
Prchala's Story

The Czech officer Prchala, now in mufti, of course, returned to Moravian Knitwear several months later. Meanwhile, Katharina had taken over his office, not changing anything, to be sure, since she was certain Prchala would come back to his job so long as nothing happened to him; Ferdinand was skeptical, and Steinhiber, the head of finance and personnel, who had turned out to be "an old Party comrade and companion of Konrad Henlein," called it outrageous.

There was a knock. Katharina reluctantly cried, "Come in," and in the doorway stood Prchala, skinny, wearing a somewhat old-fashioned hiking suit of burl tweed. He asked her not to make a big fuss about his return, he would report to Ferdinand right away. Ferdinand, though unwilling to admit it, was alarmed; he would rather Prchala had remained in oblivion. Prchala had not expected him to react otherwise, but he did not offer to resign, which Steinhiber had hoped for and then eventually demanded.

Prchala did not talk about the period behind him, the defeat of the Czech army, the arrival of the Germans, the establishment of the Protectorate. He told Katharina she didn't have to move back to the antechamber; if she had no objections, he would work at the small desk, and she could take over his desk; that would correspond fully to his present position. She noticed that all the German workers and some of the Czech workers no longer addressed him as Herr Direktor, they simply used his last name. The factory degraded him with no outside help. He didn't seem offended.

Ferdinand left him out of many meetings. It happened despite Katharina's protests; she felt Prchala had to be supported now of all times.

Although Prchala belonged to the Circle, and she had been working with him for years, she knew little about him—only that he was an inveterate bachelor and loved driving his car (a powerful Tatra), he had an apartment in the city, right over Meindl's store, and went fishing every Sunday (he had leased a pond right near the Mazocha), often accompanied by Jan Waldhans, who seemed to be his best friend.

Prchala never spoke about private matters.

During the early time of the occupation, Katharina had been infected by Ferdinand's optimism: He kept stressing that the atmosphere had been purified, life was easier and more lucid; there were no more problems about orders now that they were primarily working for the Wehrmacht. He was certain there would be no excesses against Jews in the Protectorate.

The twins served eagerly in the Hitler Youth, gushing on about evening meetings, working on the Bann; they were familiar with all kinds of weapons, made fun of Tommies and Frenchies, and Peter lectured Katharina about all the harm caused by world Jewry throughout the centuries.

The discussions in the Circle had become torturous, for Dorothee Neumeister guarded the inviolability of the Doctrine. Practically all they talked about was movies, plays, travels; they avoid politics. Camilla, who had become a pig-headed teenager, occasionally astonished the group by reciting chauvinistic poems; she thundered out *Der Deutsche Rat,* which always delighted Dorothee Neumeister anew. The first time, Katharina was horrified, fearing that Jan and Ana Waldhans and Prchala would henceforth stay away, but they did nothing of the sort, they smirked whenever Camilla began to recite.

Katharina's fear began to wane. Ferdinand's confidence was catching. She adjusted; she found everything "not so bad anymore." She viewed Reich Protector Neurath as a decent man. However, the Party people with whom Ferdinand occasionally got together acted pushy and gross, and she vanished into her room whenever they visited.

Mummi now left her apartment as good as never. Gutsi maintained contact with Katharina, dropping over every day.

Until the war broke out.

It changed everything.

Not the twins, not Ferdinand, who saw themselves vindicated from victory to victory, not Dorothee Neumeister, who now controlled the

Circle, usually bringing guests whose presence made the Czechs fall silent for good. Dorothee advised Katharina not to invite Waldhans and Prchala anymore. She wouldn't dream of leaving them out, said Katharina. They had been meeting for more than ten years.

Mummi received the news from Dresden that Uncle David had committed suicide. She wanted to set out instantly, to attend the funeral. They told her absolutely not. Since even Gutsi warned her she'd be arrested at her brother's grave, she changed her mind. She wept for days on end, there was no way to calm her.

Uncle David had written:

> I feel sorry for everything, girl. People try to convince me that I'm thinking Jewish. Well, I'm an old man, and I think what I think desperately. If I wonder why I feel a draft in my back, am I thinking Jewish? Am I thinking Jewish when I think: Go out today, David, and do something nice for yourself? Or when I think, while singing, your voice doesn't carry Brahms anymore, am I thinking Jewish? I am a Jew, an old Jew and I have done harm to the Germanic world. To whom and when? Is a censor reading this too? I ask you amiably and with the Hitler salute to bear in mind, *mein Herr,* that we are thinking about whether I am thinking Jewish. Don't be sad, girl. You're Aryan, I know it. And your children are certainly Aryan. Your husband anyway. Let me think Jewishly that all time passes. Love and kisses from your 'foster uncle' David.

Ferdinand was angry when he read the letter. The old fool was endangering the family. What did he mean "girl"? After all, she was thirty-nine.

I am a girl, she said emphatically, and Uncle David knows it.

She heard that the Jewish laws would now be applied in the Protectorate too.

Here begins Prchala's story.

The ground opened up under Ferdinand's feet; it was all her fault. Not that he would have said so, they had grown closer again, and Annamaria was his favorite. But he avoided visiting Mummi or inviting her over; he had fired the only Jewish bookkeeper in the firm without consulting Katharina and with Steinhiber's approval; he had "purged" the library and he seldom took part in the Circle evenings—all these actions proved to her how vulnerable he felt. She had thought about it—she asked him, trying to sound perceptive, sympathetic:

Isn't it time we separated?

He walked out of the room, slamming the door behind him.

When they drove to the factory the next day, he abruptly stated that he loved her.

Our love is strange. She kissed him on the forehead. I don't believe we understand each other. But still, I don't know whom I could love more than you.

She had suggested confiding in Prchala. Do you happen to know his first name?

Why do you ask? Do you want to flirt with him?

Of course not, but he's never had a first name for me. He was always "Prchala."

His first name is Bedřich, Frederick. Why did she want to confide in Prchala?

He probably knows that Mummi's Jewish. I imagine he could help us.

Soon he won't be able to help himself.

I'm going to ask him.

Prchala was late for work; he apologized. He usually wore his curious hiking outfits. His thin, blond hair stood out over his ears, a sparse tonsure. She told him she had to consult him about something, a difficult matter. It would be better if they spoke outside the building, for she didn't know whether Steinhiber didn't hang his ears out everywhere.

Prchala laughed: It was funny, he said, picturing Steinhiber's ears like that. Hundreds of gigantic, fluttering, listening Steinhiber-ears on walls and doors.

They took the trolley to the Opera Café.

Do you know?

He knew everything.

He sat there tensely, ignoring the many uniformed men who alarmed her.

Say nothing, he said. Are you going to see Traviata on Saturday? He loved Verdi; he could, if asked, recite whole passages from Verdi's letters, from Franz Werfel's book on Verdi. This had earned him Gawliček's mockery.

Don't worry.

He said he couldn't advise her, answer her on the spur of the moment. Did she know the wafer bakery near Winterholler-Platz—its fragrance spread far into the park.

Yes, she said, the chestnut trees smell like cinnamon. Why do you ask?

He said the baker was a friend of his. He visited the bakery on Sunday mornings and would wait for her there.

All at once, such conspiracies struck her as ludicrous.

Ferdinand asked her what the upshot of the conversation was.

She replied that Prchala had left things up in the air; she said nothing about the appointment at the wafer bakery.

They saw one another at the opera and said hello; Ferdinand exchanged a few words with him, then abandoned him in order to pay his respects to the district leader (he had been principal of a tiny elementary school in some Sudeten German village).

Waldhans had talked about concentration camps, about Terezín. He said he had received letters from there.

He said they were being successively killed.

No, that's not true.

The Führer knows what he's doing—that was Paul's comment to every major or minor event, every bit of war news.

She had said she was meeting Ana Waldhans in town. Ferdinand distrusted her.

I'll explain everything to you this afternoon. I probably won't be back for lunch. I've already told Božena.

What is there to explain?

Don't act silly, Ferdinand.

It was true: the park was redolent of pastry, cinnamon, anise, and ginger, and the morning strollers were reveling. The door to the basement bakery was locked. She was hesitant about knocking, so undecided that she didn't even notice Prchala standing behind her. She jumped when he placed his hand on her shoulder. He laughed. That's how far we've come. He whistled the oboe motif from Dvořák's *New World Symphony*, and the door opened; a giant, swelled up even more by the white baker's apron, greeted them and led them through the baking room, with its numbing smell, into a tiny cabinet, then left them again after pushing an envelope into Prchala's hand. He said everything had gone well.

The aroma, the queer situation released her feelings. "I was floating again. I could have done anything, no matter how foolish. I had been seized with a naive joy in cloak-and-dagger doings."

What is going to happen, Herr Prchala?

He drew papers from the envelope.

These are new documents for your mother.

She took the I.D. pass, leafed through it, shook her head: This is impossible.

It's our only chance. We've also found a refuge for your Máma on a farm near Vyškov. The people are reliable.

And now she's Susanne Wüllner, née Schneider?

That's her name now.

And I?

Some of your papers have vanished, others will have to vanish too. Could you take care of that?

I can't.

Then who can?

I don't know, I can't tell you.

Can we count on it?

We'll see. I think we can.

When does Mummi have to leave?

Someone will call for her the day after tomorrow.

What about Gutsi?

She'll have to stay with you.

You regulate my life so easily.

I don't.

She was home earlier than Ferdinand had expected. She told him what would happen.

If it gets out, then no one can help us, he said.

Someone *has* helped us, she said.

In late 1941, Ferdinand was told to dismiss the Czech Bedřich Prchala without delay; Prchala's shares were taken over and held in trust by a Herr Karl Sigwart. This measure was necessary because the firm was only manufacturing products vital to the war effort, and it was inadmissible having non-German elements in the management of such factories.

Prchala was prepared.

Ferdinand had been reeducated.

The twins obtained their high school diplomas by the skin of their teeth. Both were determined to volunteer for the Wehrmacht; as Hitler Youth leaders, they had been repeatedly invited to the air base, and they were inspired equally by the courage of the pilots and by their privileges: much better food and endless supplies of chocolate soda. They were ordered to report for basic training in Berlin.

Ferdinand wondered how he could thank Prchala. He was reluctant to offer him money. Waldhans, in whom he now confided, although cautiously, suggested that he start a textile shop and hire Prchala as a salesman; with his background in textile engineering, he could make himself useful. The shop was allowed to open, but with the stipulation that they could sell only to tailors and not to the general public.

Prchala moved into two rooms in an apartment house near the railroad station; hunched up between textile bales, leafing through fashion journals, he waited for customers three hours a day. Katharina visited him frequently. In the narrow space, his charisma was greater. His calm attracted her. She talked to him about the twins and their blind militarism; they were alien to her although she constantly worried about them: "No longer my children, simply young men whom I know very well." Couriers brought her news of Mummi; she went to him when she was notified about Ferdinand's death; it was he who helped her after the arrival of the Soviet troops, who restored her and Mummi's earlier identities, who said goodbye to her, with whom she began to use the familiar form too late, who told her when they left Czechoslovakia: You'll never come back, Kathi.

She never forgot his voice. Whenever she heard music by Dvořák, years later, she would say, That's the way Prchala spoke, and no one knew who that was.

It turned out that Prchala had been at the center of the Moravian resistance. He was celebrated, he traveled back and forth between Prague and Brno, and, after the death of Foreign Minister Masaryk, he emigrated to Canada, which infuriated Ana Waldhans, who had pledged her life to the Communists.

What he had fought for was nothing but a figment. He had been forced to realize it. He couldn't stand the new order. So they all went their separate ways.

35
A Page from the Diary

October 1943

Everything I have loved is doomed. Why are we trapped inside ourselves, unable to get out? I once believed I could love. Can I really? Ferdinand is far away when we make love, when I touch him, when he touches me. Perhaps I am incapable of giving myself fully. But that cannot be.

Time is dashing through me. I absorb too little. When the Stalingrad drama ended in January, with Ferdinand and the girls glued to the radio listening to Goebbels, I wandered around the house, longing for Mummi. Gutsi was a good substitute. We sat together, not speaking a word. General Paulus and General Seydlitz surrendered. Ferdinand came with the news. Why was he weeping? Because so many men had perished? Or because we had lost? I felt like crying too. But only because I understood none of it. This reality does not reach me. I think I am dependent on another person, who transmits reality to me.

After a long hiatus, I have finally received another letter from Dieter; he is in a labor camp in Salzgitter. The letter has come to me through some messenger and by way of three other addresses. In 1940, when the Wehrmacht discovered that he was half-Jewish, he was demoted and then given a dishonorable discharge. Ernst is supposedly in Italy. I care for my brothers, but their lives, their feelings are different from mine; my commiseration is hypocritical.

196

When I think of them, I am afraid—afraid for myself, not for them, and I can only see them as boys, fleeing, always moving, next to Elle, whom I convince myself I loved.

Peter and Paul visited recently. Their new language makes them unfamiliar to me. They are my sons; I gave birth to them. They wear uniforms and talk about their Messerschmitts as if they were their mistresses.

I rammed right in, nuts and all, said Paul, telling us about a dogfight, and he laughed when I was dismayed by his choice of words. They are my children.

I notice that I am trying to sum up.

Language is difficult. I do not mean what I say. I cannot say what I mean.

Ever since Ferdinand was drafted (we thought his work would keep him indispensable to the war effort) and Camilla is working in Pomerania (she has written that she plans to marry), I cannot run the house properly. I most likely never could, I was merely deceiving myself. Annamaria, Gutsi, and I have remained, Božena is laboring in a factory. I am very close to Annamaria, she resembles me more and more, according to Gutsi. Three women in drydock.

At the first air raid, we acted indescribably stupid. We were so wrought up we did not manage to get into the basement. When bombs hit, we left everything we had gathered and we dashed down. No sooner had Gutsi arrived in the basement than she ran upstairs again: she had a rabbit in the oven, and she did not want it to burn. To stave off want, she raises rabbits and chickens in the garden, I am beginning to feel grateful to her for it. Everything I do takes place in a state of numbness.

36
Adam Wagner

In November 1943, Katharina Perchtmann was notified that her husband had fallen in combat for "the Folk and the Fatherland." Several weeks later, she learned that her son, Aviation Cadet Paul Perchtmann, had died a "hero's death." Her brother Ernst Wüllner, she heard, had committed suicide in an Italian village. Gutsi could not comfort her. Dorothee Neumeister came by and disavowed her heroism. Wagner sometimes took her to the theater; his wife had run away. Katharina did not tell her mother about any of the deaths, and she made sure that Gutsi and Annamaria held their tongues.

She played the piano a lot. She spent more time with Annamaria. Afternoon tea became a strict ritual for the two women and the girl. They would discuss the happenings of the day, the events at school, tomorrow's menus. Annamaria had told her she looked good in black, instantly adding that it was a tactless compliment. Oh no, Katharina had replied, you don't have to apologize, one likes to be beautiful in mourning too.

She couldn't get used to being alone night after night; she began to masturbate. The ruined surroundings barely shocked her now. She decided she was becoming "morally corrupt." The Circle now consisted of Dorothee Neumeister, Ana and Jan Waldhans, Dr. Gürtler, a young, badly wounded lawyer from the Reich, occasionally Prchala, and always Adam Wagner, who unsparingly revealed his wife's adventures: She had most likely cheated on him a few days after the wedding, she was both charming and incapable of love. He had soon found out and confronted her. It didn't help. I waited for her to walk out on me. It took her long enough. And now, odd as it sounds, I miss her. She had written him a poignant Dear John letter. Ana Waldhans was repelled by the whole business.

Wagner kept visiting her more and more between the Circle soirees. Katharina felt he had changed for the better after his wife deserted him, he acted more self-confident. Wagner had always held back during the conversations, but, albeit somewhat vaguely, sided against Dorothee Neumeister; he was no German chauvinist, but a down-to-earth businessman, who found political emotions disagreeable. Moreover, his was an old, established family; he dealt with Czechs, Slovaks, and Jews as a matter of course; his Czech had no trace of an accent. Katharina preferred tall, slender men or small graceful ones like Father. Wagner, in contrast, was not tall, but stocky, almost fat; his movements were awkward, cautious. His face was remarkably smooth for a man over fifty; the forehead, the "little cheeks," the round chin, which he had recently started concealing behind an Assyrian beard.

It was Wagner who first made her familiar with the city. She had been living in Brno for twenty years, seeing and getting to know the city in fragments; but during her strolls with him, in the daytime, and especially in the evening, the townscape came together, already perforated by ruins, bomb craters, temporarily closed streets. They often stopped in a wine cellar by the old town hall, behind the passageway where the dragon hung from the ceiling. They became steady customers here and, even when the shortages began, they were still served "the finest." Adam Wagner was a supplier for Sedláček, the proprietor.

She slid into this affair, no talk about fire, about passion, she never deceived herself about love—their intimacy increased, giving her a sense of closeness, protection, and that was enough for her. Gutsi accepted the relationship, but Annamaria was annoyed. The fifteen-year-old reacted mulishly, avoiding affection. Katharina meant to have a talk with her, but never got around to it. Time was faster, it took Adam Wagner away.

She was received by his secretary, a fat, milky-pale girl, whose upper thighs cracked together when she walked. This creature, Katharina imagined, must smell of sour sweat. Herr Wagner sent his apologies, the girl said; an electric oven had gone out in the bakery, they had called him. He would hurry. Katharina's first visit here was obviously doomed. She had been reluctant to come, since in order to reach his office she had to pass through the store, where she was known; the salesgirls had all greeted her cordially. And one of them had handed her on to the doughy secretary.

She does not sit down, she wanders about the room, with its old-fashioned furnishings, where the smell from the bakery has settled in, for years now, yeast and sourdough, hot flour, and something sweet, voluptuous blends in. I couldn't stand it here, she thinks to herself. She has walked in through a door; the room has two other doors. She walks through one of them, it is dark inside, she gropes for the switch, and when the light comes on, she sees countless bookcases with nothing but candied fruit in piles of jars and crates. A sugar den, in which the children could eat themselves to death. In the middle of the war, when the simplest foods have become rarities, Adam Wagner is heaping up sugar-coated delicacies that will survive the collapse, green towers of lemon peels, crystal cherries and plum mummies, yellow-brown cliffs of candied orange peels, plus almonds, sorted into bitter and sweet, all kinds of nuts, raisins, currants. She starts nibbling, presses a cherry between her lips, follows it up with a piece of lemon peel, orange peel, stuffs her face full of currants, bites into a bitter almond, spits out the remnants between the congealed fruits, chews walnuts and hazelnuts, chomps, rubs her sticky hands. Wagner pulls her out of this temple of eternal fruits. Wasn't the door locked? Not at all. No one was to find out about this; these were his reserves.

How can you bake without flour?

I've stocked up on flour too.

I misjudged you, Herr Wagner. You've truly got a baker's mind.

Does that bother you?

No.

She finds the term "baker's mind" nasty and apologizes.

You simply have a touch of arrogance, he says.

She had told him about Ferdinand, Paul, and Ernst. She had liked his tact, and now she had offended him.

That terrible, sweetened wealth had made her childish, almost crazy. She grabbed him, kissed him. He barely reacted. Those damn candied cherries, they're so powerful, she said. Eventually, he laughed. "He kissed like an adolescent, like Eberhard."

She didn't dare suggest that he sleep with her. Nor did he. That evening, they sat with Sedláček in the wine cellar. He drove her home, shyly kissing her good-night. He said he would drop by tomorrow.

Later on, when she slept with him, in his apartment, it came out of intimacy. She assumed he was comparing her with Swetlana, as she was comparing him with Ferdinand. "Compare" wasn't the right word: For twenty years, she had not been with any man but Ferdinand. She did not count her fantasies, her heated dreams. Wagner was perhaps more prosaic than Ferdinand, more constant in his affections, more relaxed in his work.

Wagner advised her to allow the Nazis to manage the factory. She had been forced to make Steinhiber general manager. Without Ferdinand and Prchala, she felt chilly in the offices of the management wing, even though the old employees outdid one another with their kindnesses. She attended two or three more board meetings. The money was sent to her punctually.

Now and then, Adam Wagner would spend the night with her. Each time, Annamaria's tacit rebukes hurt her, so that Katharina preferred staying in his place until late at night, leaving Gutsi alone with the child. Katharina knew that Annamaria had told Peter and Camilla about their mother's relationship with Wagner. A palpable barrier arose between Katharina and the children, leaving her helpless: she was unable to make them understand. She would have liked to tell them: I'm not just your mother, I'm a human being, I'm alive, I want to live, especially now in an era that makes it clear how insignificant life is. I'm still young, I love and suffer no differently from you, even though you think mothers should be mothers and nothing else.

She took this freedom upon herself.

She reproached herself only if she wasn't at home during an air raid. The basement of the house, as experts had predicted, was unsafe. Adam's bakery cellar, a labyrinth of corridors and niches, was incomparably safer. She enjoyed an unwanted advantage.

During the times in the basement, she became increasingly apathetic. Previously, she would have denied being particularly fearful; she considered herself courageous, equal to challenges. Her fear became physical, numbing not only her mind. If she was in her own cellar, she fought against her fear so as not to alarm Annamaria and Gutsi. But in Wagner's cellar, she let herself go.

Whenever they went outside the house after the all-clear signal, she looked at the flames, the devastation, the teeming throngs of firemen, soldiers, people digging for their belongings, as a living extension of the horrors she had previously fantasized about.

Once, after such an evening, Adam Wagner had asked her to marry him.

No, Adam, I can't

Aren't you being overly considerate of your kids?

I wasn't thinking about them.

Then I don't understand.

It's hard to explain: I'm not free of all my memories. I'd be a burden for you.

You're imagining that.

Perhaps. Aren't we also the things we imagine? And I need time.

You're forty, you're no longer young.

Sometimes I think I'm still the girl who ran away from home.

The city was inundated by refugees, transients. The law and order that the Reich had so greatly valued was dissolving. She oriented herself in the chaos. She didn't have to practice, she could cope with it; so could Gutsi, who desperately kept everything in its place. Annamaria seldom had to attend school.

When the front came closer, Wagner, threatened with being drafted into the *Volkssturm* like all the boys and old men, made up his mind to flee.

She asked: What will become of your sugar paradise?

Take it home.

I'll take the cherries.

He told her to join him along with Gutsi and Annamaria.

No, she said, she'd stay. Prchala had advised her to.

He's not omnipotent either.

No one's omnipotent now, not even the Führer.

During the last night, he was unable to make love with her. She was obsessed, stroking his naked back, clinging to him, but she did not feel him.

I'll try to find you after the war.

It's no use, she said.

What do you mean?

We won't belong together in a different era.

Did she really associate love with an era?

She said she couldn't see it any other way. She'd be different too.

37
Confusion or The End of
Katharina Perchtmann the Factory Owner

She had been overlooked. She had made herself think she was free,
she had cheated her way out of her fear, she had perceived only the
closest things, reacted only to them; but she had barely been touched by
the fact that a world was changing and going under. Ferdinand, the
twins, Uncle David, Prchala, Waldhans, even Mummi had been involved. But not she. She had been devastated by some of the events:
When the war had broken out, she had wept, and also when Ferdinand
had died in action, and when the news had been released about the
attempt on Hitler's life—she didn't even know whether she was weeping
because the attempt had failed. She had never feared that the flimflam
with Mummi and her could come out. She had protected herself by
dealing only with the things closest to her.

Now, everyone was leaving her—Gutsi and Annamaria during the
day, and often at night; they were working at the railroad station,
distributing milk and soup to refugees. At the factory she saw only
strange faces (Steinhiber and the Nazi protector had resigned). And now
she began to act, albeit without a plan or a goal.

Prchala, who had vanished for several months, no longer attending
the Circle, had suddenly shown up again and told her to bring Mummi to
Brno, since the Russians were already in Ostrava. She discussed the
expedition with Gutsi. Gutsi wanted to wait with her in Brno. Katharina

decided against it; the three of them would go to Mummi; whatever might happen, she didn't want them to be separated. Gutsi agreed.

Katharina asked Annamaria to get a train schedule, the child roared with laughter: There've been no train schedules for a long time now.

"I locked up the house. I realized that even if I came back here with Mummi for a few days, it would no longer be our house. It had given us up."

They waited at the station for three days, until there was a train going to Přerov. They were told the front was getting closer; no one could say how far the train would get.

She braced herself against a torrent of plunging, dissolving faces, mingling voices, a permanent murmur occasionally disrupted by shouts; in the overall haste, language lost its meaning.

Annamaria trusted her again. When the girl slept, she put her head in her mother's lap.

Traveling circuitously, past many stations, they finally reached the farm. Katharina's mother, who had not been notified, received them as if she'd been expecting the small party of travelers. She served them tea and Danish pastry in her room.

You don't have to pack much.

Do I have to sew the Jewish star on my coat?

You're not Jewish.

Not even now?

You'll become Jewish again when the war's over.

Will they allow it then?

These few sentences hooked into Katharina's memory. Sometimes, when conversation would turn to the war, to future wars, she would recite those sentences, bridging the years, repeating an instant, in which time, which she had not accepted, condensed for her.

The farmers who, induced by Prchala and his friends, had braved all danger by taking Mummi in, accompanied them silently for a while. When they bade farewell to the old woman, she kissed them on their foreheads, and the farmers passed from their silence into a new wordlessness.

The women walked long distances. Katharina took care of her mother, whose strength, however, surpassed hers. Eventually, fleeing soldiers took them along on a truck, all the way to Brno.

The house did not welcome them. Now, as outlaws, they were no longer able to live in such houses. The factory had stopped operating. When Katharina went there to pick up documents and empty the safe, she walked through a wasteland. Only one of the bookkeepers held the fort; he bowed to her, kissing her hand, and said he couldn't imagine that everything was going under. It is, she said, it is.

On the way home, she saw that many of the houses had been wiped out by bombs during her trip. There were few people in the streets. Many people had dumped their Christmas trees through their windows down to the sidewalk. The city was cowering, waiting.

The succession of air raids was almost continuous. The women moved down into the basement, made do as best they could, mummified themselves in order to look old when the Russians came; they had heard that girls and young women were not safe.

She had no idea whether Camilla and Peter were still alive; she didn't know where they were.

She often thought of Uncle David, and whenever the mood hit her, she would leave the basement, even during an air raid, go to the grand piano in the living room, and play some of the songs he had sung.

You're getting crotchety, said Annamaria.

I didn't realize that cellar bugs could get crotchety, she said. She felt that Uncle David's answer would have sounded like that.

Mummi told Annamaria about Klotzsche; Katharina wasn't listening. She had sloughed off her skin, none of that belonged to her anymore.

"No more. How often we say 'no more.'"

The Soviet troops were nearing the city, but Prchala turned up first; to her amazement, he wore a uniform. He was accompanied by several men; they stood in the living room, like conquerors, already the new owners. Prchala kissed her hand, and also Gutsi's and Annamaria's; smiling helplessly, he said that much as he regretted it, they had to leave the house immediately—it was being requisitioned for officers of the Red Army. However, he said, in order not to inconvenience them, he had an apartment ready for them, in the same building as his shop; a Reich German, he emphasized maliciously, had given it up. Moreover, Frau Wüllner could use her old documents again, they would presumably be useful. Naturally, he would help them out if they had any problems.

Must we leave right away?

As I said, immediately.

The Czech militiamen helped them pack and loaded the bags and bundles on a wagon.

You'll have to ride along.

We'd rather walk.

That was impossible, he said, they might be stopped by Red Army men in town. Women had been raped.

They crossed the threshold without looking back.

"Prchala really did help us," Katharina wrote in June 1945. "The note on the apartment door alone protected us. It said in Russian and Czech that we were a family who had been persecuted by the Nazis and already investigated and cleared by the Národní výbor. I'd never been sick a day in my life, now I got pneumonia. Gutsi was about to take me to the hospital. I refused. Prchala got hold of a good doctor. The news of Hitler's death has reached us belatedly. We hear he has taken his life; others say he has managed to escape in a submarine. I cannot imagine it. I assume he was cowardly; perhaps he thought everything would end with him. I once believed that about myself. Annamaria is not allowed to attend school. We are Germans. Our, or rather Mummi's, being Jewish helps us to some extent. Most Germans were rounded up; they had to march south. We understand that many died en route. Supposedly the Czechs treated them cruelly. When I asked Prchala about it, he did not deny it. He said not only the people had been freed, but also their anger and hatred, their thirst for blood. He seems languid, more melancholy; he is no longer radiant as during the first few days after the Russians marched in. He is completely absorbed by his work, he says; he sees no light at the end of the tunnel. We are laboriously pushing through the garbage, he says. Mummi and I are afraid to go out. Božena, who found refuge with relatives, looked us up, she brings us the essentials. We are afraid of any noise on the staircase; fear increases as the footsteps come closer. Prchala has said we cannot have the apartment permanently. He is signing us up for a transport of privileged people going to the Reich. Mummi is happy, she wants to go to Dresden. Prchala said that unfortunately he cannot determine where the transport is heading."

They had been assigned places in a passenger coach rather than in one of the freight cars. Božena had wanted to come to the station, but she did not show up. "I've spent a lifetime with that woman." Katharina asked, and she asked too late, why Božena had never married. Did she have any boyfriends? Gutsi didn't want to hear the questions.

The train rattled torturously along the tracks. Annamaria leaned out the window.

There's Franzensberg with the cathedral.

Yes, yes.

Why didn't you ever come along to the Spielberg casemates?

I don't know.

You can even see the roof of city hall.

Yes, yes.

The view disintegrates like an aging decal, a dazzling whiteness breaks through the colors, nothing more, a memory gap.

Katharina looks away from the window, she gently places the back of her hand against her mouth.

38
The Third Mirror Image or
An Anticipation of Obscenity

When Katharina looks into the mirror, she conceals what still remains to be told.

Or else it is all arranged in a row, splinters of stories, tales, reactions—beginnings of actions that are not continued. The transport becoming an odyssey through a kingdom of ruins, along more and more dead tracks, bleak railroad stations with bizarrely twisted bars of glass roofs arching overhead, places of shards; hunger growing worse and worse, thirst and hunger crushing the passengers, forcing them to lie, to steal; haggling for cigarettes and bread, for dry marmalade and powdered milk; the rifle butts of the accompanying troops dividing the clusters of people, knocking them apart; harried, not knowing how long the train would stop, humbly relieving themselves by squatting alongside the railroad embankment: Susanne Wüllner, at seventy-seven, becoming their ringleader, the only one not giving in to the chaos, enduring the hunger; the faces and voices changing, scarcely perceived, no longer registered, nameless passengers traveling toward an unknown destination until they arrived somewhere; reaching the German border one evening and seeing nothing of the Promised Land but the silhouette of a water pump and the familiar patterns of tracks in a station; strangers squeezing in among them, leaping on, riding illegally, vanishing again with their secrets, leaving conjectures behind; Gutsi becoming a black marketeer within a few scant hours and doing well; Katharina Perchtmann, née

Wüllner, a manufacturer's wife from Brno, traveling through weeks of filth and rampant scabies, finding the other Katharina, Katharina the proletarian, smashing with words, pushing through, ignoring challenges unless they aim at her life, using all her strength, rearing up and learning to get her way, knowing nothing but this present moment that is caked with filth.

One of the illegal passengers, who had jumped upon the train step, was Werner Rossmann. He remained in the compartment with them, against Mummi's and Annamaria's wishes. He remained with them.

She lives in the basement apartment where she cannot be as yet. They have been allocated two rooms. Mummi, Gutsi, and Annamaria live in the larger one, she and Rossmann in the other.

The tiny mirror hangs over the chipped enamel sink and doesn't take her in fully until she steps back and lies down on the bed.

Sometimes she offers herself to the mirror. Sometimes they make love in the mirror.

She lies down in the mirror and waits for Rossmann.

She is forty-four years old.

She has stopped pulling out gray hairs.

She stretches in the mirror.

Her breasts have become heavier, conspicuous on the thin body.

Her hands feel up the body piece by piece; it only wants to be a body and nothing else, it waits.

Until the man lies down next to her and grins into the mirror.

He has driven Eberhard, Skodlerrak, Ferdinand, and Wagner out of her memory.

She sees his body on hers, the tensing and relaxing muscles, she sees her arms and legs embracing him. Her skin is paler than his.

Half concealed by a male shoulder, the face of a woman giving herself—she still must get to know it.

He moans.

She says: Be quiet, remember who's in the next room.

But then he fills her up and she screams.

She doesn't care if her mother or her daughter despise her. She is alive.

PART THREE

(Stuttgart 1946–1970)

39
A Love Story

After four weeks of traveling, no one felt like looking at other faces—they were distorted by filth, repainted by it. The men grew beards, disguises that they usually desired. The tall man, wearing an undefinable uniform, pushed his way into her compartment in a forest shortly after Furth. He managed to grab a spot, among feet, in the corridor, sitting there with his legs drawn in, his arms crossed over a knapsack. He was ignored as an intruder.

He was constantly bothered by the tips of the dirty shoes of women. He slept most of the time, his chin on his pack; he was trained to sleep in any position, a man experienced in homelessness.

He was the one she took up with.

She wasn't prepared, she was busy keeping up the morale and good spirits of her group, tending Annamaria, who had caught a bad cold during the trip, and especially supporting Gutsi, who finally collapsed. Katharina scarcely noticed the intruder. He must have had a strenuous time behind him for he mostly slept during the first few days—that death-like military sleep—which depressed her. He disappeared during one of the long stops, returning after a while (they had all hoped he wouldn't come back); he had two loaves of freshly baked bread, which he tore apart and distributed. He began to gain favor.

She was awakened by a hand stroking her leg from the ankles to the backs of the knees, sometimes clutching her leg, sometimes grazing her with the fingertips.

The dim light blurred the contours of the sleepers, motionless cloth lumps. After three weeks, they had gotten accustomed to the rhythm of the wheels; Katharina could barely imagine ever leaving the train again. They were heading in any direction, toward any goal. The train often moved back and forth, apparently turned away, following a new route. They had long since given up asking the various train escorts where they were going, since the answers were always evasive and usually contradicted by the subsequent route.

She pulled her legs back, pressing them against her seat. After a while, the hand followed, reaching for her ankles, holding one foot tight, drawing it slightly forward against her resistance. Katharina did not dare speak, for Mummi was a light sleeper, and would kick up a fuss if she found out about the silent man's advances. Besides, with his stubborn intimacy, the man was flattering his way into her fantasy, arousing pent-up feelings, a desire for tenderness, that had nothing to do with Mummi's consolations or Annamaria's childlike hugs. Time had liberated Katharina, this trip would go on forever. She could try all kinds of beginnings. Nothing tied her to the Katharina who had had a home and a family. She leaned back, drew the blanket in more snugly, pretended to be asleep, and yielded to the caressing hand, which became more and more eager, more and more greedy, briefly pausing behind the knees, then reaching between her thighs. The daredevil intimacy made them allies against the others, releasing her, at least briefly, from the obligations that made her suffer: having to know everything better than the other three women, being ahead of them, feigning confidence when none existed.

When the hand became impatient, trying to force the thighs apart, she intervened. Her skirt had slid down to her hips beneath the blanket; she shoved it down to her knees together with the alien hand, which suddenly felt hard and chapped. However, she did not let go of the hand. For a while, they kept still; then the stranger became restless. They communicated silently. He got up without a sound, helped her out of the blanket tube. He opened the door without a sound and drew her along, squeezing her hand to signal obstructions: sleepers in the corridor, people brooding in the darkness, cigarettes glowing fitfully.

He abruptly pushed her against the wall, kissed her. She didn't resist; she snuggled against him, holding him close. His beard stubble hurt her, chafing her, leaving her sore. When he tried to get under her skirt, she resisted—not here, not now—and he gave up.

The next day, when the train halted out in the open and the

engineer jumped from the locomotive, indicating that they would have to wait for a long time, she left the compartment; the man followed her, throwing his bundle over his shoulder, accustomed as he was to always carrying the remnant of his belongings. He followed her wordlessly, as though they had promised not to break the silence. His footsteps excited her—she ran faster, more impatiently. She wanted to get away from all the people who were relieving themselves or similarly seeking a place to make love in. She didn't want it like that. She threw herself down in a clearing. She could no longer play and put off, she wanted him to pounce on her. She ignored the footsteps of others who were looking for hiding places, groping through the bushes and returning. For her, the indecency of the situation was part of the transformation that she desired and that the stranger helped her attain. She would be able to forget and start from scratch.

It was only on the way back that she asked him what his name was.

He was Werner Rossmann.

She told him her name.

He found "Katharina" too complicated. He said Katja sounded nice.

She found it right for him to call her that. No one had ever called her that.

Where do you come from?

It's hard to say.

I mean where did you live before you became a soldier?

In Eger.

I know Eger.

I haven't been there for a long time.

What did you do, what kind of work?

I'm a turner.

What's that?

I worked in a factory, I turned hand grenades.

On a machine?

Yes, on a machine.

She introduced him to the other women. Susanne Wüllner ignored him, Gutsi and Annamaria shook his hand.

Katharina flaunted her affection. As soon as the train lumbered off, he sat down at her feet and took her hand.

When Rossmann briefly left the compartment, Mummi called her a whore. Annamaria contradicted her. Her conduct was vulgar, said Mummi. You can see that that man is unsuitable for you—a nobody, probably a worker, completely uneducated.

Katharina ignored her.

She waited for him from one stop to the next, and when the two of them jumped out of the train and dashed hand in hand into the woods, the thicket, everyone knew they were going to "do it." She pictured Annamaria's fantasies without reproaching herself. She had long since released herself from all obligations.

At the refugee camp in Wasseralfingen, where they had to wait two weeks before being assigned a city, she was separated from Rossmann. Men and women were housed in separate barracks.

But they had sworn they would stay together no matter where they wound up.

In Stuttgart, he moved in with them, in the basement apartment on Schlossstrasse, even though he had been allocated a room in Zuffenhausen. He quickly found a taker for his room, which got him in trouble with the authorities for a long time.

So far, they had always made love on the floors of forests, on grass. Now they had a bed, wide, with a checkered cover. They did not wait until night; they hastily divided up the apartment, closed the door behind them, and, heedless of the bated breath in the next room, they occupied this wretched space, under which no wheels sprang, and they made it livable, for themselves alone.

Gutsi listlessly told her that her mother was looking for a place of her own: She could not endure living in this den of iniquity. She would probably be given preference as a Jew.

Katharina did not bother having a talk with her mother; Mummi remained for the time being, as did Annamaria, who attended school again, spending long evenings poring over her notebooks in bad light.

If they counted the jewelry, their financial reserves would hold out for a while.

She did not think about the future, she drifted, she had little contact with the local Germans, who, as became clear in conflicts, viewed the refugees as exotics and liars. Rossmann, no doubt experienced, managed smoothly in the black market. He dealt mainly with Americans. Occasionally, he traveled to Tübingen, in the French Zone. Mummi would then hope all day long that he would get caught and vanish forever. He came back—he knew what he was doing.

They were irritated by the narrow space; they argued a lot, even Mummi lost some inhibitions, acquiring curses that would have made her blush just a few weeks earlier. Each of them shielded himself against the vulnerability of the others by striking first. It was either Annamaria's zippered skirt, which Gutsi refused to hem; or translating decagrams into grams, which caused problems for Katharina, "the simplest thing in the world"; or the available cash, which Mummi checked suspiciously, since she didn't trust Rossmann; or the personal space, which each person stubbornly defended; or Katharina's lewdness; or, nearly always, Rossmann, whose presence, they said, did not allow them to make a halfway civilized home for themselves—and all these conflicts often on the same day.

She fled, holding on to Rossmann, who was growing wild; he had mastered the laws of the underground and enjoyed prestige in the barrack taverns around Leonhardsplatz. They stayed out all night, he wheeling and dealing, she dancing, wanting to go wherever a new band appeared; she was crazed by the music, saying it expressed her state of mind, which Rossmann, an expert, corrected: It was all reprises, nothing new, and the freedom of Negroes was not her freedom.

He was wrong, she said.

They fought more, locked horns. Only their bodies were still close, needing one another. Nevertheless, she was proud of Rossmann, often hiding behind him.

If she danced too long, too close with someone else, if she forgot herself, he would tear her away, and at times he even fought the other man. Gradually, she understood the milieu, its customs, its language. She was growing coarse, as Gutsi described it. She practically stopped looking after Annamaria.

If they made love, late at night, exhausted from liquor, nicotine, and dancing, almost ready to hit one another, Susanne Wüllner would sometimes knock on the door, telling Katharina she must have lost all sense of decency, and she shouldn't forget the presence of her daughter.

She deliberately remained on the periphery, with no desire to be accepted. Mummi often spoke of Camilla and Peter (during the transport, Katharina had told her for no reason at all: You finally have to know, Ferdinand is dead, David is dead, Paul is dead, Ernst is dead, you finally have to know). Mummi wondered whether Camilla and Peter were alive and how they could get in touch with them. Katharina snapped that they were leading their own lives, goodness knows, they had learned how to do it, and they would hear from them sooner or later. Gutsi had already registered their names with the Red Cross.

It did not appear as if anything would change; she had learned to cope amid ruins and ramshackle structures, where black marketeers and people with a rage to live got together. Strangely enough, she began to read again, now of all times; she would borrow books from the American Library, spending whole days at home, lying on the bed, occasionally disturbed by arguments in the next room or by snide remarks from Rossmann, who was gradually drifting away from her.

The past, her time too, rolled by in front of her, an insane film distorted by streaks of blood. She had known the names, Terezín and

Auschwitz, she had been grazed by the fear of the potential victims, and good luck, which now seemed unbelievable, had saved Mummi, her, the children from the killers. Everything she read, she learned anew. When she tried to repeat it all to Rossmann, he was untouched. He said there had been a lot of atrocities, on both sides, and a lot of things were made up—after all, the Germans had lost. They could have killed me, she said, and Mummi is Jewish. This did not appear to sit well with him.

He mustn't go. But what else was she to give up for his sake? She had nothing left. He was bothered by anything she gained. Burrowing into bed with him, she would talk to him, often after they had fought; she would talk herself to sleep, offended by him, taking his questions and answers into her dreams.

Why is everything changing between us?

You're imagining things, Katja.

We just fight, fight, fight.

That's the way we are.

Do you want to leave?

Why should I?

Why don't you ever talk to me?

That's all crap.

What?

The books you love, the stuff you imagine.

There was a lot I didn't know.

You're too refined for me.

I?

Basically, you want to be something special, Katja.

Are you crazy?

You're just fooling yourself.

I?

With no explanation, Mummi and Gutsi moved out. Mummi said that with the help of friendly people ("They're helping you as a Jew only in order to help themselves"), she had found a nice apartment on Rotebühlstrasse.

Annamaria, left in the front room, played the consternated spectator, who, although she had looked forward to a different play, was still willing to applaud; but Katharina did not manage to pull off a single scene to her daughter's liking.

Later on, Annamaria said that her mother had looked incredibly young, but fierce, aloof. I'll never forget the way you dashed through my room toward evening in that black skirt, that black sweater with the plunging neckline, and with that swaying, expectant walk. And I hated you. I could have killed you.

That's not true.

It was.

Rossmann finally stayed away, never communicated. She looked for him in his favorite dives—no one knew where he was—until she learned he had found his family, his wife and two children; he was working in Feuerbach, and years later, she saw him, on Schulstrasse, very close, only a step away, almost unchanged, smartly dressed, a philistine, forced to suppress fragments of his past, a bit too bizarre, and afraid of her.

It wouldn't sink in, she forced Annamaria to help her look, asked her to sleep next to her. I just don't know what to do, child. Gutsi brought her a message: Frau Perchtmann was willing to take her in, there was enough room in her apartment on Rotebühlstrasse.

By now, she was ready to do anything to find a warm nook to crawl into.

40

In the Packing Department or So Much for Skodlerrak

Susanne Wüllner had guarded the remaining money for nothing. When the currency was reformed, their cash reserve melted. They received forty marks, "per capita quota," like everyone else, the rest was exchanged 10:1, and they did not own any valuable latifundia. Rossmann, induced by Katharina, had bartered most of the jewelry for cigarettes, stockings, and food. The family was broke. Gutsi was the first to look for work, and, although way past seventy, she drudged at the market hall every morning, cursing her daily sciatica. Katharina, however, refused, saying she had no training, she was useless, she'd be forced to do the worst shitwork. If only Father had let me go to the university. Yes, but she had run the factory for years. Mummi couldn't understand that a past reputation didn't count; neither did a Gymnasium diploma.

She registered at the employment office. If she wanted to, she was told, she could help with the city clean-up work, no one was being forced. She refused. Three weeks later, armed with the coveted employment voucher, she was sent to the packing department of a chocolate factory in Cannstatt. She became a packer of chocolate bars, yummy things that were unavailable "on the outside," and would remain unavailable for a while; she piled them up in cartons, and with bogus speed.

"The foreman is decent. He knows where I come from, what I was, or else I imagine he has not forgotten. I have already learned my first

218

Swabian expressions, *ha no* and *noi*. But I still cannot get it into my head that I have to be here and who knows for how long. I am a worker. I scarcely know the director, the directors, as little as our workers knew me. Sometimes I see the Ferdinands walking across the courtyard, getting into one of the two company cars, I think of our Czech workers, the one in Prague who threw me out of his apartment—earlier it was only a whim that moved me to change fronts. Now it has happened without my doing or my desire; I am learning quite personally what false notions the "lady" had. Such work is so repetitious that it makes you ill, dull, listless. By now I probably have the same thoughts as the other women: Sunday off, good food, rest, a nice dress. No one thinks about lovemaking here, although the men never leave you alone. Physical work drives out love. For my nights, when I often see my hands acting as if they were detached from me, I do not wish to have anyone in my bed."

She needed no training. She was somewhat too slow during the first few days, but she only had to practice a few twists and turns. She stood next to other women at the long packing table; at first, they teased her good-naturedly. She seldom conversed, remaining an alien, and this did not change for five years. She recoiled from the familiar form of address, which was natural for the others. She was surprised by the women's manners, their direct, coarse language (the dialect was obscure here, it took her a long time to grasp everything); she was surprised by the way they huddled together during their lunch break, chomping out of their lunch boxes.

Not that she wanted to fit in. But the environment left its mark on her. She noticed that her speech, her gestures were changing; she noticed that she no longer cared about pleasing anyone else, and that the spare movements of her daily work affected her gestures.

You're becoming slovenly, Mummi criticized.

What do you know? Gutsi and I are bringing home the bacon.

Can't you find a job in an office?

I never learned shorthand.

Then learn it now.

I don't want to.

It was true, she didn't want to, she had decided to fall. She didn't brood and dream at work, like so many others, but sometimes she saw herself as a bride, in Bad Schandau, as a tiny girl in a white dress, running through the garden; she thought of Wagner, Prchala, she saw the children, still small, she wondered about Camilla and Peter; but she never spoke about these thoughts, she never boasted about past property, she could not imagine that she would ever return; she threw away the

invitations she received for meetings of "Brünn Germans" in Ludwigsburg
or Schwäbisch Gmünd; the names, the faces, the stories vanished from
her memory.

It took her a while to realize that she could not remain the choco-
late-packer Perchtmann.

Yet the women whom she had initially scorned, who poured out
sweat when they changed clothes, the smell of physical labor, who
repelled her with their obsessively foul mouths, with their flat sexual
fantasies and their daydreams about elegant people—these women
helped her when she began suffering from menopausal complaints, sudden nausea and dizziness; unable to fill her quota, she tried to hide her
weakness, botched up her work, basically left the others holding the
bag—these women unceremoniously came to her rescue, pushing her
aside, concealing cartons, pouring the scarce coffee for her, telling her
that others had suffered in the same way—it would soon pass—she ought
to see a doctor—she had the right—you'll make it—take care of yourself.

This was the first time anyone had ever pinch-hit for her. Božena
and Gutsi had waited on her, she had never thought of checking to see
how they were, asking how they felt. She had learned, starting in her
childhood, that other people should help her without bothering her, she
had been taught that there was an upstairs and a downstairs, that some
people had to stay in the kitchen while the others dined at the table.
Granted, in Brno, Gutsi had often eaten with them, but only because
Katharina couldn't bring herself to inflict conventions on her, an aging
woman who had worked her way into becoming practically a member of
the family. These women in the factory acted without worrying about
convention or propriety. They simply helped.

"I am like them. I am concerned with political events. Fucking
denazification and fucking democracy, the women say, and some say:
Everything was better under Hitler. If I disagree with them and tell them
about myself, about Mummi, they deny reality: Well, okay, that Jewish
stuff wasn't right, and you're not really Jewish anyway. Denazification
concerns them only in regard to their own husbands. After all, the big
people will come out of it smelling like roses. And the little people will
be hanged. I learn nothing, I adjust to this way of life. Only the books I
get tear me out of it. Yesterday, the union tried to recruit us and everyone
but Opitz refused to join. People said she never listens to reason, she had
almost been sent to a concentration camp—as if that were a failing."

Sometimes, after work, she dawdles, doesn't head for the trolley stop
right away; she wanders through streets, from which most of the rubble
has been cleared, houses are being built again, or at least the ground is
shooting up out of the debris, you can buy lemonade, sandwiches with a

mustardy smear, potato pancakes; she looks into people's faces, keeps walking, she has not forgotten how to talk to them, she gradually feels herself again after the mechanical motions, stretches out her legs, draws circles in the gravel with the heels of her shoes, fears Mummi's nightly scolding or Annamaria's questions.

But I've already told you, I've lost a lot of my French, and Montaigne isn't easy.

She's become stupid. Stupid.

That's not true.

Overnight, Annamaria began calling her "Mother" instead of "Mami." Katharina was startled; she wanted to correct her, but then realized that the childish word no longer applied to her.

Relishing the autumn twilight, yielding to her wanderlust, she stood at a booth, nibbling on a potato pancake that tasted of bad grease. The tall man who impatiently pushed her aside, with a torn leather coat flapping about his calves, his gray hair in greasy strands over his ears and forehead, ordered a lemonade and two sandwiches; he was apparently a regular customer at this time of day and used to giving orders. He leaned against the wooden partition, ignoring his surroundings, eating. Each of his movements was familiar to her, as if they came from a story that she could no longer tell coherently, but from which she knew sentences, scenes. A face that had once turned to her, long ago. Her staring bothered him; he looked at her, shrugged, smiled. It was Skodlerrak.

She walked toward him, intimidated by his aloofness.

Before she could even address him, he said: Hello, Kathi.

You recognized me?

Right away?

Why didn't you talk to me?

Why?

Yes, why? It's been twenty-five years.

She knew she'd be talking to Skodlerrak only this once.

How are you, Kathi?

So-so.

Are you still with your husband, I remember him, I remember your wedding, a handsome, wealthy gentleman, your Ferdinand.

He died in action.

I'm sorry. Do you have any children?

Yes, four. Three are alive.

And your parents?

Father is dead. My mother is living here, with us.

Where are you working?

Over there, in the factory.

In the office?

No, in the packing department.

That's bad.

It's all right, Skodlerrak. You know—

He interrupts: I know nothing, you can be sure I know absolutely nothing.

What are you doing?

Nothing.

Aren't you working?

Sometimes.

She was silent.

He said: My name is Obermaier now.

Why, it's all history now.

For you.

Even more so for you. You're a Socialist.

He laughs. Socialist? You're a riot, Kathi, still the same curious, innocent Kathi.

But you were a Socialist.

I was in the SS.

That's impossible. That's not true.

Why not?

You would have had to give up everything, Skodlerrak.

Don't call me that.

I'm sorry, I didn't mean to.

It just happened that way. No one helped me, and then I helped myself.

And what about everything you thought and demanded back then?

I forgot it.

I can't imagine it. In Hellerau—

It was all bullshit.

No.

It's too long ago, so much has happened.

What happened to the others?

They caught Kasimir.

Who?

Who do you think? The Nazis.

The SS?

No, the Gestapo. He's no longer alive.

They killed him?

Yes.

And what are you planning to do?

It'll work out.

He pushed his bottle through the window, stood up suddenly, ran his hand under her kerchief: You sure have a lot of gray hair.

So do you.

Farewell, Kathi.

He ran across the street, with his name and without it, leaving nothing but a future story that would end differently, not as she had imagined.

The women elected her shop steward.

She now told herself: Some day, I'm getting out of here.

Mummi had applied for reparations, if only for the birdseed company, and she had also pushed Katharina to apply for indemnification for her property in Czechoslovakia. You've lost a great deal, you know.

Most of it can't be replaced, Mummi, she said between the stove and the table, drying her wet hands on her apron. Then, as she always did between seven and seven-thirty, she gave Annamaria a vocabulary quiz.

41
Camilla or You Can't Go Back Again

Gutsi was the only one who sometimes recited the litany of losses. She pronounced her obituaries for Elle, Ernst, Paul, and Ferdinand as if they had all passed away on the same day, and, without involving Susanne Wüllner or Katharina, she wondered where Camilla, Peter, and Dieter were. An outsider would never have guessed that these were an uncle, a nephew, and a niece, for Gutsi's grief wiped out age differences and kinship degrees, making the missing people all equal. Katharina refused to think about what might have happened to her children. Missing-person reports were made at the Red Cross. She waited and worked, she was the packer Katharina Perchtmann. Her suppressed fear penetrated her dreams.

"A Dream about the Twins" is entered in the diary under 3 March 1946: "Horrible, I was awakened by my own wailing. I was walking with Peter and Paul, not in Brno, apparently in the Great Garden; the boys were whining, they absolutely insisted on going to the zoo. I felt their little hands in mine, they let me pull them along, as they often did. I gradually noticed the change. I realized that they were growing step by step, but, although I was anxious, I paid no attention. They grew audibly. Their bones and skin were crunching and grinding. Passersby halted, walking next to us and behind us. Soon there was a whole mob. The twins would not stop growing. Their hands welled up around mine, enclosing them. I did not look to the side anymore. They cast gigantic shadows. I wanted to run away—they held me tight, lifting me up. We could not advance any further, because the crowd had surrounded us. The people were speaking a foreign language. By now, the twins were twice as big as I, they were giants. Someone pulled me away from them violently. As I ran, I looked back—I saw two human towers, which no longer resembled the twins. Tanks and cannons rode past, a whole army. The people grabbed me. They showed me the cannons being set up in a row, the tanks heading toward the twins. Then they began to shoot. The gigantic figures disintegrated under the fire, individual pieces broke off, until the twins finally crumbled into a pile of debris."

Camilla is the first to turn up, she has not written. In June 1946, she stands at the door, relishing the surprise, amused at her dumbfounded mother, she then gets her husband, who has had to wait out in the street with their tiny daughter. Everything at once would have been too much. Camilla explains that she got their address from the Red Cross just three days ago, and since they live in Darmstadt, not so far away, they set out immediately.

After the excitement abates, and Gutsi apologizes for her spotty apron, and Mummi wipes away her tears, Katharina asks: What's your name now, Camilla?, and at the same moment, she sees how silly her question is. Her name, the daughter's, the name of the man who has come with her, who is probably Camilla's husband. Katharina's son-in-law, and the name of the daughter, Katharina's first grandchild. She might also have asked: Where have you been, why haven't you gotten in touch with us, what's become of you? She could also have asked what she then asks: Are you pregnant? Pregnant again?

She receives answers, many answers, which she cannot all retain right now, which she will repeat later, as if hoping they will form a story to explain everything.

Camilla says: Yes, my name, it's the same as his, he's my husband, my last name is Wertmüller, and I call him Kalle, even though he was christened Friedhelm, but no one's ever called him that, so you should call him Kalle too, this is Kalle, your son-in-law, Mami; she doesn't say Mother, as Annamaria does now, she abides by Mami; she points to the child, who has white-blond hair; this is Thea, your granddaughter, give her a kiss, I've told her a lot about you, I imagined what became of you after Father's death: Where is Herr Wagner? she asks. Wagner? Who do you mean? Katharina asks; Gutsi laughs; then Katharina says: Oh, you mean Wagner, that Wagner; I don't know. They sit down around the kitchen table.

But what does your husband do? What does—Kalle do?

He's a teacher.

A real teacher? (She's talking nonsense.)

Yes, at a high school.

So he's a professor?

They don't call them that here in Germany. He's a tenured member of the faculty.

Are you having a baby?

Yes.

She finds no words for her qualms, Camilla articulates them: It's crazy bringing a child into the world now, only Thea isn't Kalle's kid, she's someone else's, Kalle knows, we hadn't met yet, and I nearly became a farmer's wife, but I didn't because the farm was lost in Pomerania, that's where I had Thea, and I met Kalle a little later, on the refugee ship. Yes, I could tell you a whole lot, but I don't want to spoil our day, it's enough when the soldiers keep talking about having been soldiers and what it was like and where it was, do you still know?, it's awful, and now our child is coming, Kalle's and mine.

Camilla asks the two old women how they are: as usual when they have visitors, Mummi and Gutsi cannot complain; and now Katharina should talk about herself.

I'm a packer, she says, I work in a factory.

Why didn't you look for an office job?

I couldn't.

You look amazingly young, Mami, says Camilla. Annamaria, who has kept quiet all this time, holding her little niece on her lap, corrects her sister: She has watched Mother growing old, it might change again in the course of time.

You all have to visit us, Kalle exclaims when leaving, after barely managing to get a word in edgewise.

Of course, of course.

They all adjusted, like something that had been ordered but had not turned out as expected. A letter came from Peter, he was in Hamburg, enrolled at the university, "almost an old man," majoring in philosophy, working part-time at a newspaper, not an important one. He would drop by eventually. He hoped they were all well. He was married and the father of a tiny boy.

You've got two grandchildren, said Annamaria, you want to be young, younger and younger.

Katharina wishes she were somewhere else. "I lived with them, for years. Perhaps I'm closest to Mummi now (or Gutsi?). But what about the children? Did I feel 'maternal joy' when I saw Camilla again after four years? I was relieved that nothing had happened to her, and that was all."

Mummi, too, got one of her children back. Dieter. He had returned to Dresden and was employed in the city administration. He was the one I least expected to become a Communist, said Mummi, I would have expected it more from you and Elle—but Dieter?

Do you know what he went through in the labor camp?

That's all over now.

For some people it's never over.

Mummi told her she was speaking as if she had been alone all her life.

No, I was never alone.

42
An Apartment Is Renovated

Annamaria graduated from high school, developed energies, and adamantly decided to move out: having registered at the Teachers' Institute in Esslingen, she pointed out that, as a future public school teacher, she would be receiving a scholarship, which would enable her to rent a cheap room. Despite her resolution to allow her daughter full freedom as soon as possible, Katharina asked her to stay on with them at least for the first year. Annamaria was astonished: Her mother, of all people, clinging to her? Hadn't she been complaining for years about the cramped quarters, the miserable female household? Wasn't it she who had taken freedoms with no consideration for anyone else?

I'm moving out.

I can't hold you here.

You can't.

Why are you being so harsh?

Have you forgotten everything?

None of that matters anymore.

Do you remember the way you carried on with that pig, in the next room?

You've got a nasty philistine mind, Annamaria. It would be better if you did move out.

Her daughter left that same day.

The departure was a caesura.

228

Mummi grew more and more peculiar. The old woman admired Adenauer; when he was elected chancellor, it was a personal triumph for her, and also a dig at her daughter, who called Adenauer a reactionary and quoted from Kurt Schumacher's speeches. The Nazi spirit would never be driven out of this country, not in this way. She said she had to reproach her Jewish mother for that.

Susanne Wüllner had never wanted to play a role, but had always been forced to play the lead when—it seemed like centuries ago, even for Katharina—her husband was traveling or, as he put it, when he had to be "away for various and sundry reasons," when Georg Wüllner lost his factory, and Susanne had to fill pouches with birdseed, when, after Wüllner's death, Hitler began to persecute the Jews and Susanne Wüllner became a victim. She had always been forced to lead a life that others invented for her; and now she turned away once and for all, twisted around something that had been twisted for her anyhow, and she played pranks on the people who seemed more capable. First, Mummi, who was in charge of running the household, began hoarding the monthly foodcards, which she believed were valid indefinitely; and then when Gutsi and Katharina found out, Mummi still refused to hand over all the stamps for the current month. She was never satisfied with anything the other two women did. She swept up after Gutsi, she criticized dishes that she had only just previously admired, she turned on the gas after Gutsi shut it off, and Gutsi, no longer steady on her legs, had to keep watch constantly.

During the first years in Stuttgart, Susanne Wüllner occasionally went out alone, to the theater, where, to her delight, "the old Dresdeners" Theodor Loos and Erich Ponto were performing; but now, Gutsi never let her out of her sight. Recently, Mummi had begun to specialize in graveyards, especially the Prague Cemetery, which she visited almost daily; she was familiar with the rows of graves, a connoisseur of deceased clans, and she sometimes chatted with headstones. She didn't want to be buried "among the Russians in Dresden," Dieter would certainly not tend her grave and a transfer of her body would be exorbitantly expensive anyway, so she selected gravesites in the Prague Cemetery; of course, they were then taken by others, which infuriated her: Too many people were dying, she said.

She confused a lot of things; her memory hunted far back, her stories, uniting the living and the dead, brought Uncle David to the present, a small boy, her brother, whom she can call when she needs help, who, a bit later, is a student in Leipzig, and whose songs she hums when she allows Georg Wüllner to court her. She treats Katharina like a naughty six-year-old; with Gutsi, her conversations travel through a long life. Strangely enough, Annamaria is the only one she excludes, leaving her out of the drifting state that blurs eras. The girl's visits gave Mummi a chance to surprise Gutsi and Katharina "with reasonable behavior"; she asked her granddaughter about her work, her studies, where she intended to teach, and why she wanted to get married so early.

One morning, she refused to get up; she did not leave her bed. Her dying lasted a long time. A doctor, summoned against her will, said one could chart her decline on small-meshed graph paper: the old woman was tough, she wanted to live.

Katharina and Mummi now talked a lot, while Gutsi sat at the foot of the bed, occasionally drying the sweat from the old woman's forehead, dabbing away the saliva from the corners of her mouth, setting the pillows right, washing the patient carefully every morning and evening. Gutsi would be losing her companion, a person to whom she had voluntarily bound herself for life.

They conversed when Katharina came home from work in the evening; they talked for hours, sometimes stopping, then resuming again. Childhood intimacy had been restored, a tenderness that Katharina had missed, that she may not have wanted since her marriage to Ferdinand.

Mummi was haunted by Rossmann; it was obvious she had held back her objections, she had felt left out. Now, she made up for it, asking certain questions, without bitterness.

Did you love him?

Who, Mummi?

Well, that man.

You mean Eberhard?

I mean the soldier.

Werner Rossmann?

Yes, him. Did you love him?

Why are you bringing him up? You really wanted to kick us both out, didn't you?

Perhaps. We were in your way, you wanted to live alone with him.

I might have thought about it, yes.

Don't talk your way out of it.

That's not what I'm doing, Mummi.

It was the time. He wasn't suitable for you.

That's not true. The time may have been more suitable than the previous time.

You couldn't take care of the children so well. You always needed Gutsi.

And you didn't?

Not like you.

Then, as if needing an answer for her end, the dying woman asked an insidious question, which confused Katharina, and which she took time to answer:

Be honest, Kathi, whom did you love the most?

Susanne Wüllner waited. Katharina tried to think of everyone—the men, the children, her parents, people she had encountered casually, friends like Prchala and Waldhans, and the harder her memory concentrated on individuals, the more difficult her declaration of love become.

She said: Uncle David.

You amaze me.

Do you understand me, Mummi?

He preserved your childhood for you.

I often dream about him, even today.

Because he could dream.

Mummi's voice became weak, they had to lean over to catch her words.

Don't remain alone, Kathi, she said.

No.

You're unable to anyway.

That's true.

This was the first time Katharina had ever watched a person die. Many people she had known, had liked, were dead, but they had never died in her presence. She realized her mother had accepted death at a moment that could not be determined precisely: The old woman became virtually weightless.

Katharina and Gutsi did not stir for several hours. They sat by the bed.

She was overprotective of me, said Katharina.

That's nonsense, Gutsi replied.

She did not ask even Annamaria to come to the funeral. She and Gutsi walked behind the coffin, along with two old women who spoke about Mummi respectfully. They said they had met her in the theater and occasionally gotten together at the Café Marquardt. Susanne Wüllner had never invited anyone to her home.

The pastor spoke, Katharina did not listen.

From now on, she would be alone.

She threw earth and flowers on the grave and supported Gutsi.

I won't stay with you, Kathi, Gutsi had told her, sighing constantly, I can't. You never needed me, you can get along by yourself and find someone. I've got a place in the Municipal Old Age Home.

The pastor said: Susanne Wüllner, née Eichlaub, passed away in her eighty-fourth year.

That hit her: "How old am I? Why do people we know stop aging for us after a certain point! Because we grow older with them? Or because we don't want to grow older?"

She helped Gutsi move.

The few belongings.

I've never had more than that.

More and more lives explain themselves, making it clear to her how negligent she was.

Gutsi died four months later, at the age of eighty-four. Katharina began painting the apartment on her free evenings. Some-times Annamaria dropped by; they got along better now.

43

Erika Opitz or
The Things We Can't Learn from One Another

It was Erika Opitz's fault that Katharina virtually jackknifed, becoming a sectarian for certain people, especially her three children. Peter said she had lost control during the war and had been drifting ever since, subject to anyone's influence. In Stuttgart, he said, she had not found her way back into her old milieu. It was sad to see a woman of her background and experience letting herself go like that. There was no helping her. Peter had first visited her in 1949 with his wife and two children, while Mummi was still alive. He had told Katharina he was going on for a post-doctoral degree, his adviser was encouraging him, and, if everything went well, he would be tenured in five years.

He said she had dealt with this plan as if they were discussing the vocational prospects of a drugstore assistant.

She told him not to be annoyed, she was glad about his career, but she hadn't had anything in common with professors for a long time, and besides, it made her melancholy that all her children were becoming teachers, Camilla not in practice of course, but at least through her marriage.

She was getting odd, he said.

She said she didn't deny it.

Katharina had avoided Erika Opitz for a long time. She was afraid of the disheveled woman's aggressiveness, yet she was drawn by her voice. Whenever she spoke, the alarm bells clanged. Erika Opitz would bitch about the slightest abuse and confront the foreman. She was known as a real scourge, you had to watch out for her. Besides, they said, she was the only Communist for miles around. She had been hired in 1945 only out of special mercy, charity, which Erika Opitz corrected: Under pressure, back then the Communists still had a say.

She would tell her life story without being asked, in one breath, in a few sentences, a life that hadn't yielded much and that had flowed without confusion: Her father was a Communist, they had lived in Stammheim, and he had worked at the gas plant. In 1937, he had been thrown into a concentration camp, and later sent to Auschwitz, where he had been murdered. Her mother had committed suicide in 1939. Erika had had to take care of her three younger sisters and brothers. She had never concealed her Communism, even under the Nazis, which was why the Gestapo picked her up and grilled her three or four times. But they couldn't prove anything, even though she had slipped pamphlets into letter boxes at night. She hadn't had any chance to learn much. Or to find a husband. And now, she said, it looked like the Communists had to fight in this country again.

She was as partisan as she was practical. She had never read Marx, but the Party pamphlets told her how to behave.

When the women elected Katharina to represent their department, against the votes of Erika Opitz and the foreman (who considered it inappropriate to have a refugee in this position), Katharina and Erika nevertheless reached an understanding. Erika Opitz, refusing to calm down about this "fraudulent election," was rebuked by the foreman, who threatened to dismiss her. He said he'd make sure of it. Katharina defended her: Opitz could voice criticism; she, Katharina, didn't know much about politics, nor did she particularly care for it, but the rules had to be observed. That, Erika Opitz remarked afterward, was bullshit, but nice. Thus began Katharina's Perchtmann's political awakening, thanks to Erika Opitz.

If it *was* politics.

If it wasn't sham that the two women got involved in.

Each one had learned, in her own way.

And they never stopped arguing with one another.

For Erika Opitz, Katharina remained a bourgeois, trapped in conventional ideas, with no understanding of workers. Katharina disagreed: Wasn't she as angry as Erika about the gap, visible once again in Germany, between the haves and the havenots, about the piecework pressure, about the debates between the Christian Democrats and the Social Democrats, about Adenauer's conservative arrogance? What separated them? Words above all, which allowed Erika to crow: Katharina's tongue was too fine, she didn't want to burn it on the truth. Also blind obedience. There was nothing that could not exist for the Party's sake, including the labor camps, which Katharina read about, and which she hated, no matter who set them up.

Mind your own business, said Erika Opitz, that's our concern.

Yours? Do you live in the Soviet Union?

That is a matter for International Communism.

You're talking in slogans.

There's no helping you, Katharina. I wonder why I make such an effort.

Much to Opitz's annoyance, Katharina did not join the Party. Had Erika read the arguments between Sartre and Camus, about the camps in Russia, and whose side was she on? Katharina asked, hoping they could agree at least on this issue. But Opitz sided with Sartre, and Katharina with Camus; they repeated sentences, grabbed hold of notions, exchanged rebukes of humanity and inhumanity, until they could no longer stand each other, slamming doors, cursing, making up again because they were alone and no politics annulled their loneliness.

But the others were suspicious of both women. Their zeal aroused distrust. The foreman had urged Katharina to break off with Opitz: That woman would never listen to reason, she was a burden on the company.

She told him to go to hell, she wouldn't dream of abandoning Opitz, even if she didn't agree with everything she spouted. There was a lot less she liked about him, she said. And the joint stank.

That was no way for a shop steward to act, he said.

Then he ought to see to it that she was voted out of office, just let him try.

Erika Opitz was called in by the head of personnel; she was not told anything definite, just concealed threats—she didn't know what to do, the man complained about her unruliness. Katharina tried to shed some light on it; she went to see the head of personnel, asked him questions, and received lame answers. She bluntly asked whether they wanted to fire Erika Opitz because she was a Communist.

Why, that was the farthest thing from their minds.

Well, what was on their minds when they were leaning on her?

No one was leaning on her.

What *were* they doing?

She obviously suffered from a persecution complex, like Frau Opitz.

Perhaps she *was* being persecuted; she could not discern any complex.

Resistance was enough.

Do we have to put up with everything?

She left the large, elegant room in which Ferdinand might have sat, not she anymore, no, not she anymore.

When the company introduced new cartons, which had to be folded in a different way, requiring different maneuvers after three years of mechanical manipulation, Opitz failed. She simply couldn't do it: her hands were used to the old motions, her head had forgotten the hands. She got badly tangled, disrupting the flow. The foreman saw a chance to get rid of her; the women, annoyed by her many digs, her scorn, were not willing to help. For three days, Katharina fought against Opitz's inability and the foreman's wiles. She managed to make a few women aware of how vulnerable they were: It could happen to any of them, and since it could happen to any of them, any woman could be broken out of this dismal group. Opitz arduously retrained her hands, and once they had readjusted, the new convert said to Katharina: You've learned a lot from me—which infuriated Katharina.

You've been taught something.

You'll never learn, replied Erika Opitz.

They both took part in the first Easter March. Katharina was easily won over for demonstrations against nuclear death, against war, against rearmament. She liked being with others in such situations: hurrying arm in arm, singing, becoming young, and she noticed how old she was, since her memory always joined in when anything was said.

Opitz was accustomed to getting lost in the crowd; Katharina wasn't. They stood close together; a boy had placed his arm around her shoulder; they listened to speeches, didn't listen, talked with one another, hummed songs they had previously sung loudly, they felt powerful in their sensible stance, in their humanity.

The young man kissed her on the cheek, saying, You're great, Mama, it's good to have you here.

He had, lovingly, pushed her off into old age.

I'm leaving, she abruptly told Opitz.

Her friend didn't understand, viewed her as a deserter.

What are you gonna do?

Nothing, I just want to be alone.

She got together with Opitz even after she switched over to the office, adjusting, making a career, as Erika Opitz put it; which was stupid, said Katharina, after all, a person has to use his abilities; for whose sake?; my own; once again, according to Opitz, she had learned nothing.

Katharina had needed Opitz. Both were responsible for losing sight of each other, and Katharina learned about her death belatedly: Their experiences were dissimilar, they had been friends in need.

Opitz died an inappropriate death. She took her own life, as Katharina heard, not because she was being forced underground again as a Communist or because she couldn't cope with the Party, but because the man she loved and had lived with for a while left her without any explanation.

Her death brought Katharina close to Opitz, but it was too late.

44
A Woman Goes for a Walk

That could be her; it's not her; she's only playing her. Fine, she's got money again, she's settled in nicely, she knows the children are all taken care of—if only they were still children. Adults whom she needn't worry about anymore.

She strolls. She runs her fingers along wire fences, wooden fences; her open hands touch the wooden braces of a bench, she rubs the back of her hand on stone. Why does she feel things only now, see them, hold them, discover what she knew but never perceived; now she sees what she never saw: the soft leather of the pony saddle, the bark of the pine tree, paint peeling on the garden fence, porcelain, rustling, fragrant textiles, the tweeds that Ferdinand preferred, the flannels that Wagner wore, Rossmann's tarpaulin jackets, stone balustrades, stair landings, the summer-warm metal of Ferdinand's Tatra, the handle of the baby carriage, a strange, usually sticky rubber, the bomb splinters in the garden, shards, glass shards, the noise of the bombs, the swelling howl, the clattering tank tracks—she makes up for the past, gathers.

That's her too.

She does not part with things, she takes possession; it is a possession that concerns her alone. Sometimes she says: My soul is learning.

Some things she no longer plays.

Now when she strolls, a woman of fifty, still conspicuous with her youthful face, with her impatient walk, she has given up being a wife and

238

mother, given up remembering. She is free, she was freed, bit by bit, and she endures her freedom. She is alone, but knows it could be different. Sometimes she feels old age. She doesn't know whether she'll ever have a man again. Her body begins to forget. She leafs through photo albums, perusing her past. There's no one to whom she can say: You know, here, this photo, Ferdinand took it when we went skiing in the Beskids. She scrutinizes herself, at twenty, at thirty, she can't imagine she is no longer those ages. No one has photographed her for years.

She has advanced quickly in the office. First in the typing pool, then as secretary to a senior clerk, now as secretary to a head of department. She feels her work is appreciated, but whom can she tell. She is not close to anyone, doesn't talk much to her female colleagues. There is no Opitz there.

She frequently goes to the theater, the opera.

She talks to herself. She gets along with herself.

45
Annamaria or A Son Is Made Up For

The town no longer looks jagged. It is being rebuilt; the remaining ruins have entered the eyes of passersby as the present. A second install-ment of indemnity for her lost property has enabled Katharina Perchtmann to prepare for old age without anxiety. She gave the children only their due portions, nothing more; they had never concerned them-selves with her, so she didn't have to idemnify anything. She visits Mummi's and Gutsi's graves more often now.

In June 1957, she writes in her diary: "If someone does not come and talk to me soon, I will go dumb or deaf, or suffocate. I believed I could be alone. I am unable to be alone. On bad days, when I cannot endure the apartment and I walk or I sit down in a café, I actually envy the old hookers on Leonhardsplatz because men speak to them. At least they hear things, whole life stories. And if they have nothing else, they have their bodies. My body only collects small pains, that is all. Some-times my back aches, sometimes my legs ache. If things go on like this, I can imagine that I will take my own life. I need people."

She comes back with Achim. Annamaria, who resembles her most closely, who lives in Friedrichshafen with her husband and child, can't manage: school in the morning, the child in the afternoon, her husband in the evening. She shows her disquiet; "she's inherited it from her

240

grandfather, from Ernst, from me"; she writes desperate letters after a long interruption, complains about her husband, whom Katharina has met only a few times, casually, finding him unloving and pallid, one of those weaklings who exploit the people nearest them—Annamaria confesses to her mother that she has been having affairs with other men, no great loves, no, until she finally finds one whom she "really" loves, but who doesn't offer her heaven, he walks out on her. It's over, I can't go on, I'm going to run away, I'm going to drown myself, help me, Mother—and Katharina instantly wires: Come.

She comes with Achim, disrupts the peace and quiet, chatters, swears, curses, makes Katharina feel terribly helpless, she wasn't prepared for these wounds: her daughter on the edge like this, barely capable of a clear thought.

The eight-year-old boy is intimidated, he doesn't have the nerve to speak; he sits on the sofa, his hands folded in his lap.

She asks Annamaria whether she needs a doctor.

A doctor couldn't help.

Katharina tells her she looks awful, like a drowned rat.

Leave me alone, Mother.

Is that why you came here?

No.

They drink coffee. Achim explores the apartment, approves of it. Better than our place.

He likes it, says Annamaria.

What happened? Tell me.

But Annamaria tells her only that night, when she can no longer stand Gutsi's former room, where Katharina has put her and Achim up; she joins her mother in bed, as she did ages ago.

And this is actually Mummi's bed, a monster, a wooden platform on high legs, a ship on which one floats through the night, high above everything else; Mummi found the rather demolished frame second-hand, on Hauptstätterstrasse; ignoring Gutsi's protests, she took it to a carpenter, who fixed it up for her, saying the material couldn't be killed, it would certainly last a lifetime.

Annamaria falls asleep first, then Katharina.

Annamaria's fingers, touching her cheeks, her forehead, wake Katharina.

Tell me. What happened?

Annamaria speaks softly; Katharina has to make an effort to understand her. The sentences do not take their time, do not even care to make the story intelligible. I was already unhappy when I married Kern.

She never used his first name. You barely know him. He was born dry, Mother; all he knows is order, calm. He's old, inexperienced. When I made love with him, I embraced a lizard. I'm not like that. I can't do it.

Did you ever tell him how alien he was to you?

No. I hardly spoke to him anymore. Within six months, we weren't living together, we were living next to each other, and that was fine for him.

What about when Achim came?

He likes the child.

But it didn't change your relationship in any way?

I couldn't stand him. The child and I were a single cell, which he didn't penetrate.

Why did you stay with him?

He insisted, he felt he couldn't afford to get divorced in his position, the chief engineer. And he's Catholic. He didn't even like my working at the school again.

And the other men?

I couldn't stand it. I went to bed with anyone who so much as caressed me.

You poor thing.

What do you mean, Mother?

I don't know. I mean it affectionately.

You're still crazy.

And what happened next?

I kept going off with other men, the last time I thought it would all work out, Kern said I should become a hooker and he'd train to be a pimp. He didn't understand.

You're ill, Annamaria.

Oh, stop.

You've never taken care of yourself, you were too scared and hungry. You've always looked for yourself in someone else.

That's not true.

Now you're starting to reprimand me.

Do you want to stay here for a while?

She said—and I was frightened by her tone of voice: No. I only want to leave Achim here. I asked her whether she had a new boyfriend. She denied it. She said she didn't want to live under my tutelage. That was one thing she couldn't say about me, she said. You always attract everyone, Mother, and if you don't, then you forget them, which is even worse.

She kept her daughter another three weeks, her reasons were sound: she'd take Achim in, she didn't care for how long, but she had to make certain arrangements; since the child mustn't stay alone, she could work only mornings, while Achim was at school; you think it's all so simple, Annamaria, you deposit your child here and then you skedaddle. You'll have to put up with me for a while, and you can please take care of the red tape—stop carrying on.

Katharina was demoted at the company, people in responsible positions could not work part-time, so she sat in the typing pool again with fourteen other women, her head numb from the droning of the typewriters, and she picked the boy up from school at twelve-thirty every day. She promised she'd take care of him; now you can go, Annamaria, I can do it, I'm fifty-five—am I senile, am I feeble, am I stupid? And don't think I'm doing it for you, I'm doing it for myself, just so you'll know, the child has come to me like a present.

Annamaria never returned for the boy.

She visited him every six months; a few years later he was allowed to visit his stepfather's home on holidays, but he refused to assume the man's name. It took Annamaria a long time to find this man, although she was troubled because he was cold and unloving; but now she was the wife of a manufacturer, as her mother had been.

A few days after Annamaria left, Katharina set down one of her first conversations with Achim—her grandson, her fosterchild, her new companion:

> I picked him up at school, he ran toward me, calling me Grummi, as he still does today, he grabbed my hand; I was moved by this throwback: walking with a child, going home.
> I asked him: Was it nice?
> It's better at home.
> Do you like living with me?
> Yes.
> Why?
> Because no one shouts at me and—
> And?
> Because it's right.

46
The Second Ferdinand

Katharina still loses patience very quickly. Achim has to get used to her abrupt decisions. He knows that when Grummi goes out in the evening, she'll come back, just as she's promised.

When are you coming back?

I can't say precisely.

Tell me sort of precisely.

Just go to sleep.

Are you gonna come back?

I'm coming back. You know I am.

Are you leaving?

I'm leaving now.

She often doesn't know where she's going. She has a few acquaintances, she can accept invitations that bore her. She sits in a movie theater, but, as she says, she sees the movies after she's seen them and she can spend hours talking about three scenes that she says epitomize her life, or she could explain it like that if it didn't sound too theatrical, or that's how she wants to see herself, if she thinks of Dreyer's Joan of Arc—that moment in the cell when the face, haggard from waiting, looks toward the light pouring in through the embrasure, just that one turn—or The Children of Paradise, the way he crashes against the mob in the last scene, the furious merriment swallows him up, devours him, he goes down in it, drowns under jerking, cheering bodies, or the way the guards in Potemkin stalk down the steps, power, a woman with a child bracing herself against the air that has turned into iron, you see her all at once, steel that you can't breathe, and before the woman falls, she pauses, understands everything—that's me too.

That's *not* you, you're exaggerating.

Why should I explain it to you?

The second Ferdinand simply sneaked in without her even noticing.

The light between spring and summer had always been her favorite, April light, fickle, driving along cloud shadows, or shiny. She was waiting impatiently for Achim, who should have been back from school long ago; he was probably dawdling again, rubbing his nose along shop windows, gaping at people, an attentive dreamer, the teachers have nothing good to say about him, which doesn't bother Katharina in the least. He's not stupid, she usually said, wiping aside the pedagogical objections: they planned to go to Denkendorf, wander across the fields; cloudbursts in April don't trouble us at all. They hiked across farmland, along country paths, talking, remaining silent, the boy next to her, clutching her hand at times, a companion in whom she confided anything. Achim was accustomed to her speaking to him as if to herself, sometimes extending conversations into soliloquies.

They sat on a bench outside the Denkendorf Monastery. "The elderly man occupying part of the bench with a backpack and an array of utensils barely glanced up; but he then look surprised, said good day, and went back to his snack. I thought perhaps I knew him from Stuttgart, I had previously noticed that impossible baldness with the fringe of thin gray hair."

Achim and she talked about their hike so far, and Achim, expressing himself in the most involved way, suggested that they stop somewhere and take a later trolley home. It's no fun sitting around here. Okay, said Katharina, we'll stop at the Sonnenhof. The bald-headed man caught them unawares; they hadn't really noticed him, they stood up, Achim put on Katharina's jacket. He danced; look, Grummi; she said, You're making the jacket dirty. They left without saying goodbye and the man called after them: Auf Wiedersehen, Frau Perchtmann. She was startled. She said: So I *do* know you. But from where?

We live in the same building.

That's impossible.

Not at all. I moved in three years ago.

That can't be.

If you say so. Please don't let me hold you up. Auf Wiedersehen.

He's weird, said Achim.

He's probably alone, said Katharina; look at me, I'm old and peculiar too, aren't I?

You, Grummi? Achim laughed, his laughter delighted her. Nevertheless, they greeted one another in the building. She found his wardrobe too outré; he drove his own car to a job she could not picture—probably in an office or a government agency—he left in the morning, returned in the evening; he obviously lived alone, as she conjectured. He held back, but his restraint became a challenge: They conversed on the stairs, mostly about Achim, whereby the man, discreet, did not ask about the child's mother; they talked about the unfriendliness of their neighbors, about the sweep-up schedule so adamantly observed in Swabia—each tenant had to take turns cleaning the halls and stairways, so that she eventually made him an offer, reluctantly, but to keep their conversation going, she said she'd take over his cleaning duties, he was just making a fool of himself. But he protested, not without irony: In Stuttgart, he explained, a man becomes perfect only when he outdoes a woman by becoming a stickler for cleanliness—that's how it began.

During their first meeting on the staircase, the man introduced himself as Ferdinand Novotny from Znojmo: a refugee like yourself, or, as the term goes nowadays, a neo-citizen, whereby the *neo* always gives me the creeps, as if people like us were artificial human beings or something of the sort.

Achim bristled. He called the bald-headed man old and slimy. Novotny actually did gesticulate unrestrainedly, comically; he would grab the other person during a conversation, a habit that Katharina found as unbearable as Achim did, and Novotny's dialect, which Katharina was familiar with, sounded horrible to Achim, who spoke Swabian; there was something all too placating about Novotny's regional phrases, something sticky. She realized she mustn't get into any political discussions with Novotny, for after a few conversations she had noticed the Teutonic rubbish that she had forgotten. It was partly because of Novotny that she frequently thought about Waldhans, about Dorothee Neumeister, Prchala, and Gottgetreu. She scrambled everything and everyone in her imagination. She did not avoid Novotny; she talked to him more and more with no special aim; she got used to him. Even Achim put up with Novotny's visiting her almost every evening or with Grummi's going out, he put up with the man's gentle advice, so that after months, Novotny's question almost sounded like the most natural thing in the world: Wouldn't it make more sense if he gave up his apartment and moved in with "you, my dear Katharina"; she listened to these final words of a very long, twisted, convoluted sentence.

Why not? she replied.

Thus Novotny became the "Second Ferdinand."

She learned of his past in fragments, he preferred talking about the glorious moments of his life, but she managed to piece the rest together: he had grown up in Znojmo; his parents had "not exactly been blessed with worldly goods"; he had studied law in Prague, entered the administrative apparatus, became a judicial executive official "at a youthful age," and joined the storm troopers after the Führer marched in.

She told him: I'm half-Jewish. This bewildered him; he answered, That doesn't matter anymore. She asked, Would it have mattered back then?

He was almost one foot taller than she.

Achim, who made fun of their difference in height, told her that first of all she had shrunk with the years, and secondly if a woman is beautiful she doesn't have to be tall because she looks taller to everybody else—that's what things had been like earlier.

You're beautiful, Grummi, but small.

She had been embarrassed about undressing in front of Novotny; she had feared the first night with him—an aging woman, fifty-seven, with an aging man, sixty,—she had retreated into the bathroom, telling him to lie down, read something, she needed time, and he, standing outside the door, had answered that he understood; her clothes rustled more than normal, everything was louder, more concrete, painful. She bathed, glanced very casually into the mirror, went to him; the lamp on his nighttable was on, she used the shadow: Don't look at me, I'm not such an appealing sight anymore; and he replied: Oh, go on: she lay down next to him, kept aloof, he put out the light, turned toward her, began to caress her cheeks, her throat; her resistance ripped like skin, she embraced him, snuggled against him, he kissed her, she said, You smell of cigars; he asked, Do you find that unpleasant?; she said, I don't really like it; he asked, Should I brush my teeth?; she said, Oh, just stay here; he drew her nightgown over her head, took hold of her, rolled on top of her, tried to penetrate her, but she was dry and tight; she said, I can't do it anymore, forget about it, he shook his head, saying, It'll work out; she said, No, it's over, I don't know what it was like or how to do it, that's all, where should it come from anyway, do you understand. He said, It doesn't matter, we love one another; she said, In any case, we're together now, like this, side by side in bed.

He asked her why she never called him by his first name.

I can't, if I call you Ferdinand, I'll always see the other one, you're the second, after all. You know what: I'll call you Second.

He said she was making him look ridiculous.

Well, if you can't take even that. . . .

She had to be a little understanding, he said.

Don't be silly, Second.

Just listen to the way it sounds.

I like saying it—do you understand, Second?

When he left for the Ministry of Justice every morning, the Herr Regierungsdirektor (Chief Executive Officer), she was proud of him. She had come to terms with his past: a Nazi, classified as one, not just a fellow traveler.

"Everything is topsyturvy with me. Back then, I would have never gotten involved with a Nazi. Now that the Hitler period has been over for such a long time, I find one."

Novotny questioned her little by little; she concealed, revised the past.

He said he'd heard of Moravian Knitwear. It's a prestigious firm.

It was, she said.

Yes, was.

Novotny crammed as if learning foreign words—children and children's children—he gradually understood what Katharina meant when she talked about "Gutsi" or "Mummi" or "the twins" in her monologues.

Peter the eldest, Paul's brother, Professor of Germanic Studies at the University of Kiel, married to Dietlind, father of Tobias and Alma,

good, says Katharina (and he eventually met all of them), Camilla, the second oldest, married to the high-school teacher Felix Wertmüller, nicknamed Kalle, in Darmstadt, mother of Thea, Susanne, and Friedhelm,

good, says Katharina,

and Annamaria and Achim, and you.

Achim comes to terms with Novotny.

He just happens to be here, the old man is here, and the older the boy and old man get, the more fatalistically they accept being allocated to Katharina; if either let go of the other, suspected the other, she would be furious with them, driving Second into his room and grounding Achim: You can't pull that nonsense on me, not on me!

They would not marry, they had agreed not to, even though Novotny had coaxed her and gotten Achim's permission. Achim had said it wouldn't change anything if Uncle Novotny married Grummi, but it would sound silly if her name were Novotny instead of Perchtmann.

I think so too.

That's the only reason?

It would take a lifetime, she said, to explain the rest.

Nevertheless, Novotny did manage to get his way sometimes: Softening her with his caresses, he talked Katharina into giving up her job; he gave her a piano for her fifty-ninth birthday, saying it made no difference that it wasn't a round number; she played a lot, driving the gout out of her fingers with Schubert, as she put it; they lived, the day had its rhythm.

47
The Sixty-fifth Birthday

Katharina had refused to let them celebrate her sixtieth birthday. I don't want to know that I've reached sixty, she had said; what kind of celebration is that anyway, what can it be, and Novotny had given up. But when she turned sixty-five, he insisted: Why don't you let us throw a party for you—you need it, you're always living for other people. Not for others, she had retorted, only for myself, you're wrong, all of you, even when things went badly, it was my business—what do you think? The children had been reluctant, complaining about the long trip; if they were going to celebrate, then all the grandchildren had to be present, Katharina put her foot down. It was so much trouble, Peter wailed. The reluctance changed Katharina's mood. Now she insisted on her party no matter how much they'd bitch and squawk, except for Annamaria, who would come with her chauffeur, of course, flaunting her wealth; Novotny, driven to distraction by these mood swings, refused to discuss it with her; he prepared for the big day, with Achim's support. They asked her only crucial questions. She said she didn't want to have anyone in the apartment, she had waited so often for letters during the past few years, for visits, and had been put off with quick visits, people dropping by or passing through, which she understood perfectly, she said, for what can you do with an elderly woman who can only remember their childhoods and complains about the present. So she refused to let them into her home, aside from Annamaria, they should find some decent tavern or restaurant—there were so many, for instance The Old Coach or The Stag in Möhringen or The Grape in Pflieningen or The Ox in Stetten, but, if they were going to have a wild time, then she wanted to be surprised: Leave me alone until the day has come.

Nevertheless, she cleaned the apartment spic and span, just in case, and with Achim making fun of her.

She wanted to escape, avoid the rumpus, that temporal slash, an age that she was indifferent to because she didn't feel it, because it hadn't settled in her. "Since I am a little younger than Achim, who's eighteen," she had written to Annamaria, "we have no problems with one another, we get along fine. What he does is none of my business, and if ever it does concern me in any way, I can sympathize—whatever we call 'sympathy,' or maybe it would be better to call it 'empathy' or even better 'understanding'—it is hard to find the right word."

Nevertheless, for the first time in years, she had ordered a dress, admitting that she certainly enjoyed the expenditure. Layer by layer, familiar scenes were stored up again—for instance, when she went to the seamstress, embarrassed, not with the self-confidence of the thirty-year-old (the seamstress had been recommended by the mother of a friend of Achim's); she hesitated on the all-too-elegant staircase, which was decked out with *haute couture* posters. She was reluctantly reminded of earlier visits, in Prague and Brno, oddly summery associations; she felt fabrics in her hands again, heard the female chitchat. When she called for the dress after the last fitting, she felt almost like a traitor. She hadn't lived like that for years and she didn't want to go back. But she liked the frock—it was white, interwoven with silver threads, reaching down to her ankles; it was beautiful; she tried it on in her room for several evenings before her birthday; she enjoyed the sense of "being different, not ordinary."

The winter—damp, not especially cold, with quickly changing weather—had been a strain on her. On some mornings she was unwilling to rise; she got out of bed late, remaining grumpy all day long. Ferdinand and Achim stayed out of her way, until the boy accused her of behaving like an old woman—if she was really sick she ought to say so, but these moods were unbearable. So for his sake, she again was the first to rise, ignoring the pains in her limbs, making breakfast for the men, sending them out of the house.

The birthday party had to be scheduled for a weekend, since, as Peter wrote sarcastically, "the children will not be excused from school even for such an important occasion."

Fine, she said.

That tone, she said.

Four days prior to the event, Novotny told Katharina he had prepared everything, but he did not want to take part in the festivities; there were many reasons, he preferred going away all weekend, hiking on the Alb. She said that if he did that to her, she would cancel everything at the last moment. It was only for one evening, after all. Achim also talked to him, trying to make him change his mind. Novotny gave in. If the Perchtmann children kept carrying on like that, he said, then she ought to know there'd be a commotion. Achim said she'd probably enjoy it, this was a splendid harmony.

Where was the party going to take place?

Novotny had reserved a room at The Ox in Stetten.

That's fine.

Then she said she wanted to complete the day's program.

It's your birthday, Katharina.

She refused to pick the kids up at the station, she said: They knew what hotel they'd be staying at (the Royal, wasn't it?), and since Annamaria and the Wertmüllers were driving, they'd have no problem getting to Stetten. The day belonged to her, she said; she would go walking alone with Achim in the Rem Valley if the weather didn't upset her plans.

What about me?

She hugged Novotny, caressed him. You'll arrive a little before the others, darling, and you'll arrange the entrance of the gladiators.

Sometimes you can be peculiarly heartless.

You think?

It was cold, a little snow was falling, when she went to the station with Achim (she had written a note, excusing him from school).

What are you planning, Grummi?

It's a surprise.

They took the train to Endersbach.

So, now we'll start our hike.

In this weather—are you crazy? What if you slip and fall, and break a leg—first of all I'll have to carry you, and secondly, there won't be any party.

Let's risk it.

They walked along the road to Strümpfelbach for a while, then through the vineyards. She did slip occasionally and, in order to help herself and amuse Achim, she played the frail old lady. Achim was a head taller than she and sometimes, breathing heavily, she looked up at him: You're gonna be carrying me soon. Oh, c'mon, Grummi, where are we going, do you know?

I know.

Then tell me.

Maultaschen!

Then we're going to The Lamb.

You're a sly little fox.

Tell me a story, he begged, that'll make the distance seem shorter, but she was struggling for air: No, later, when we're nice and comfy. You haven't congratulated me yet.

I'll do it tonight.

It's already my birthday.

You're really childish.

You have no idea how much that helps me.

They reached The Lamb around one. It took her a while to move her fingers again.

We're staying here, she said.

They ate, drank.

This wine tastes good only if you drink it here.

You're really drinking it too, Grummi.

Do you mind, grandchild?

What if you're drunk tonight?

She began to tell him stories, incoherently; the boy listened, not always attentive, it was all the same to her.

You have no idea how far back I can remember, five lives, six—this has not been one life, no.

Don't drink so much, Grummi.

Leave me alone, Achim. And what became of them all? I could cry.

Please don't.

Don't interrupt. Birthdays, oh Lord, all the presents I've gotten, and all the things that were taken from me. What is something worth? Now, I have nothing, and perhaps it was only the pony that delighted me five hundred years ago.

You're drinking too much, Grummi.

I tell you, five hundred years ago—you haven't the foggiest idea how many lives a life can have—when Father, in a time that wouldn't be my time if it were described, when I could still dream, when there was nothing but a bundle of feelings, that was all, my boy, and happiness, and a pain that was much larger than I or my shadow on the lawn in front of the white house, now I'm by the house—yes, I wonder if it's still standing, it can't be like that anymore, it's gone—I'm rebuilding it in my mind—and here comes Father, with the pony on its halter, and he places the red saddle in front of small white shoes—you know, I say "small white shoes" as if they hadn't been my shoes, as if they hadn't squeezed my feet, white patent leather—and a little girl whom I see, who was I, and who is happy, she throws her arms around her father—how old have I become?, I don't know, six, five, seven, we play with little years and talk about centuries.

You people were real plutocrats.

That's nonsense, we inhabited a mirage, we lived in Father's visions and Mummi made them comfortable—what nonsense you young people talk—it's all gone, it will never happen again—or do you want to make yourself at home in a fairy tale, Achim, that's what it was, do you want me to summon a king for you, David—you'd laugh your head off at me—but he visited me many times, and his singing was incomparable, he stood at my cradle and blessed me and he took along his kingdom, where, I can't imagine, I'm not religious, I was always merely playing—tell me, have I always merely played?

You're a little high now.

High, high, high as David's crown.

Grummi, pull yourself together.

I've been pulling myself together all my life, why do I have to do it now?

Are we gonna stay here or should we walk a little?

A taxi is calling for us at five.

Good God, you won't be in any condition for anything by then.

Listen, boy, don't keep breaking in, I want to tell you another story, one single story, then we can talk about anything you like—just this one story, you probably won't understand it, it's too important for me, but first I have to go out.

He tried to stand up; she pushed him back into the chair, walked slowly, very straight, through the tavern, and came back after a short time.

Do you feel nauseous, Grummi?

You're a dear, silly child.

Then tell me.

Not in the least.

You were going to tell me a story.

You tell me one.

You said just this one story.

Yes, that's what I said; she leaned across the table, gazing at him like a conspirator.

I can't get it together.

Yes, you can.

It's not a story, it is—how shall I put it?—a narrated experience. Imagine someone like me, but don't stick to me, it's important for me that you say to yourself: a person similar to Grummi, but not Grummi, do you understand?, and what she has on her mind, what she thinks of every day, what she remembers, sometimes it's a lot, sometimes nothing, very seldom her whole life—this person lived and suddenly she discovers that she has been lived, that she herself did little to lead her own life; it was usually other people; perhaps she only acted like a loving person, and if she weighs it, it was also the chance things, the random events to which she yielded. She had seven lives, like a cat. And finally, much too late, she began to resist; but the people around her allow her to play the part that she has begun in her seventh life. She tries to shake off everything and everybody, forget them, for she would like to begin. That's probably what it is. But one feels one's own life so differently. That's all, Achim. She raised the glass and said, In your Swabian dialect, you'd probably want to say: I don' unnerstan' nothin'.

You're a little confused, Grummi. It's your big party. He stood up, took her head in his hands, and kissed her on the forehead, paying no attention to the other people in the tavern.

She ordered another carafe of wine and a grape juice for Achim.

Stop it, Grummi.

This is the last glass. The taxi's coming soon.

Promise me.

You are probably my last love, Achim.

You're nuts. He made up his mind to watch her carefully tonight.

The car drove them to Stetten. She sent Achim into the tavern to bring her the carton containing her evening gown. She said Novotny was taking care of it. She changed clothes in the toilet, struggling against a growing dizziness.

She waited, had trouble with the zipper; a young woman helped her. Her nausea subsided; she dabbed some cologne on her temples, fixed her hair.

Pull yourself together, she said. Go to your children and the second Ferdinand, review the parade of your grandchildren.

Novotny walked toward her through the tavern. After three steps, she noticed she was slipping into the role she would maintain all evening.

Novotny scrutinized her and was satisfied; they were all waiting in the next room, so few and yet so many, he took the lead. She saw for the first time that his right foot dragged slightly, or was he too under great strain? She steeled herself, he opened the door—they were all standing around the table, talking, adults and children. They fell silent. She took a few very short steps, halted. We haven't seen one another for a long time, she said, my goodness but you're solemn, if Gutsi were still alive she'd be blubbering into her handkerchief.

Annamaria and Achim were the first to congratulate her, then the others; she was surrounded, her hands were shaken, she got kissed on her cheeks and forehead. She was surprised at the altered faces—they were fatter, uglier, she looked into unfamiliar eyes. I can't understand, she thought to herself, why Peter, who has made something of himself, is still so clumsy at the age of forty-four; that must be Thea, yes, that's Thea, she's pretty, she knows it, I ought to ask her whether she's got a boyfriend, whether she's already run away from men—why have I thought of that necessarily, I'd love to be starting out like her, she knows a lot already. Why does Camilla treat Wertmüller so horribly—after all, he did get her out of the mess she was in; the little girl is Alma, she's delightful, slightly cross-eyed, and she keeps holding on to her mother; God, is she skinny, she must have gone on a crash diet, I can't remember her name, something Germanic, oh yes, Dietlind, you feel like softening her up in some way.

Come, said Ferdinand, this is your seat.

The hubbub of voices quieted down. She heard Peter read the menu to his wife, carefully emphasizing: smoked trout filet, Flädle soup (that's Swabian!), pheasant on cabbage in wine, poire Helène, mocha, then the wines: Stettener Brotwasser—weird name!—Uhlscher Trollinger, Kessler Hochgewächs.

Do sit down, Katharina.

They observed the seating arrangement that Katharina had dictated to Ferdinand; why should I sit next to someone I can't stand.

They're your children and grandchildren, Katharina.

That's got nothing to do with it.

So Achim sat at her left, Ferdinand at her right, Peter at the opposite end, between Camilla and Annamaria, then the others.

You look marvelous, said Annamaria.

You should, she replied, add: for your age.

Don't get nasty again, Mother.

I feel fine.

The innkeeper's wife asked if everything was all right, she congratulated Katharina, lit the candles on the table, and turned off the light.

They're overdoing it again, she said, she doesn't care to have it so festive.

Novotny put his hand on her arm; Achim said, You're the guest of honor, Grummi, there's nothing you can do.

Two waiters served the trout; Katharina sipped the wine.

You can't do that, Achim whispered to her, you have to wait till Uncle Peter proposes the toast.

Stop it, boy. She took a long draft; Peter waited for everyone to finish the hors d'oeuvre, then stood up, produced a few slips of paper from his jacket pocket, arranged them—he was noticeably excited.

The pressure of Novotny's hand on her arm grew stronger.

Don't worry, Second, she told him.

Dearest Mother, all of us, your children and grandchildren know that you were somewhat reluctant to prepare for this celebration; in the course of a long, eventful life, you have lost interest in celebrations, even though, as children, we discovered what marvelous parties you could give, and you were always the life of each party. We know that was a long time ago. And it is difficult to imagine everything you have been through. We know about your childhood chiefly from the stories we were told by Grandmother and Gutsi. It always seemed like a fairy tale. And that must be how you think of it now. However, our childhood too was rich and carefree thanks to Father and yourself. What happened later was something that you endured admirably, you were able to cope with the ups and downs, you always managed to get through. You did not have an easy time of it, and perhaps we did not make things easy for you. Forgive us our omissions. Your old age may grant you peace and quiet. And now we want to drink to your health, dearest Mother.

They all got to their feet; Peter came around the table, saying, as he struck his glass against hers, Long life to you; she hugged him, thanked him. Peter, I can't understand why you talk about old age so much.

But Mother.

By the time they came to dessert, the seating arrangement broke up; they sat down with her, went off, talked to her, asked her:

Why hasn't Uncle Dieter come?

He's not well, he could have gotten permission to come from East Germany since he's retired, but he's got a gangrenous leg from all his smoking.

Listen, Grandma, is it true that when you were a little girl you had horses?

Yes, a whole herd, giant horses, and when I visited them at night, their nostrils snorted fire. . . .

That's not true.

I've never told a lie in all my life.

What ever became of Wagner, Mother?

I had a letter from him a few years ago.

He's alive?

He's got a big bakery in Nördlingen, these salt sticks on the table may be his.

And you've never felt like visiting him?

What for?

You're drinking too much again, Grummi.

I want to get drunk, Achim, now you know, I want to survive this, do you understand?

I can't stand drunken women.

At your age, one shouldn't voice prejudices so thoughtlessly. Do you like drunken men?

I prefer them to drunken women.

How come?

You know, Mother, my husband should have come along.

Yes, Annamaria, why isn't he here?

He had to attend an urgent meeting in Constance.

Fine with me, I can't stand him.

You're awful.

Grandmother—

You can call me Granny, Thea.

Sorry.

Don't be sorry, this is a gathering of strangers who are related to one another. What did you want to ask me?

Father says you were a revolutionary when you were young.

Does he now? It would have been lovely. Do you have a boyfriend, Thea?

Yes, we're getting engaged soon.

Engaged? Do you have to? Keep him dangling for a while and try out a few others.

That wouldn't do.

Forgive me, child, I'm old-fashioned.

Grummi, watch your dress, you've spilled some wine.

It doesn't leave stains, Achim, and what if it did, I'm never going to wear this dress again.

How do you feel, Katharina?

Excellent, Second, I feel nothing, and that's good.

Have you noticed that Alma is cross-eyed?

Yes, Camilla.

Such a darling girl—it's too bad.

You should worry more about your own kids. Camilla, it's better to be cross-eyed than mindless.

You're being impossible again, Mami.

Ferdinand tapped a spoon against his glass. He said he didn't intend to give a speech.

I don't intend to give a speech. After all, I'm the only one here who's not a relative. Your mother and grandmother has sort of adopted me. You all know we're not married and do not plan to get married. In any case, I want to thank you, dear Katharina, for our home, and I want to tell you here, in public, how much I admire you and love you. The young people may not imagine that there is still such a thing as love at our age. But there is. To your health, long life to you. He bent over and kissed her.

Achim was the only one who clapped.

At the very start, she had noticed the piano standing against the longer wall: she had decided she would play; then Peter, filled with pride, had told her that Tobias had a marvelous voice, and his teacher at the conservatory thought the world of him.

Things recur, she said.

What do you mean?

Oh, nothing.

She had paid no attention to Tobias, but now she asked him to join her.

I had quite forgotten that you sing.

Didn't Father write you?

Maybe. Do you want to sing something, should I accompany you?

Do you have a favorite song, Grandmother?

Many.

What would you like to hear?

I don't know if you can do it; what voice do you sing?

Baritone.

Perhaps.

What?

"I Came Here As a Stranger."

I'll try, it's difficult.

He sang it; she accompanied him, she hadn't expected such a rich voice, she got confused as she accompanied him. When Tobias was done, she thanked him, saying something he didn't understand: Uncle David always claimed he could work magic, now I know he could.

Had Achim brought along the record player? Let's have some music and dance.

What should we play first, Grummi? Achim shouted through the room.

The Rolling Stones: "Live with Me."

She's crazy and she'll always be crazy, Camilla said to her husband.

The youngsters danced; Katharina sat facing them, her legs stretched out, she was in pain.

Achim was dancing with Susanne Wertmüller; Katharina cut in.

You sure can dance, Grummi, where'd you learn?

By watching you kids.

She danced a lot, became breathless. Ferdinand wanted to call it a night. Achim kept telling her not to drink so much; she heard Dietlind say, She's drunk, that's awful, at her age; she sang along with the hits that Achim always played nonstop at home.

Okay, I'm going—okay, we're all going soon. She asked Achim to turn off the record player. It was nice, she said, then louder: Stop, don't go running off yet! It's time for my speech; it won't be long, don't worry. I feel a bit sick; it's been a long day. I am sixty-five, the old woman's sixty-five—do you think I want you to keep believing that? I am not sixty-five. And I wonder what connection I have to any of you. I've given birth to some of you, that's all. The war—how long ago that was—took you away from me very early, and none of you has ever come back. I didn't expect that. Evidently, children assume their mothers love them even when the children are far away and offer no reason to be loved. But that's not the way it is. I just wanted to make that clear to you. You're here. Fine, I know you. I once loved you, I like your children. They address me respectfully because I am a stranger to them, because, for one instant, they are more honest than you, my children. I was not offended by their politeness. It amused me. We got together for this celebration, not because we loved each other, but for one single reason: Because my memory encompasses all of you. You are in my brain as you were and as you will never be again. And now the party is over.

They stood there, flabbergasted. Peter stuttered: You can't let us go like that, Mother. She looked at him, her head tilting sharply: Then drop by again soon.

It was snowing. They said goodbye to one another in front of the house. She perfunctorily wished all of them bon voyage, she was holding back her hiccups. Novotny helped her into his car. Achim sat next to him in front. She wasn't tired, she wouldn't be able to sleep.

Was it good, Achim?

The end was bad, Grummi.

Achim, it was—and the hiccup lurched between the syllables—a truly successful party.

48

The Fourth Mirror Image or
An Old Woman Removes Her Make-up

She holds her face close to the mirror, and when she breathes, the glass mists over. She runs her fingers over her forehead, smoothing out the furrows. The skin has become thin, cracked. The lips are shrinking too. Her eyes glued to the mirror image, she reaches for the lipstick, pulling color across the countless fine cracks.

A milky film settles over the iris.

But I can see as well as ever.

Taking a tube, she squeezes a pink paste into her hand and smears it all over her face; she pauses at the sinews in her neck.

They can't be covered up.

She dampens the handkerchief with cologne, rubs the color off her face, her lips.

Her face is growing smaller; it is still narrow, and arrogant, and it looks like the head of a girl waiting for her father, who comes back from a trip and surprises her with a gift.

She smiles. The smile produces many creases.

49
Easter in Esslingen

She kept talking about that summer, sixty-seven, calling it unique, hot, dry; there could have been a good wine, but the fall was too cold.

The disquiet came back, and Novotny said she was exaggerating as she did so often; she shouldn't bother with the young people, she was a burden to them anyway.

That's possible, Second.

But the group of boys and girls who visited Achim, sitting around on the floor of his room, filling the place with smoke, listening to music she liked—The Rolling Stones, Joan Baez, Bob Dylan, Judy Collins—talking about books she tried to read but couldn't—Adorno, Marcuse, Habermas—discussing society as if it were a synthetic product, something that could shatter when played with, discussing workers as if they were creatures of fable—and she had been dumbfounded hearing Achim say in there: My grandmother was a worker too, she knows all about it.

You know better than that, she had rebuked him.

Isn't it true?

Sort of.

One evening, when she was bored (Novotny was cursing the dreadful mess that the group always left behind), Achim asked her to come in: Tell us about the Sparticists, Grummi, you know, I forget where it was, the place you always mention. . . .

Hellerau? Child, that was such a casual business.

You were with them.

She becomes history, tells them about Skodlerrak and Kasimir, talks about the Kapp Putsch, about Rosa, whom they all loved, about their rage after she was murdered, about Liebknecht and the others.

A couple of them call her Granny and address her in the familiar form.

She permits it.

Did you guys talk about Marx?

More about Bakunin and Rosa Luxemburg.

Then you must have been anarchists.

We didn't quite know what we were, at least not all of us. Do you people know what you are?

They nodded, but offered no word of explanation as to why they were so certain.

You people are a beginning that won't admit that there were other beginnings, that many things recur, that the change you're after will be different from what you imagine. You people are so severe, she said to Achim; Achim rebuked her: She didn't know what she was talking about, she ought to read first.

Why do I have to read if I have lived?

He said she was arrogant.

Novotny rebuked him: He evidently didn't realize who he was talking to.

I do, it's Grummi.

His insolence was outrageous, said Novotny.

Achim said it was nothing new to him that Novotny was a reactionary.

Pull yourself together, Achim.

He asked her to come to his group again and again; she listened, sang the Internationale with them, came to terms with Novotny's reproaches, told the girls to take the Pill, asked them about the boys; they confided in her; Granny's okay even if she's not quite with it politically.

She wasn't, she didn't want to be. She was merely curious. And she was scared of the disappointments they were bound to suffer.

Just don't treat me like a walking history-book. I don't know very much.

Because she hadn't lived consciously, they said.

This hit home because they were right and yet they weren't. These kids had been born after the war; what did they know about living in order to survive. About the things that happen to you. When bombs drop, you don't ask about the causes, or whether Hitler or Churchill has dropped them, you just dash to the nearest basement.

But one has to try to analyze the situation one is in.

I reacted, maybe that was wrong.

It is entirely unpolitical.

She said she agreed.

Then she'd have to learn, they said.

What should I learn, that power is never just because it knows nothing but itself?

That sounds good, but it's wrong.

I guess I'm not enlightened.

Don't you want to get rid of social classes and bring about justice?

Of course. Of course.

Then why do you resist?

Because once you people are in power, then, even if you don't want to, you will claim that your class is now the only class, your justice the only justice, and you will create new elites and new injustices.

You're acting stupid, said Achim, you're cunning.

When the Shah of Persia visited Berlin, the police gunned down a student named Ohnesorg.

They formed a mob in the streets, even though the school had prohibited it, they demonstrated all through the night, holding signs, accompanied by the police.

She was worried about Achim. She had begged him not to go.

It's over, Grummi. We're gonna show those Fascists.

Her question, Do you really know what Fascists are? did not reach him; she let him go.

Novotny said: The boy's ruining you, you should send him back to his mother.

You're great, Second, when things get hot, you simply give up.

She looked for Achim, found him marching in the middle of a silent column. Several people carried torches; she threaded her way through the ranks, was elbowed good-naturedly: Who ya lookin' for, Granny, this ain' nothin' for you. She linked arms with him, had a hard time keeping up; one of the girls took her other arm.

I'll never forget this, Grummi.

She was out with him for a long time. She took several young people home in the middle of the night; they could stay over in Achim's room if their parents weren't worried, just call them! and don't sing too loud.

The excitement persisted. She realized she couldn't get anywhere with her experiences; no comparisons would help, no reference to anything that had already happened. These were children who were horrified at wars on other continents, talking their heads off about systems, but without grasping or even wanting to grasp realities, creatures of a listless peace, theoreticians of a future that was so flawless it could be endured only on a different star, but not on this earth, whose history she had learned in more than sixty years—she was superior to the children and poorer than they. Of course, she was infuriated by many of the things they said. But their exuberance always carried her away.

Novotny, who, since 1945, had viewed all politics as evil, prophesized disaster: This younger generation would ruin everything their fathers had so painstakingly built up.

Oh, your pot-belly attitude, she said. They didn't get along so well during this period.

Achim managed to graduate from Gymnasium, not without difficulty; he was going to study medicine at Tübingen, but wanted them to keep his room free.

You're not getting rid of me that fast, Grummi.

That's what you think, boy.

That winter, he didn't even come on weekends.

She began writing letters to him in Tübingen, which amused Novotny, who was now being given his due: He said he was no longer jealous of the brat; she'd be astonished at how fast the kid would forget her.

Angry at the joint administration by the Social Democrats and the Union parties, she always wrote "In the first year of the Great Coalition" instead of the date, but she did not talk politics; she told Achim about her daily life, sometimes making up minor events, and, as she wrote, she noticed that the times were gradually leaving her out.

Before Easter Achim came home several times, meeting friends whom she didn't know and who didn't value her participation; like Kasimir, they seemed to have become professional revolutionaries.

They planned to prevent the distribution of the reactionary Sunday newspaper that was printed in Esslingen.

I'd like to watch.

That's impossible.

Why?

There might be scuffles, beatings.

They won't do anything to an old lady.

Do you think anyone is going to be considerate of dear old Frau Perchtmann?

I want to see it.

Achim let her have her way. His friends made fun of him: If things got hot, he wanted to take refuge behind his grandmother's petticoats.

They drove to Esslingen in three cars, parking at the edge of the industrial lot; they walked in small groups to the printing plant, where many people were sitting in at the gate; Achim told her to remain on the periphery and to run if there were any clashes.

She leaned against a fence, making sure to keep away from larger groups, she cringed under shouts she didn't understand, hummed along when several people sang the Internationale.

The police cars had focused their searchlights on the demonstration and on the blocked trucks in the courtyard, the lights sketched gigantic shadows; voices and noises were muffled by the night; it was an artificial space in which rage, belligerence, and violence were lurking; "that was probably how generals used to work up their soldiers for a battle—with campfires, songs, who-goes-there shouts, a growing tension"; a few students were talking to policemen; when their faces moved into the light they all looked the same, young and wrought up.

Slogans were chanted, ebbing and rising.

When the police reinforcements arrived, she suddenly realized the hatred of the young people. It was like an assault by dark, nocturnal satraps. In leather and sparkling helmets, they leaped from the cars, seeking shadows, listening to orders, creating a realm of violence and fear. "There are noises that are quite simply brutal, martial, creating resistance or surrender. Hitler too employed these night people. But the young policemen do not know this. Perhaps they enjoy being camouflaged by the half-light, feeling power and flaunting it."

There were yells from the courtyard. The newspaper truckdrivers attempted to smash through the living barrier. They were answered by screams, shouts, slogans.

Metal clattered on the asphalt.

The orders shouted by the policemen became louder.

The young people sang the Internationale; she joined in loudly. A water cannon was driven up. The wall of bodies swayed to and fro; a few people detached themselves, vanishing into the darkness, a few faces came into the light.

The instant the jet of water hit the young people, stones cracked against metal. The police raised their shields.

Someone took her arm and said, This isn't for you, Grandma, get away, fast, get away.

She saw the clash, heard shrieks.

She began to run, didn't know where, it couldn't be far to the railroad station, a car stopped next to her, policemen, one of them asked whether they could give her a lift, yes, to the station, she said, breathless, she was pushed into the back of the car, sat next to one of the uniformed men, shifted away from him; he laughed, wondered what she was doing here, was she one of the revolutionaries; if you keep on like this, she said, then maybe; at your age, said the policeman, you ought to be smarter.

She slept all day. Novotny tiptoed through the apartment; there was no helping her, he shouted at her that evening.

You people are not winning anything, she told Achim, you're losing everything.

He said she'd been discouraged by just one demonstration.

She said that all her life—and she knew he wouldn't understand—all her life she had feared people who lose sight of others because of their own decreed hatred. That probably has nothing to do with politics.

It doesn't, said Achim.

50
Annamaria's Letter

Stuttgart, 12 May 1970

Dear Camilla,

I brought Mother home from St. Catharine's Hospital. She's recovered from her pneumonia with no permanent damage, but as her
doctor explains, her overall condition is not good. She's been losing
strength ever since Novotny's sudden death. Six months ago, I
suggested that she move into a nursing home, but she wouldn't hear
of it. She said she had to be here for Achim. Yet ever since the boy's
been studying in Berlin, he barely stirs, and she carries on because
he never writes. My son—actually he's not mine, he's hers. Inciden-
tally, today he arrived with his girlfriend and welcomed Mother in
the apartment. She was blissful. She likes the girl. Everything goes
on, she said.

I'm writing you for an important reason. Achim, her favorite,
has managed to do what I couldn't: He has gotten Mother to agree
to move into a nursing home in Sillenbuch. A rather expensive
place, it's run like a hotel. She has to buy her apartment there
outright, but she doesn't have the money. We children are supposed
to pitch in. Achim threatened that if we refused, he'd collect money

from his fellow students and embarrass us in our avarice. You'll have to contribute about five thousand marks. Is that all right? I feel sorry for the old woman, and she needs care, she's not so steady on her feet anymore.

I am sitting in Novotny's former room, I hear her laughing next door with Achim and the girl. Mother is indestructible. When she saw Achim in the doorway of the apartment, she threw her arms around him, and for an instant she looked like a young girl.

We didn't have very much from our Mother, that's true. She always went her own way. And I still can't understand her, even in her old age. Perhaps it was the right thing for her to take in Achim. She always needed people who required her love.

So, please send the money soon. We can't leave Mother alone in this apartment, which is in a terrible state. It looks like after the war.

Love and kisses,

Annamaria